Narrating Nomadism

Narrating Nomadism

Tales of Recovery and Resistance

EDITORS

G. N. Devy
Geoffrey V. Davis
K. K. Chakravarty

Routledge
Taylor & Francis Group
LONDON NEW YORK NEW DELHI

First published 2013 in India
by Routledge
912 Tolstoy House, 15–17 Tolstoy Marg, Connaught Place, New Delhi 110 001

Simultaneously published in the UK
by Routledge
2 Park Square, Milton Park, Abingdon, OX14 4RN

by Routledge
711 Third Avenue, New York, NY 10017

First issued in paperback 2018

Routledge is an imprint of the Taylor & Francis Group, an informa business

© 2013 G. N. Devy, Geoffrey V. Davis and K. K. Chakravarty

Typeset by
Star Compugraphics Private Limited
5, CSC, Near City Apartments
Vasundhara Enclave
Delhi 110 096

British Library Cataloguing-in-Publication Data
A catalogue record of this book is available from the British Library

ISBN 13: 978-1-138-66398-5 (pbk)
ISBN 13: 978-0-415-81180-4 (hbk)

Dedicated to

*The indigenous peoples in all continents
who know that they belong to the earth,
not that the earth belongs to them*

Contents

List of Abbreviations

ACLALS	Association for Commonwealth Literature and Language Studies
AIDS	Acquired Immuno-Deficiency Syndrome
a.k.a.	Also Known As
APB	Aboriginal Protection Board
BRPC	Bhasha Research and Publication Centre
CE	Common Era
CT	Criminal Tribe(s)
CTA	Criminal Tribes Act
DMSC	Durbar Mahila Samanway Committee
DNC	Denotified Community
DNT	Denotified and Nomadic Tribe
DNT-RAG	Denotified and Nomadic Tribe Rights Action Group
DP	Displaced Persons
FM	Frequency Modulation
HIV	Human Immuno-Deficiency Virus
HOA	Habitual Offenders Act
ILO	International Labour Organization
ILTD	Indian Leaf Tobacco Development
JSS	Junior Secondary School
KBC	Kenya Broadcasting Corporation
NGO	Non-Governmental Organization
NSDF	National Slum Dwellers Federation
PTSD	Post-Traumatic Stress Disorder
RAG	Rights Action Group
SDI	Slum/Shack Dwellers International
SPARC	Society for the Promotion of Area Resource Centres
SSS	Senior Secondary School
TAG	Technical Advisory Group
UN	United Nations
UNESCO	United Nations Educational, Scientific and Cultural Organization
US	United States

Introduction

♋

The essays by scholars and activists from various countries brought together in this volume include some presentations made at the Second Chotro Conference held in Baroda in 2009 as well as some presentations made at the next Chotro held in 2010 at Delhi and Shimla. Companion volumes of essays based on the Third Chotro are being brought out by Routledge under the titles *Knowing Differently: The Challenge of the Indigenous* and *Oral Traditions: Local Knowledge and Global Transformation*. Previously, two volumes, based on the First Chotro held at Delhi in 2008, have been published as *Indigeneity: Culture and Representation* (Devy et al. 2009) and *Voice and Memory: Indigenous Imagination and Expression* (Devy et al. 2011). The Chotro conferences of 2009 and 2010 were hosted jointly by the Bhasha Research and Publication Centre (BRPC) and the Association for Commonwealth Literature and Language Studies (ACLALS).

While the participants of these Chotro events included eminent scholars from the fields of literature and social sciences, the focus of the presentations and interactions remained the indigenous communities from all parts of the world. The intellectual engagement in these confer-ences, and in the publications resulting out of them, has not been akin to that in any established branch of anthropology or previously practised form of literary studies. The idea of Chotro had taken birth in the middle of hectic social activism, and the issues addressed in each of the Chotro conferences had vital links with social thought, though the presentations were based on long reflection quite akin to academic research. It may be useful for the readers of the present volume to get an idea of the gen-esis and the nature of the concept of Chotro that has brought together over 300 distinguished scholars to share ideas over the last four years. Towards this end, I draw upon the following three paragraphs from my 'Introduction' to *Indigeneity* (Devy et al. 2009):

> Recognized as 'Aborigines' in Australia, as Māori in New Zealand, as 'First Nations' in Canada, as 'Indigenous' in the United States, as 'Janajatis'

in India, or as 'tribes' in anthropology, as 'Notified Communities' in the administrative parlance of many countries, as 'Indigenous People' in the discourse of Human Rights, and as 'Adivasis' in the terminology of Asian activists, these variously described communities are far too numerous and dispersed in geographical locations to admit of any single inclusive description. It would be simplistic to perceive them as divergent victim groups of any shared epochal phenomenon such as colonialism, imperialism, modernity or globalization. In their ethnic, cultural and linguistic attributes, they are so varied that it is almost impossible to speak of them as a common constituency. No single term can describe them with any degree of semantic assuredness, nor can any universal definition of an invented descriptive term stretch without fatigue beyond the margins of a single nation or continent. The term 'indigenous', for instance, as employed by the ILO[1] and UNESCO,[2] seeks to represent over a thousand different communities spread over all continents. Obviously, it would be preposterous to lump all of them together. Even if one were to accept this or any similar term for the purpose, its normative frame may run up against numerous contradictions with the strikingly divergent history of every community. Though terms like 'colonized' or 'colonizers' have learnt to perform at least a degree of communicational theatre, a scrutiny of the entire range of signification that the term 'indigenous' is expected to cover brings home that most discursive concepts are perennially contestable.

The *Chotro* series comprising global conferences organized for literary scholars and social scientists engaged in a variety of 'indigenous' communities in their own continents and fields of study, was set up with a very clear understanding that it had no business to go overboard and start looking for any pre-conceived set of cultural or historic convergences. What was expected to be shared was not a set of conclusions and concerns, but just a space for articulation and expression. The series of conferences was conceptualized as a *place* where an inquisitive and serious audience would 'listen', internalize, learn, imagine and empathize, rather than as a forum where one was expected to 'speak', argue, present and score points. In other words, Chotro was not designed for expanding the frontiers of any specific field of knowledge, it was organized as an exercise in reducing our collective ignorance about the communities generally described as 'indigenous'. Moreover, even if convened for listening to or listening about, the indigenous peoples from various continents, Chotro was not intended to be 'a celebration of diversity', as the cliché goes. In the context of the communities and cultures that were the focus the expression 'celebration' would amount to a travesty of the existential

---

[1] International Labour Organization.

[2] United Nations Educational, Scientific and Cultural Organization.

disasters that these communities have been facing everywhere. However, Chotro was not organized as a mourning marathon either. It was not meant for foregrounding the activists fighting for the rights of the indigenous. While discussions in Chotro displayed a profound recognition of the importance of activism, it was by no means planned as an ideological intervention. Chotro was not organized by any local or global professional or occupational organization, nor was it aimed at creating any such organization.

Considering these definitional difficulties, it was felt that it would be best to avoid calling the unique convergence of scholars, writers and members of the communities, a 'conference'. When Geoffrey Davis and I started discussing the possibility of convening such a conference, it became evident to them that the term 'conference' would be quite inappropriate to bring home the spirit of what they were to embark upon. Therefore, we chose the term 'Chotro' while announcing the event. In many varieties of the Bhili language group, 'Chotro' implies 'a place where villagers gather', 'a public platform', 'a centre for dispute resolution' and 'a place for announcing news' (Devy et al. 2009: xi–xii).

In 1996, I started work with migratory labourers moving to metropolitan centres in search of wages. They would work without any holidays throughout the month, except the new moon day. My colleagues started bringing them together on that day every month. We asked them how they would like the meeting to be named and they promptly answered, 'Chotro'. In these meetings many stories surfaced. These were narratives drawn from cultural memory and allegories based on contemporary social reality and conflict. There was quite a polyphony of literary tones, some in music and song, some in prose and even just gossip. 'Chotro' gradually came to mean a literary form for those tribals, a form such as their tradition did not know but one that their lives in the context of modernity had created. Therefore, when we were looking for a suitable title for an international conference on the literature of Indian tribal people or the Janajatis, Australian Aborigines, New Zealand Māori, Canadian First Nations and American indigenous people, we were thinking not of a discipline but of a rich polyphony. Hence, 'Chotro'.

In response to the essays included in *Indigeneity* based on the first Chotro conference, I had remarked that the essays

make it evident that there are major areas as yet waiting for scholarly exploration. They include the study of numerous marginalized languages, their literary traditions, the aesthetic framework of those traditions, the origins of the communities, their mythologies and histories, their visual representations, artistic practices and art criticism, and the politics and the ideologies of these communities (Devy et al. 2009: xiv).

The papers included in that volume had taken up for discussion specific histories of conflict and annihilation; the loss of language and neglect of intellectual traditions; the exclusion from knowledge transactions that the indigenous have to face; the question of representation as 'savages' from an external perspective; their deprivation of natural resources; denial of access to education and other measures of social justice; their excitement with life and the expression of their joy; and the creativity of the indigenous communities. The aim of the Second Chotro conference was clearly different. Its focus was the plight of the nomadic communities. In the backdrop of that conference was the major human rights campaign that BRPC had run since 1998 for drawing the world's attention to the long overdue issue of the denotified communities in India. Some discussion about the nature of the issues and the trajectory of the campaign will be in order here.

I moved from the field of post-colonial literary studies to a study of the languages of the indigenous communities by giving up my university job in 1996. The work with the languages of the indigenous took me from village to village and from community to community. However, it was not until March 1998 that I became fully aware that there exist in India a large number of communities described by the rather hackneyed expression 'Denotified and Nomadic Tribes', or the DNTs for short. Not that all of these can be called 'indigenous' or Janajatis. The DNTs have a population of approximately six crore, though there are various claims and no way of knowing the exact figures.[3] Some of them are included

---

[3] When I was working on the Technical Advisory Group's report, I found a vast divergence of views and subjective claims regarding the DNT population in the country. The Advisory Group accepted 60 million as the most sensible estimate, which was based on the estimate provided in the May 1998 issue of the Budhan Newsletter, published by the BRPC, Baroda, which in turn was a figure based on the estimate presented by Dr Milind Bokil in an earlier study of DNTs with reference to Maharashtra and some other states. Dr Bokil's statistics were extrapolated by combining some of the reports produced for the Maharashtra government and the Census of India, 1931. It is likely that the Census of India, 2011, as and when the figures are released, will give some idea of the population of the DNTs, provided again that a complete list of the castes and communities 'notified' and 'denotified' gets fully compiled.

in the list of Scheduled Castes, some others in that of the Scheduled Tribes, quite a few in Other Backward Classes, and a few of them are not included in any of these social benefit lists. What is common to DNTs is the fate of being branded as 'born' criminals.

The story of the DNTs goes back to the early years of colonial rule. In those times, whoever opposed the British colonial expansion was perceived as a potential criminal. Particularly, if any attempt was made to oppose the colonial government with the use of arms, the charge of criminality was a certainty. The British did not understand the communities that were non-sedentary. Therefore nomadic communities became suspect in the eyes of the colonial British rulers. The colonial government drafted a unique piece of legislation in 1871, which they thought would tame the nomadic communities. Many of the wandering minstrels, fakirs, petty traders, rustic transporters and disbanded groups of soldiers were included by the British in their list of criminal groups. During the first half of the 19th century, the tribes in the North West frontier were declared 'criminal tribes'. This category became increasingly open ended, and by 1871 the British had prepared an official list of Criminal Tribes. An act to regulate criminal tribes was passed in that year. For instance, the Bhils who had fought the British rule in Khandesh or on the banks of the Narmada and were convicted under section 110 of the Indian Penal Code were to be recognized as criminal tribals. The Criminal Tribes (CT) Act made provisions for establishing reformatory settlements where the criminal adivasis could be kept in confinement and subjected to low paid work. They were required to report to the guard rooms several times every day, so that they did not escape the oppressive settlements. By 1921, the CT Act was extended to cover numerous other tribes in the Madras Presidency, Hyderabad and Mysore. Thus, about the time Indian politics saw the emergence of Mahatma Gandhi as the leader of the freedom struggle Indian society mutely witnessed the emergence of a new class of people who were branded as born criminals. This legislation was called the *Criminal Tribes Act*. The CT Act passed through a series of revisions till 1924. It provided for confiscation of land and other possessions of the so-called criminal tribes and a forced internment. Special areas for confining the 'criminals' were created. They were called settlements. Nearly 200 nomadic communities were brought under the provisions of the CT Act. After Independence, the notification issued during the colonial regime was repealed. Therefore, these communities came to be known as Denotified Tribes. But the stigma attached to them persisted. The members of the public and the police continued to look at them as criminals.

And the police in particular used this situation in an exploitative manner. Little solace was ever offered by the state governments or the central government to the DNTs since they were randomly distributed between the Scheduled Tribes, Scheduled Castes and Other Backward Classes.

Soon after Independence, the communities notified as criminal adivasis were denotified by the government. This notification was followed by the substitution of a series of Acts, generally entitled 'Habitual Offenders Act' (HOA). The denotification and the passing of the HOAs should have ended the misery of the communities penalized under the CT Act. This however did not transpire as the HOAs preserved most of the provisions of the former CT Act, except the premise implicit in it that an entire community can be 'born' criminal. The police forces as well as the people in general were taught to look upon the 'criminal tribes' as born criminals during the colonial times. That attitude continues to persist even today. One does not know if the police training academies in India still teach the trainees that certain communities are habitually criminal; but surely the CT Act is a part of the syllabus leading to the discussion of crime-watch. The result is that every time there is a petty theft in a locality, the DNTs in the neighbourhood become the first suspects. The ratio between the arrests and the convictions of the DNTs needs to be analyzed to see the extent of the harassment caused by the police to this most vulnerable and disadvantaged section of our society. The land possessed by the 'criminal' tribes was already alienated during the colonial rule. After Independence, various state governments have done little to restore their land to them. Schemes for economic uplift do not seem to have benefited them. The illiteracy rate amongst the DNTs is higher than among the Scheduled Castes or the Scheduled Tribes, malnutrition more frequent and provisions for education and health care almost negligible, since most of the DNTs have remained nomadic in habit. Above all, there is no end to the atrocities that the DNTs have to face.

Being illiterate and ignorant of the law of the land, the DNTs know very little about police procedures, and so they often get into difficult situations. The onus of proving innocence rests with them. Mob-lynched, hounded from village to village, starved of all civic amenities, deprived of the means of livelihood and gripped by the fear of police persecution, the DNTs of India are on the run. Freedom has still not reached them. Attempts in isolated pockets made, at best, in a piecemeal manner will not bring about any significant change in the lives of the DNTs in India. For that to happen a radical change in popular perception must occur, and the state will have to squarely own the responsibility of the empowerment of these hounded communities.

In March 1998, Mahasweta Devi was invited by BRPC to give the annual Verrier Elwin Memorial Lecture. She had chosen the DNTs as the theme of her lecture. Laxman Gaikwad, the author of a celebrated autobiography *Uchalya* (1998) (literal meaning: a petty thief), who belongs to one of the denotified communities, was present in Baroda for the lecture. It was a deeply moving lecture. The following day, Mahasweta Devi, Laxman Gaikwad and I decided to form a national forum for the DNT rights which we called the DNT Rights Action Group (DNT-RAG). In order to mobilize the DNTs, we started travelling to various states in India, visiting their habitats, talking to them and listening to heart wrenching stories of the atrocities they have to face. We took up cases of custodial deaths, mob-lynching, rapes and other brutalities to the National Human Rights Commission, the Ministry of Home Affairs, judicial authorities and every possible forum where they needed to be heard. Between 1998 and 2006, the RAG had to plead for justice in several hundred cases of atrocity. It was through these instances that the DNTs of India started voicing their agony in an organized way. Here is an example of a Chhara woman questioning the police authorities, presented as a random sample (BRPC 1998: 14):[4]

Ramilaben Rajubhai Rathod (Chhara), Mahajanwas, Chharanagar, Opp. S. T. Workshop, Jhajijpur, Naroda Road, Ahmedabad, dated 12-10-98, to, The Honourable Chief Justice, Mumbai High Court, Mumbai

SUB: A writ petition to plead for justice on the death of my husband Shri Rajubhai Narubhai Rathod in police lock-up, after he was brutally beaten up.

Honourable Chief Justice *Saheb*,

My husband was arrested on 28th September '98 and locked up in Kandivali Police Station, Mumbai on charges of mere suspicion and was on remand till 7th October '98.

During this time, the police brutally beat up my husband and did not give him anything to eat or drink. As a result, my husband died an unnatural death on 3rd October '98 at midnight in police lock-up. We came to know

---

[4] From the archives of the DNT-RAG, Bhasha Research and Publication Centre.

of his death on 4th October when the *Mumbai Samachar* published the news. I left for Mumbai, with some relatives on the night of 5th October and reached Kandivali Police Station on 6th October. We contacted the Deputy Commissioner of Police, Crime Branch, Shri J. N. Naike and Police Sub Inspector Shri Dipak Katagare. They refused to give us any kind of information. When my brother requested for another post-mortem report, the officials behaved very badly with him. All the relatives submitted a written application for re-examining the case but it was rejected. We were subjected to a great deal of mental stress and the body was handed over to us after great difficulty.

We belong to the Chhara community, considered backward and certified as a Denotified Criminal Tribe. The Police treat us as born criminals. I have three small children — Kajal, age 12 years, Hetal, 9 years, and Jigish, 7 years old. I humbly request you to order a C.B.I. investigation to grant this poor woman compensation and to take the strictest measures against the police officials responsible for this crime and thus grant me justice. I do not have money to hire lawyers. And if somehow I manage to come to Mumbai to file a case, the police may harass me. Please treat this letter as a writ petition and take appropriate action.

I thank you very much.

Yours sincerely,
Ramilaben Rajubhai Rathod

Many writers, painters, filmmakers joined us in these efforts. Several little magazines dedicated to the DNT issues started appearing and various theatre groups took up plays based on the real life stories of the DNTs. Newspapers started reporting our meetings. Films and video documentaries on the life and conditions of the DNTs started circulating among students. Several scholars from other countries took up writing research papers inspired by the work of the RAG, seminars and workshops of activists to discuss the DNT rights started getting organized. In August 1998, Gayatri Chakravorty Spivak visited Baroda and travelled with us to various 'settlements' (previously, 'reformative jails') of the DNTs, and on her return to New York, wrote a petition to the United Nations. I quote its concluding paragraphs:[5]

---

[5] From the archives of the DNT-RAG, Bhasha Research and Publication Centre.

The old settlements have grown into ghettos where outside light hardly penetrates. No educational or employment opportunities worth mentioning are available to the ghetto dwellers. At the same time, there is ample scope to commit crime and to get deeper into it. Organised gangs, in collusion with the police, are eager to recruit them into their armies. As for the communities which were not kept interned during the British regime, they still wander carrying out odd jobs, which have practically lost relevance in the present day world. Most of them are forced to wander into cities in search of livelihood, which is hard to find, as they are not trusted by the public. Police make it more difficult by representing them as dreaded criminals. Avoided by the public, harassed by the police, and occasionally lynched by mobs, their existence is threatened from all sides.

It is unthinkable that a section of people who are among the earliest occupants of this sub-continent, constituting about 6% of its population, should be deprived of a dignified life, and persecuted in the most inhuman manner even after half a century of Independence. During the British period, though confined and used as captive labour, efforts were made to take them away from crime; now, on the other hand, police and vested interests have kept them engaged in criminal activities alone. Both the national and state governments have completely ignored their rights to live decently. Being unorganised and not easily identifiable, they seldom appear in the electoral rolls, and hence, do not attract the attention of political parties. Organisations like the National Human Rights Commission and the United Nations are therefore the sole arbiters to help these communities to achieve justice and regain dignity among the peoples of India.

Though the repugnant Act has been repealed, the perception of the police towards the DNCs [Denotified Communities] has not changed. Both in training and practice, they continue to hold on to the old concept of branding the whole communities as born criminals. The Action Group that has visited some of the surviving settlements has found that they still live a socially isolated life. Further, the *Habitual Offenders Acts, which* the States have passed almost immediately after the repeal of the Criminal Tribes Act, are being used by police to harass the communities. It is necessary, therefore, to initiate action through the Government of India in order to provide Constitutional guarantee for the protection of the human rights of the Denotified and Nomadic Communities.

The Denotified and Nomadic Tribals Rights Action Group has represented this matter to the National Government and the National Human Rights Commission. In many instances of violation of the basic human rights of individuals belonging to Denotified communities, the Rights Action Group has moved High Courts in various states. It has networked with Denotified Communities throughout the country and initiated legal aid services. However, the magnitude of the problem is so enormous that nothing short of full Constitutional guarantee for protection of the inalienable human rights in accordance with the UN [United Nations] Charter of Human Rights is required.

We hope that the United Nations will treat this submission with the seriousness that it deserves and will take the necessary and appropriate steps to advise the Government of India in this regard. We will be happy to furnish further information and documentary evidences to you if necessary (BRPC 1998: 39).

The initiative inspired so much social energy that the RAG soon became a major social movement. During the course of the movement, we were required to meet V. P. Singh and Chandra Shekhar, both of whom had been prime ministers, and Atal Bihari Vajpayee and Dr Manmohan Singh, while they held the office as prime minister. On 14 January 2006, as a small group of her friends had assembled in Delhi to celebrate the 80th birthday of Mahasweta Devi, we received a call from Dr Manmohan Singh to see him. During that meeting, he agreed to take up the DNT issue on the government agenda. Ten days later, one of our associates was invited to chair the National Commission for Denotified, Nomadic and Semi-nomadic Communities. Three months after the DNT Commission was constituted, I received a call from the Prime Minister's office to suggest names for a small committee to function as an advisory group to the Government of India on the DNT issues. The group was called Technical Advisory Group (TAG), and I was made its chairperson. I submitted the TAG report to the Government of India on the International Human Rights Day — 10 December 2006.

It was in January 2007 that Prof. Geoffrey Davis, who was at the BRPC as a Fellow, and I started thinking of creating an innovative international conference of scholars engaged in post-colonial studies so as to bring the life and culture of the indigenous into focus. We met Dr K. K. Chakravarty in August 2007 to seek his collaboration in the effort. The three of us felt that after the inaugural Chotro planned for January 2008, we should invite a Chotro conference devoted to the theme of 'Nomadic Communities'. The present volume of essays is a result primarily of the Chotro-2009 held with this background, strengthened by some essays drawn from the Chotro-2010.

The essays included in the volume should make it clear that for over the last three centuries, the world has increasingly become insensitive to the perspective of the nomads since, as Dr K. K. Chakravarty has often stated in his lectures during the DNT movement, 'to turn the citizens to a sedentary life-style has come to be seen as the mission of the

State' (Chakravarty 2008: 4). Whether this forced transformation of the subject-citizens is to be seen as a purely colonial feat of social engineering or whether to read its pathology in terms of the growth of a capitalist vision of economy and ecology, is a question that needs a far greater study. The record of even the anti-capitalistic nation states on the question of the rights of the nomadic communities has not been any different. The Gypsies have suffered alike in a Fascist regime as in a Communist regime in Europe, and Democracies have not shown any strikingly different approach to them. It was perhaps natural, therefore, for the British colonial government in India to be suspicious of the nomadic communities. Mahasweta Devi writes:[6]

> I think people, who from the time of the *Rigveda*, did not cultivate, or, were not given land, people who were free to choose their own professions and remained contented with very little, who loved to protest and fight and joined the small feudal chiefs, were suspects to the British. The forest dweller and other tribals were something they failed to understand. Even today, one is afraid of people whom one does not understand. So, the Regulation Act xxii of 1793, the same as 1836, the IPC Act of 1861 were not enough. So the infamous Criminal Tribes act of 1871 had to be made. This Act was not enough, so in 1910, and 1920 two other Acts were passed. Throughout India, more than 150 tribes and castes were notified to be criminal tribes. Hunters and fishers, street singers and herbal medicine practitioners, wandering tribes who sang and danced and also made excellent *zari* embroideries, were perceived as 'criminals'.

The story of the listing of the communities, placing them under a scanner of suspicion, formulation of the legal instrument that gave the police unchecked powers, the detention of the communities listed under the colonial law and their brutalization through several generations of exclusion, has not so far been presented from a post-colonial perspective. The text of the Criminal Tribes Act, 1871, and the texts of later modifications to the CTA are included in the volume as a special section so that scholars and activists engaged in re-writing the approach to nomadic communities can find in these otherwise uninteresting legal documents a 'mirror of history' reflecting the 'defacement' of the love for freedom and beauty that the nomads of the world have contributed to the human civilization. The editors would like to hope that this volume of essays

---

[6] From the archives of the DNT-RAG, Bhasha Research and Publication Centre.

provides an impetus to an area of research that will have an immense importance in entering the social imagination of colonialism.

G. N. Devy
Baroda, May 2011

References

Bhasha Research and Publication Centre (BRPC). 1998. *Budhan, Newsletter of Denotified and Nomadic Tribes — Rights Action Group*, October.

Chakravarty, K. K. 2008. 'Communities, Culture and Conservation'. Academy Foundation Lecture, Bhasha Research and Publication Centre, 17 November.

Devy, G. N., Geoffrey V. Davis and K. K. Chakravarty. 2009. *Indigeneity: Culture and Representation*, New Delhi: Orient BlackSwan.

———. 2011. *Voice and Memory: Indigenous Imagination and Expression*. New Delhi: Orient BlackSwan.

Gaikwad, Laxman. 1998. *Uchalya*, New Delhi: Sahitya Akademi.

I

Identity, History and Protest

CT/DNT in Literary and Social Texts in India

Vibha S. Chauhan

I

The year 1871 . . . The English laughed . . . Criminals by birth . . . The Act
was implemented — The professions of groups like Kabootara, Moghiya,
Kalander, Sansi, Pardi, Mampat, Auidya began to be treated as crime . .
. They were tied down by the pen of the British government . . . Yet they
smiled fearlessly and said to each other — we are not lone twigs but bound
together in bundles impossible to break. We will endure the penalty of
being the companions of Maharani of Chittor as well as Rani of Jhansi.
Yes, we shall endure everything. We have become slaves of the register
in the police station and cannot go anywhere without putting our thumb
marks there. We are especially watched during nights, with the village
headman and the police daroga becoming incarnations of the omniscient
God . . . Naked bodies, severe cold, scorching heat and rains that cracked
the skies were their companions. Who bothered about how many of them
died or how many survived? The police registers turned into records of
Yamaraj, the God of death. These are the people — like ghosts and spirits
— whose feet leave behind no marks, their footprints disappearing from
the footpaths (Pushpa 2004: 130–33).

Thus goes the narration in Maitreyi Pushpa's Hindi novel *Alma
Kabootari* about a group of nomadic people — known as 'Kabootaras' —
branded as criminals at birth (ibid.)! Tribes like the Kabootaras were notified as criminals at birth by the infamous 'Criminal Tribes Act' (CTA)
formulated by the colonial British government in India in 1871. This

was accompanied with the preparation of a list of communities that were primarily nomadic and/or inhabited the forest. The British government had by then already legitimized its authority on forest land by passing the Indian Forest Act of 1865 that granted it control over forest land and produce. This led to a loss of grazing land as well as forest produce for a number of communities. Several nomadic communities that were not tied to the forest were traders who carried goods to remote corners of the country.[1] These communities too were adversely affected by the introduction of the road and rail network in the country during the 1950s that made the transport of goods much easier even in far-flung corners of the country. Bereft of sources of livelihood many of these forest-based and nomadic communities resisted the British policies that weighed heavily in favour of the settled and agricultural communities. This preference of the British government for the settled communities was to be expected, for the coffers of the British government were filled by the tax paid by them on land. Nomadic communities on the other hand, fell outside the net of tax collection. Moreover, the colonial powers found it difficult to administer groups of people who were always on the move. It was with the intention of tightening their noose over the nomadic communities that kept slipping out of their control, that the British passed the CTA. The Act stipulated that the members of the communities 'notified' under the Act register themselves with the police. Restrictions were imposed on their movement and place of residence. A large number of these communities were forced to live in 'settlements' where they laboured like low-paid slaves. It was in 1952 that the Indian state repealed the CTA and 'denotified' the communities listed under it. The story of shame and pain, however, did not finish here. The government passed another piece of legislation in 1959, known as the Habitual Offenders Act (HOA) which continued with several features similar to the CTA and was often used to repress the Denotified and Nomadic Tribes (DNTs).

The novel *Alma Kabootari* describes the travails of the group of the Kabootara men and women living in the Kabootara *basti* (poor neighbourhood) with its makeshift shacks precariously existing on the margins of a village with its own dynamics of familial and caste morality (Pushpa 2004). Despite the apparently unbridgeable social divide between the village and the Kabootara *basti*, the lives of people from these two conglomera-

---

[1] Refer to the discussion about Koravars — the community trading mainly in salt — in Radhakrishna (2001).

tions are intertwined in a web of complex personal and group relation-ships. These were further embedded within the political and historical context representative of the unequal power relations that continue to exist in contemporary Indian society with its contradictory trends of lib-eral democratic framework coexisting with categories like caste, creed and community. The narrative of *Alma Kabootari* explores the tensions generated through the presence of a domineering state and police and various strategies through which the Kabootara men and women nego-tiate with the state to eventually unsettle the existing social order and generate a trajectory facilitating their movement from the periphery of society towards the centre of social and political control.

Such transformation in personal and social relations is worked out in the novel through various means that the Kabootara community adopts in an attempt to adjust and accommodate with their extreme degradation (ibid.). At an imaginative level they continue to hold on to the memory of a glorious past that is often a stark contrast to their lived experience. This aspect of preservation and continuation of a *srishtitatva* (creation myths) generally rooted in divinity or narratives of a lost magnificence, is a common feature of a large number of marginalized communities. These become significant for providing these communities with a perspective through which they look at their past as well as their present; the pres-ence and absence of social status; their duties and rights; their values and ethics. Though existing in the realm of imagination, these memories and myths do not exist as mere fancies but often play a dynamic role in the creation of individual and community identity. While some scholars consider the continuation of community identity as a major deterrent in the growth and evolution of an egalitarian democratic system in India, others perceive it as holding the possibility of engendering politically active pressure groups within parliamentary democracy, with commu-nity identity getting to play an important role in the democratic process of Indian polity. The debate goes on but what gets established in the process is the extremely volatile inter-connectedness between mythical community identities and the social, cultural and political assertion of marginalized groups.

The nomadic communities — with their proverbial 'homes on their backs' — make up as much as 7 per cent of the population in India and probably belong to the lowest rung of the deprivation ladder even amongst the impoverished communities. The DNT — approximately six crore in number (Devy 2006: 21) — within this group of nomadic com-munities are even more vulnerable than others due to their stigmatized past that continues to haunt them. However, their imaginative resources and a talent to tell stories is something that neither the sedentary society nor the state and the police could seize from them. Many of these apparently whimsical stories are actually articulations of identity assertions and protests against the hegemonic social order that has kept these communities tied to their depressed status. Imaginative constructs have often become agents of social and political transformation with boundaries between myth, fiction and reality often getting blurred, making it impossible to distinguish one from the other. The concepts of truth being stranger than reality and fiction being more real than fact really hold true for the DNT whose lives, characters and livelihood have been controlled and constructed by a bizarre piece of legislation rooted in the irrational dogma of their being born as criminals. Swaddled in a phantasmagoria since birth, existing as 'ghosts and spirits' — 'whose feet leave behind no marks' (Pushpa 2004: 133) — the DNT have been living in a physical and emotional no-man's land. They are, however, not phantoms but flesh- and blood-creatures sensitive to pain and humiliation. Their repressed existence over generations may create the impression of an absence of change or protest, yet these communities, like all human beings, are not immune to their oppression. The necessity to assert their self-respect and identity has found expression sometimes through their cultural constructs like narratives of the past, myths and rituals, creation of iconic figures, and in recent times through the creation of a political space in the political realm of parliamentary democracy.

This chapter will attempt to discuss the various forms of protests, through which the nomadic communities and especially the DNT have used their cultural resources and political potential to challenge the hegemony of socially powerful classes and castes. This will be based on a close study of literary as well as social texts that are inextricably mixed to create personal and social histories that have been denied to these groups. History provides a way of looking at one's own location within the social network, and an absence of history, or having a history generated by groups that seek to reproduce repressive relations, is bound to reinforce marginalization. A search for identity and dignity often begins with a search for history. This may happen through a reinterpretation of myths and stories of origins that provide the deprived and repressed communities with imaginative constructs like myths. History and the creation of histories through myths and stories of origins are often as much an articulation of degradation as an attempt to make sense of the irrationality of extremes of deprivation that seems to be the irrevocable fate of these communities. Many scholars, however, interpret the myths of repressed communities as being the only mode of protest and subversion available to them. It is within the mythical time and situation that these communities can challenge the order of the dominant social groups that is difficult, if not impossible, to challenge in their lived experience.

While it is true that myths are complex social creations that sometimes assist individuals to adjust with their deprivation by reinforcing community ethics and norms, it is equally true that they may also possess elements of defiance. Resistance, however, needs to transcend the mythical universe and dialectically impact socio-political structures of power to bring in any change in lived relations. A strong sense of shared history and myth can result in a reinforcement of identities that may become the cohesive force for constituting pressure groups within a democracy. This creation of a political space, in turn, can then lead to a further strengthening of the community identity.

This chapter will try to investigate these various forms of protest. Starting from the protest inherent in imaginative constructs of some of the DNT communities, the chapter will move on to examine the various strategies that these communities — along with some other deprived communities — adopt to create new histories and new mythologies resulting in the creation of new structures of political power with a substantial space for themselves. The analysis of these issues will be based on literary sources, historical records, autobiographies, and political movements occurring in the past as well as in contemporary India.

II

Ranajit Guha (1985) sees myths of marginalized groups as an expression of subversion and protest against myths of the socially dominant groups. An appropriate entry point into the discussion would be the enquiry regarding what constitutes marginality and what factors determine the marginality of specific groups of people or narratives. Guha in 'The Small Voice of History' (1996), which discusses the concepts of 'marginalization' and 'hegemonic', says that 'some discrimination is quite clearly at work here — some unspecified values and unstated criteria' (ibid.: 1) are used to determine what is dominant/mainstream as well as its opposite, the marginalized. He goes on to suggest that, 'the nominating authority is none other than an ideology for which the life of the state is all there is to history [substitute the term 'history' with dominance/hegemonic/mainstream]. This creates a place for itself through its availability and appeals to "a reading public, progeny of the printing technology'" (Guha 1996: 2). Guha goes on to say that the marginalized groups have 'small voices which are drowned in the noise of statist commands . . . They have many stories to tell — stories, which for their complexities are unequalled by statist discourse and indeed opposed to its abstract and oversimplified modes' (ibid: 2–3; for parts of the discussion, see Chauhan 2005).

It is such a story of a 'small' community with a 'small' voice that the Bangla novel *Nagini Kanya* (Bandopadhyay 1992) tells about the community of the Santhali snake-charmers, a forest-based nomadic community of about 30 huts 'in the grasslands on the banks of Bhagirathi' (ibid.: 22) in Bengal.

> Their journey begins soon after the festival of *naag panchami* . . . Their clans and families have traveled around for ages. After crossing spots like Hangarmukhi, Magarkhali and Hanskhali, the boats of the snake charmers form rows and float on the waters of Mother Ganga. The boats carry baskets with snakes, clay pots for cooking, and monkeys, goats and humans for street shows. Not just the Santhali snake charmers, there are many other groups of snake charmers too who travel around. Some on boats and others on foot carrying the *bahangi*[2] on their shoulders. This wandering is the law of their community — their *dharma*, the rule of their caste . . . They travel from village to village, putting up shows like the snake dance, and games of the monkey and the goat for the householders. They keep moving from one area to another. Months pass by and then one day, they return back home (ibid.: 37).

However, even after they return 'home', the Santhali snake-charmers cannot cultivate land because of their community ban against cultivation. Whether at 'home' or while travelling, the Santhali snake-charmers are dependent on the forest produce and the settled community for survival. The men and especially the women hold shows even during their travels.

> After tying their boats to the shore, the women leave their group and come away. They take the snakes, monkeys and goats and playing on their drum, go from door to door calling, 'Oh! My dear mistress, may your husband live forever! You, with gold and good fortune! With moonlike children!

---

[2] A *bahangi* is a bamboo pole with two baskets hanging at both ends to carry material.

Come and see the snake charmer's show! Come and see the black *nagini*.[3]
. . . The women leave their chores and come running. They cannot stop
themselves. These black women are very mysterious. It's probably true
that they know magic (ibid.: 46–47).

The distrust about the snake-charmers is something that is not limited
to them but has plagued the nomadic communities since colonial times.
Street entertainment began to be seen as a threat to public order. The
large crowd that collected around performers like singers, dancers and
acrobats made the local authorities nervous (Radhakrishna 2001: 11).
Moreover, with the concept of work excluding all but routine, paid
wage and agricultural labour — the kind of 'work' that could ensure
a steady increase in colonial collection of tax — serious accusations
about the nomadic communities being 'idle, lazy and not keen to work'
(Radhakrishna 2008: 16) began to gain currency. Booth Tucker, head of
the Salvation Army (ibid.),[4] in India writing about the 'criminal tribes'
wrote, 'When we asked them to till the land, or work in a factory, they
were shocked. Work? they said; we never work, we just sing and dance'
(ibid.: 16).

This comment is rooted in the understanding of work being possible
only in sedentary living and overlooks the culture, mythology and history of nomadic communities, ignoring the fact of a strong community
identity of the members being a prerequisite for the existence of the community itself. This is reinforced by strict social codes that evolve out of a
shared past and from the association of myth with divinity that grants it
a status that can neither be challenged nor violated. Community ethics
and morality being generally rooted in mythology, it is inconceivable for
the members of the community not to comply with these. If the Santhal
community were banned from cultivating fields, it would be a serious
lapse for them to do so under any pressure whatsoever.

This divide between the nomadic and the settled communities is
reflected in several cultural practices and reversals of dominant values,
for instance, the main deity of the snake-charmers' community in *Nagini
Kanyar Kahini* is not Shiva, one of the chief gods of the mainstream Hindu

---

[3] A *nagini* is a female snake.
[4] Meena Radhakrishna in her book *Dishonoured by History* (2001) discusses
how around the second decade of the 20th century, the Salvation Army — a
missionary organization — was put in charge of some nomadic communities in
India which had been declared 'criminal tribes' a few years earlier.

trinity but the female goddess Manasa (Bandopadhyay 1992). While it is true that Manasa has been assimilated into Hinduism and is worshipped by Hindu women, especially in Bengal, the Manasa of the snake-charmers is entirely different from the classically beautiful Hindu goddess who is born from the lotus and sits on it. She has 'the smell and colour of the lotus — and the same pity and love' (Östör 1984: 69). The snake-charmers' Manasa has soaked up all the poison that she rules over.

> [She] sits on a throne decorated with snakes, drinking poison and spitting it out. In a split second this poison increases a million times. The blue sky absorbs that poison and turns black. The breeze gets loaded with poison. This breeze burns the body (ibid.: 108).

The pot of Manasa worshipped by the snake-charmers is a simple ordinary clay pot, very different from the ornamental pots decorated with statues that are worshipped in the Hindu Manasa temples.

> The most elaborate Manasa *bari* [pot] incorporates . . . an image of the Goddess surrounded by all the characters of the Manasa legend. The whole complex is built of clay, with layers placed upon layers, as limbs of a tree, branching out of a hidden, central tube . . . [Some others are] many storied representations of the whole *purana* reaching a height of seven feet (ibid.: 40)

There also exist many differences between several narratives of the 'statist' Hindu society and the 'marginalized' nomadic communities like the Santhali snake-charmers. The popular story about the victory of Krishna over Kaali Nag exists in a very different form in *Nagini*. In the story in *Srimad Bhagvat* (Shastri 1948), Krishna as a young lad, while playing, jumps into the Yamuna river to get back his ball. He has a battle with Kaali Nag under water and emerges victorious, standing on the Nag's hood playing his flute. Krishna, the incarnation of Vishnu, becomes the undisputed master of Kaali Nag.

The snake-charmers however believe that things happened very differently:

> They say the Nag did not accept defeat in the battle. After a long battle the Nag said to Krishna, 'I will die but not accept defeat. I will do that only on one condition, which is that you must become my son-in-law. You must marry my daughter. I will accept defeat only if you do this.' The cunning Kanhaiya agrees. The music of the wedding starts playing in Naglok. The Nag bends his head in defeat. Krishna takes up the Nag's most deadly

weapon, the jewel on his forehead and promises to come back. 'I will soon be back', he says and goes away. But he does not return (Bandopadhyay 1992: 140).

Some scholars would interpret both the form that the Santhali Manasa takes as well as their version of the story about Krishna's victory over Kaali Nag as expressions of subversion and protest against the dominant mainstream culture by the community of the snake-charmers. This approach certainly confers the element of agency and protest upon the snake-charmers but appears to be contradictory to opinions of some historians like D. D. Kosambi. He discusses the process of social development in which the ancient matriarchal society gave way to the patriarchal and the evolution of food-gathering stages into settled, food-producing societies. Kosambi describes how the change happened only after a great deal of protest from the matriarchal, food-producing societies. He quotes the following lines from the *Rigveda* as an example of the repression that patriarchy had perpetuated against matriarchy:

> This heroic and virile deed didst thou also do, O Indra, that thou didst strike down (or kill) the evil plotting woman, the daughter of heaven. Usas, verily the daughter of heaven, the great, to be regarded as great didst thou crush, O Indra. Usas fled from the shattered wagon in fright, when the Bull (Indra) had rammed her . . . she fled to the furthest distance (Kosambi 1972: 63).

The battle referred to is fought between the goddess of the dawn Usas and the young god, Indra. Usas is an ancient goddess in spite of her youth and virginity, and Indra the new leader displaces her in an open conflict. Kosambi questions why Usas was attacked at all by Indra. Moreover, when attacked, why is she not killed but driven to the furthest distance? Kosambi offers some answers himself in his writings which are replete with strong evidence of the existence of a matriarchal system and its gradual, though unwilling, surrender to patriarchy. The root cause for the open conflict, for instance, between Usas [a prominent goddess in *Rigveda*] and Indra is explained by Kosambi as lying 'in a clash of cults, that of the old mother-goddess being crushed . . . by the new war-god of the patriarchal invaders, Indra. That she survives after being "killed" can only indicate progressive . . . assimilation of her surviving pre-Aryan worshippers' (ibid.).

A conflict similar to the one between Indra and Usas occurs between Manasa, the principal deity of the Santhali snake-charmers, and the patriarchal god Shiva. The battle is however, a proxy one between the followers of the two deities and involves deceit and hoodwinking as well. Before their defeat, the worshippers of Manasa, the Santhali snake-charmers were renowned curers of snakebite and enjoyed status and respect in society. They were no untouchables. They had the right to wear the creeper of the poison-killing plant like a *janeu*, the holy thread,[5] around their shoulders. And they also resembled the ascetic bauls. Since the knowledge and cure of poison is priceless, they took no money to cure snakebite, just a small gift of charity (Bandopadhyay 1992: 20). After their defeat in the battle, the snake-charmers lose everything. Shiva's command ensures that they lose their 'caste, respect, wealth . . . that nobody touches them and nobody allows them to stay with them' (ibid.: 22).

It is then that the snake-charmers begin their long journey and settle down in a few huts on the banks of the Bhagirathi river. However, they carry the pot of Manasa and continue to worship her as their main deity. The ban against cultivating land continues to exist, resulting in their dependence on the forest and the settled society for survival. 'They continued to be the people of the past. . . . They maintained the tradition of the forest' (ibid.: 119). However, their community collapses when the external world intrudes.

We thus find that if we consider the simple shape of the Manasa *kumbha* (pot) and the story of Krishna winning over Kaali Nag with deceit as being representations of protest, we would be privileging the ornamental pots in Hindu temples as well as the narrative of Krishna's victory over the Nag in the *Purana* as being original, authentic and older, a fact challenged by historians like Kosambi who would interpret the events in *Nagini* as a fictional representation of the violation of the matriarchal custom and appropriation of the older matriarchal deities into 'Shiva's or Vishnu's household (and also) enlist food gathering aboriginals into a much greater food productive society' (1983: 39). What we view therefore is theft of knowledge, custom, culture and tradition of the nomadic tribe by the settled society, who also modify it to suit their ideology of dominance, and then use this to create the 'dominant values of the state' which become the norm against which the nomads are eventually measured.

---

[5] A symbol of traditional high caste.

The discussion so far must not be taken as an attempt to establish the fact of absence of protest by nomadic communities against repressive social structures. In fact, these communities are the ones who put up the most severe resistance against the colonial state (see Chauhan 2009). That, in fact, became one of the reasons for the colonial government to trap these communities in the tentacles of the CTA (see Radhakrishna 2001). Protest against the repressor, however, becomes visible when it moves out of the mythical imagination to impact the lived relations and the socio-political power structure. The mode of such a protest would be largely determined by the form of discrimination practised against the communities. Protest against a colonial power, for example, would vary in its strategy from that which is carried out within a democratic system. It is here that myth and the creation of new myths and histories can play a significant role in cementing the identification of specific groups with the potential of contending with ideologies of dominance.

III

The transcendence of protest of 'small' groups like the nomadic communities from the realm of mythology to the world of inequities and repression influences relations of power if it manages in some way to impact the state structure. It is this process that can be traced in literary narratives as well as the political sphere in India since colonial times.

Protest often originates quite unexpectedly from unremitting repression in most unexpected situations and moments. It is such an expression of discontent and solidarity that grew out of the slave-like conditions of several settlements being managed by the Salvation Army. The inmates followed a strict routine. One of them who had stayed at the Bhatpurwa settlement has said in an interview that 'there was little scope for demonstration in the settlement' (quoted in Shankar 1979: 139). The unrelenting discipline of the settlements was intended to stamp out any danger of challenge, to inculcate the ability to perform and value routine labour — either in the fields or the private production units that the government was committed to encouraging — and to break down the community into families infused with Brahmanical and Victorian moral values. Settlements allotted land to individual families and slowly exposed them to settled life. It was after this that inmates in some settlements were sent out to work in factories as wage labourers. It was this trajectory that the Stuartpuram settlement in Guntur followed, where from 1913 onwards, about 6,000 Yerukulas — the Telugu branch of the Korava community who were declared a Criminal Tribe in 1911 — were sedentarized (Radhakrishna 2001: 128).

The Salvation Army actually worked as an arm of the British government and keeping the colonial economic policies in mind, decided to accrue income both from agriculture as well as factory labour. It was decided that men should be asked to stay back in the settlement for cultivating land and the female population be employed in the Indian Leaf Tobacco Development Company (ILTD). The Salvation Army had the support of government laws that enabled them to apply curbs on any aspiration for any form of personal privilege or entitlement for the inmates. The families could cultivate land but could not possess it and within the ILTD factory, Section 27 (limiting the working hours per week) and Section 28 (limiting the working hours per day) of the Factories Act were revoked. This equipped the ILTD management to impose double working shifts on the workers.

The legislation, however, did not succeed in controlling the inmates. The resistance against the repressive policies took the shape of a cooperative society in the settlement and a workers' union in the factory. The men organized themselves and got ready to spend their own money to irrigate the land with the ambition of having a right over the produce. In an attempt to stem this movement, the Salvation Army discharged a large number of men, many of whom found work at the ILTD factory.

The long hours of work at the ILTD factory was back-breaking but it brought a bargaining power to the workers who soon realized that it would be difficult to substitute them. Double shifts at work had led to no turnover of new workers, which became the management's weakness and the workers' strength. There was a prolonged strike in 1938 that ended only after the management agreed to the demands of workers like maternity benefits, facility during monthly periods, place and time for tiffin, the presence of a woman doctor and more and better crèches.

What was remarkable was that the community identity of workers as 'Criminal Tribes' (CT) — that was an identity given to them by the British — was utilized by the union to consolidate itself. The CT identity became a strong reason for mobilization and solidarity of the workers. The following comment about the cohesiveness of the Yerukula community made at least a decade earlier by the author W. J. Hatch proved to be true at this time:

> Trade unionism of the most thorough-going kind and united action was necessary in [their] tribal existence . . . [They practised] group thinking

and believed in group action . . . they formed themselves into a closed brotherhood and would on no account betray their fellow clansmen (Hatch 1928: 67, quoted in Radhakrishna 2001: 127–45).[6]

It is this community identity of the DNT community that is a curse for the Kabootaras in Maitreyi Pushpa's novel *Alma Kabootari*. It describes the extreme deprivation and discrimination the community lives under. Kadambai, a Kabootari, describes the lives of their community when she tries to persuade her young son Rana to accept and live the life of a Kabootara:

> To get beaten and to beat, to get killed and to kill — that is what life means to us. The quack, the witchdoctor, the panchayat head, and police are our gods. People from privileged castes are our guardians and masters. Hunger and thirst are our companions. When our body begins to burn in hot weather, we take a dip in the pond on the sly. When the bones begin to crack in the cold, we steal some dry twigs from the jungle and heat our bodies. All we desire is that people must forgive us (Pushpa 2004: 99).

The narrative of the novel moves on through time and concludes with a political event that sees Alma — the character from whom the novel takes its title — located at the centre of it. Alma is the educated daughter of Ramsingh, a Kabootara who had been educated by his mother Bhuri in the hope that education would ensure a better life for him. Ramsingh, however, is never accepted by a society that believes him to be a born criminal. He manages to get selected for the job of a policeman but is not allowed to join when it is discovered that he is a Kabootara, since the police believed that '[t]he Kabootaras were worse than even the dacoits and murderers who committed crimes out of no choice and not as a profession' (ibid.: 212). He eventually does manage to become a schoolteacher and soon realizes that he had got the job because it brought no 'power' or control to him. 'Making him a teacher does not change anything much. He will continue to be under control of the villagers. Even the government understands this well' (ibid.: 102). Ramsingh also discovers soon that despite his education and the job, he continues to be subservient to the police. 'He had to give a part of salary

---

[6] All the other facts regarding the settlement at Stuartpuram and the ILTD factory are also from the chapter 'From Itinerant Community to Industrial Wageworkers: Stuartpuram Settlement' in Radhakrishna (2001: 127–45).

in the police station and another part in the development office . . . He was not free from the suspicion of the police. The jail was kept ready to receive him any time' (Pushpa 2004: 101–2).

The novel moves on and we find that despite having a burning desire to work for the upliftment of the Kabootara community, Ramsingh ends up at the other end of the spectrum. Trapped by the police, he reaches a point where he becomes a pawn in the hands of the police, leading them to innocent Kabootara men who are killed in false encounters. It is not long before Ramsingh himself is killed and Alma, his 17-year-old daughter, kidnapped by the agents of major politicians. She is imprisoned in a house in Jhansi where she is repeatedly raped by politicians. The words 'Alma Kabootari' are tattooed on her arm as a constant reminder of her fallen state, her lack of all rights and complete vulnerability. Alma, however, manages to escape and reach the house of Sriram Shastri, the Minister for Social Welfare in Madhya Pradesh.

The novel never lets us forget the impoverished condition of the Kabootaras. We are told that the

> Kabootara man never possesses any land or fields. He has no right over the well and the pond. Yet one must live on. To do that one must steal and collect whatever one can. Train yourself to sleep under the roofless sky. Achieve mastery over seasons (ibid.: 113).

Despite this, we are not allowed to forget that the Kabootaras do have a space — however technical and/or ineffective — within a democratic political system. 'They may be rejects of society but they do continue to be voters' (ibid.). It is realized even by the powerful exploiters of the Kabootaras that they could win elections with their support. The police and the privileged castes see this as a threat to their hegemony.

> They were afraid that very soon the police may stop getting not just the weekly commission but even their salaries. Right now the Kabootaras may use reservation as a crutch but soon they would shake themselves awake . . . [The police and their accomplices] had become nervous about the possibility of awareness about their rights taking root in the Denotified Tribes' (ibid.: 105).

And it is exactly this trajectory that Alma's life takes. Her identity as a Kabootari was indelibly branded on her arm with the assumption of reinforcing her inferior identity as a member of the DNT. It is this, however, that becomes Alma's major strength in the political situation that she manages to enter through her marriage with Sriram Shastri, who is eventually shot down by his political rivals. Alma comes to realize the power of numbers through several deprived communities who were willing to support her because of their identification with the tattoo. She also understands the need for self-representation and how their impoverished condition had been exploited by

> the city people and debates on paper. They get excited by watching the films they make about the repressed and the deprived. This is also one of their pleasures. They of course know nothing about the wretched agony of real sores. The real job of social welfare is to throw a veil over the wounds brimming with pus (ibid.: 372).

The political parties too recognize the value of having a candidate like Alma. After Sriram Shashtri's murder, 'the ruling party announces the possibility of having Srimati Alma Shastri as their candidate for elections' (ibid.: 390). This is where the novel ends and the possibility of Alma bringing about a change in the condition of the DNT and other deprived communities is left in the realm of conjecture.

However, autobiographies of some major writers and activists belonging to the DNT establish the significant role that education and awareness of rights through education has played in their protests against discrimination. Laxman Gaikwad in his autobiography *Uchalya* (Marathi) translated into Hindi as *Uthaigeer* (2000) describes the extreme deprivation that he lives through. In the Preface of his autobiography, Gaikwad discusses how the community of Uthaigeers that he was born into has been spurned by 'the *varna* system as well as the social organization' (ibid.: 5) existing around him. He goes on to describe the degradation that he saw around him since his birth and how his protest and activism have grown out of the pain of this humiliation:

> Since my childhood, I have been a witness to the poverty, helplessness, agony of hunger and extreme deprivation of the Uthaigeer community. I gradually evolved into an activist. As a member of this community, I identified with the ache that each one of them lived through . . . I have written this [autobiography] with the purpose of bringing the distress of these people in front of everybody (ibid.).

Uthaigeer establishes that the act of writing a deprived community into existence is itself an expression of protest. Described as 'narratives of pain' these become a means of consolidating various repressed communities through their shared experience of discrimination. Not only do these autobiographies create an autonomous space within the literary texts, most of them also discuss ways of resistance and the evolution of a new social order.

Gaikwad's strategy in *Uthaigeer* is to form an alliance of all deprived groups to fight against discrimination. He talks about the resistance that he builds up amongst the workers in the cotton mill. The workers worked under extreme oppression.

> The jobbers used to beat up the workers. Did not give them attendance. Used to send them home if they were late even by a couple of minutes. Even for minor reasons, they banned their coming to work for a fortnight. Eight hours of work was recorded only as four . . . Workers doing night shifts found it difficult to wake up even after the siren went on . . . The jobbers used to brutally beat them with wet wooden sticks (Gaikwad 2000: 113).

Gaikwad starts a union of the workers that eventually goes on strike for fulfillment of their demands. Gaikwad goes on an indefinite hunger strike. Finally the union wins the battle. Gaikwad then moves on with the hope of using his experience in organizing the DNT. His ambition is to consolidate these communities, to stop sending children for theft and put them in school . . . It was decided that a conference of these communities be organized and this resulted in the first conference of the DNT in 1978 (ibid.: 134).

He goes on to say,

> I began to strive towards opening an educational institution on behalf of [my group] *Pathroot Samaj Sangathan.*[7] After trying for very long I was successful in registering an education institution for the Denotified Tribes at Kathwa in 1979 (ibid.: 140).

The facts regarding Stuartpuram settlement and Gaikwad's *Uthaigeer* reveal two parallel processes at work. The effort of the members of the CT/DNT to free themselves of the stigma of being criminals at birth goes hand-in-hand with the construction of a community identity that binds and consolidates groups not merely for reasons of similar forms of oppression they are forced to live under but also because of a common history they share. This, however, is history that is unwritten and unrecorded. Ramsingh in *Alma Kabootari*, while narrating what he calls 'the story of our ancestors . . . our personal history' to Rana and Alma, says once: '[o]ur history has not been recorded anywhere' (Pushpa 2004: 126). Yet,

---

[7] Pathroot (name of the place) Social Organization.

this 'personal history' has been carried down the generations orally and offers the rationale for their present situation. At complete variance with the 'official' version, the memory of this historical past establishes the historical contributions of these communities to the process of nation-building and confers upon them the right to demand their space in society. This agency of orality and imagination in the creation of history has the potential of generating dissent and becoming an emancipatory force through intervention into democratic structures. It is this process that the next and concluding section of this chapter will briefly examine.

IV

Ramsingh traces the history of his community to Rani Padmini of Chittor, who — it is believed — decided to perform *jauhar* (jumping into the burning pyre) to save her chastity. However, he says that this is the story generated by the privileged castes for whom 'it is the duty of a woman to perform *jauhar*, with the women from the Rajput caste burning themselves to ashes rather than allowing another man to touch their bodies. This is what they call a chaste life' (Pushpa 2004: 128). The Kabootaras however believe this to be far from the truth. Ramsingh continues to say:

> My mother used to say that Rani Padmini did not die. My mother heard this from her grandmother, and she in turn from her grandmother . . . Padmini had managed to run away with some of her female companions and soldiers. All status and respect had vanished. Life had taken away everything from her. She felt that the most valuable thing that remained with her was her life . . . The Rani crossed many frontiers. The small group of people went ahead day and night crossing hills, rivers and valleys . . . This endless running away sapped strength out of many of her fol-lowers. The food finished and the weapons started giving way.
>
> Rani ordered her wilting followers, 'Let it be deceit now! Rob the food being carried for the Sultan. Enter the camps of soldiers and steal their weapons. Attract the soldiers and then stab them.
>
> The Rani moved ahead . . . Babies were born on roads, hills and banks of rivers . . . They [grew] to be handsome and strong . . . The children of Rani Padmini! . . . The battling generations that ran away from Chittor, roamed through the forests.
>
> Those who brought rations were called Banjaras; those who sang and danced, Kabootaras; Moghiyas were knowledgeable about herbs and medi-cines; those who were experts in crossing rivers and valleys became Nats; Gudiya Lohars forged weapons; those who earned a livelihood through performance of bears and monkeys became Kalanders (ibid.: 129).

The story connects the communities with their past and their refusal to compromise with the Sultan. It gives details of the immense ordeal they lived through only to maintain their liberty. Padmini for them does not represent the values of decorum and chastity of the privileged castes. She becomes an icon of freedom, courage and tenacity — the qualities that she transfers to her descendants.

Another icon for these communities is the figure of Jhalkaribai, a close companion of Rani of Jhansi Laxmibai. Jhalkaribai is believed to have saved Laxmibai while continuing to battle with the British till she died. Her story is narrated thus in *Alma Kabootari*:

> Jhalkaribai resembled Rani Laxmibai. Pooran Koeri and Bhau Bhakshi (both belonging to deprived castes) were demolishing the British army. The battle had reached its peak. Rani felt she was in danger. A Koeri woman named Jhalkaribai, who served the Rani, managed to smuggle Rani out of the Bhanredi Gate, along with a handful of trusted soldiers. [Jhalkaribai] came to the front and gave up her life fighting (Pushpa 2004: 289).

A survey done to study the legends, myths, heroes and icons of poor and underprivileged communities in the small towns and villages of Uttar Pradesh revealed an immense popularity of several heroes at the grassroots level, with Jhalkaribai being prominent among them (Narayan 2006). The story of Jhalkaribai being the true warrior instead of Laxmibai as popularized by the nationalist historians actually becomes a narrative of the marginalization of the Dalits and their culture. The story of Jhalkaribai has however, continued to live in folk stories, folklores and conversations, with many people believing her to be divine. Jhalkaribai and her courage is a common subject of songs of many devotional Dalit groups. Many like the following verse were composed as retaliation to the songs about the bravery of Laxmibai:

Jai Jhalkari Durga, Kali
Jai, Jai Ma
Angrezon ka garba tune
Chur, chur kiya

(Hail Jhalkari Durga, Kali
Hail, Hail Mother
The pride of the British
You shattered to smithereens) (ibid.: 118).

The song is evidence of the resistance against the hegemonic culture that has pushed the disempowered castes to the periphery of social control and respectability. The Koree/Koeri caste to which Jhalkaribai is supposed to have belonged is one such caste. Jhalkaribai has gradually evolved into an icon of contesting histories of Dalits and other oppressed groups that have entered the arena of political mobilization and social control. This reinvention is based on a reconstruction of the past — though neglected — glory of the Dalits and unfolds the creation of the culture of dissent that plays a prominent role in ideological construction in the democratic context.

The Kabootaras too preserve Jhalkaribai as a character in the narrative of their own 'personal history'. Her entry into the world of politics — like that of Alma — has brought in self-representation of the marginalized sections of people. Yet, unlike Alma, the hope for change does not exist only in the world of conjecture but has begun to take shape in the realm of socio-political power. We can just hope that assertiveness of a large section of people, including the DNT would result in empowering those who live like 'ghosts and spirits'. May their footprints not just leave behind marks but also construct new roads leading to a world without discrimination.

References

Bandopadhyay, Tarashankar. 1992 [1952]. *Nagini Kanya*, trans. Gauri Banarjee. New Delhi: Bharati Bhasha Prakashan.

Chauhan, Vibha S. 2005. 'Mythical and the Real: Protest and Marginalisation', *Journal of the School of Language, Literature and Culture Studies*, 4: 133–43.

———. 2009. 'Crystallizing Protest into Movement: Adivasi Community in History, Society and Literature" in G. N. Devy, Geoffrey V. Davis and K. K. Chakravarty (eds), *Indigeneity: Culture and Representation*, pp. 55–69. New Delhi: Orient BlackSwan.

Devy, G. N. 2006. *Nomad as Thief: Reflections on Adivasi Silence*. New Delhi: Orient Longman.

Devy, G. N., Geoffrey V. Davis and K. K. Chakravarty (eds). 2009. *Indigeneity: Culture and Representation*. New Delhi: Orient BlackSwan.

Gaikwad, Laxman. 2000 [1987, 1992]. *Uthaigeer* (*Uchalya* in Marathi), trans. Suryanarayan Ransube. New Delhi: Sahitya Akademi.

Guha, Ranajit. 1985. 'Career of an Anti-God in Heaven and on Earth', in Ashok Mitra (ed.), *The Truth Unites: Essays in Tribute to Samara Sen*, pp. 1–25. Calcutta: Subarnarekha.

———. 1996. 'The Small Voice of History', in Shahid Amin and Dipesh Chakravarty (eds), *Subaltern Studies IX: Writings on South Asian Histories and Society*, pp. 1–12. New Delhi: Oxford University Press.

Hatch, W. J. 1928. *The Land Pirates of India*. London: Seeley.

Kosambi, D. D. 1972 [1970]. *The Culture and Civilisation of Ancient Indian Historical Outline*. New Delhi: Vikas Publishing House.

————. 1983 [1962]. *Myth and Reality: Studies in the Formation of Indian Culture*. Bombay: Popular Prakashan.

Narayan, Badri. 2006. *Women Heroes and Dalit Assertion in North India*. New Delhi: Sage Publications.

Östör, Ákos. 1984. *Culture and Power: Legend, Ritual, Bazaar and Rebellion in a Bengali Society*. New Delhi: Sage Publications.

Pushpa, Maitreyi. 2004. *Alma Kabootari*. New Delhi: Rajkamal Prakashan.

Radhakrishna, Meena. 2001. *Dishonoured by History: 'Criminal Tribes' and British Colonial Policy*. New Delhi: Orient Longman.

————. 2008. 'Laws of Metamorphosis: From Nomad to Offender', in Kalpana Kannabiran and Ranbir Singh (eds), *Challenging the Rules of Law*, pp. 3–17. New Delhi: Sage Publications.

Shankar, Gauri. 1979. *Born Criminal*. Varanasi: Kishore Vidya Niketan.

Shastri, Pandit Ram Narayan Dutt. 1948 [1934]. *Mahabharata: Pancham Khand, 'Shantiparva'*. Gorakhpur: Geeta Press.

2

The Lost World of Chernovicz

Memories and Revisitations

Eckhard Breitinger

Bukovina — the Beech Tree Country — was for centuries the contested territory between the Ottoman Empire (the Orient), the Czarist Empire (the East), and the Habsburg/Austrian Empire (the West) (Hausleitner 2005: 31). Its population constituted a rainbow mix of classes and peoples: Polish landowners, Armenian traders, Hungarian and Austrian administrators, Turkish and Bulgarian shop owners, and Russian businessmen, but the bulk of the population with 20–30 per cent each was Romanian (Unitarian Orthodox), Ruthenian/Ukrainian (Russian Orthodox), German (Roman Catholic and Lutheran) and Jewish. The capital of Bukovina, Chernovicz, was a centre of Jewish philosophy and learning — known as the Jerusalem of the East — and a centre of publishing and journalism; it was the home and inspiration of a large number of internationally acclaimed painters like Marc Chagall, poets like Paul Celan and Rose Ausländer, and novelists like Manès Sperber and Joseph Roth. It is one of the ironies of intellectual history that the international impact and creative output of Bukovinian artists occurred only after World War I, that is,, after the collapse of the three imperial powers, in particular the Habsburg Empire that had controlled Bukovina until 1918, and only after the cosmopolitanism and universalism of the former 'boarding house of peoples' (as opposed to 'the prison camp of peoples' on the adjacent Russian side in Bessarabia and Transnistria) had been overtaken by the provincialism of nationalist policies with the ensuing restrictive and narrow-minded language policies (Rychlo 2005: 26–28). Outstanding works such as Joseph Roth's novel *Radetzkymarsch* (1932) — a three-generation family saga that moves through the key border areas of the Habsburg empire (Northern Italy, Slovenia, Bohemia and finally Bukovina/Galicia), the famous poems of Rose Ausländer and the fantastic dream images of Marc Chagall all look back to the pre-World War I period. They were all written or painted in the 1930s and 1940s (Braun 2005: 86), looking back to and recreating the already lost world of Bukovinian multiculturalism. The year 1945 became the historic watershed, when the old-time cohabitation of peoples was replaced by the division into a communist East and a capitalist West. During the hottest phase of the Cold War, the formerly celebrated multiculturalism of Bukovina, and of Chernovicz in particular, was deliberately silenced and erased from the international agenda of cultural and literary criticism, since it appeared incompatible with the unifying and homogenizing tendencies of Soviet cultural policies. Since the Fall of the Berlin Wall and the disintegration of the Soviet empire in the 1990s, Chernovicz has been rediscovered as a model of multiculturalisms and ethnic cohabitation and a series of pictorial documentations, and ethno-historical and literary historical essays have been published (Osatschuk 2008: 178).

This new interest in a historically closed phase of multi-ethnicity and multiculturality has to be seen in connection with the rise of new nationalisms in south-eastern Europe and on the fringes of the former Soviet Empire. But it also relates to a new perception and a fresh perspective on minorities, on minority status and a concept of nations within nations. Within a society of migrants and minorities — the Saxons in Transylvania came more than 500 years ago, the Swabians in Banat 300 years ago, the Jews three or four generations ago — the personal memoir, the autobiography, served a dual purpose. It narrated an individual life story as an exemplary life, which stood for the whole of the group, defining the ethnic group as distinct and specific, but it also related the individual to the broader society. The personal memoir depicts how the ethnically determined individual interacts and relates to other ethnically defined individuals and groups. It tries to capture the individuality within an ethnically mixed collectivity.

The autobiographical texts which we want to consider here differ in their perspective, orientation, and intention: from Moses Rosenkranz's chronological reconstruction of the years of his childhood through Gregor von Rezzori's design to recreate his life through the reconstructed and remembered images of those within his family who had been closest to him and most influential in the formation of his personality, to Eginald Schlattner's fictional portrayal of the last six months of a multicultural and multi-ethnic Transylvania immediately before the occupation by the

Soviet Red Army in 1944. Personal memories — looking back and remembering decisive aspects of one's own personal experience — are located within a broad historic, ethnic and geographical context embedded in a very distinct and specific aesthetic of landscape. These attempts to recreate the essence of Bukovina and Transylvania share certain commonalities. All these memoirs seem to look back to life in Bukovina with a sense of loss, with a sense of nostalgia, but also with a certain pride in having been part of an experience of a multicultural cohabitation or togetherness that was, and still is, unique in the history of central Europe. And even Daniel Mendelsohn — a second generation, American-born Jew — attempts to reconstruct the lives of the Mendelsohns in the Ukraine 50 years after the *Sho'ah*, apparently driven by the urge to rediscover a society and a collective experience of pre-lapsarian harmony as summarized by Gregor von Rezzori:

> *Ich liebte das Land und seine Schönheit, seine Weite und Ursprünglichkeit, und ich liebte das Volk, das dort lebte — das vielgestaltete Volk nicht nur einer sondern gleich eines halben Dutzends von Nationalitäten; nicht nur eines einzigen, sondern eines halben Dutzends von Glaubensbekenntnissen; nicht nur einer, sondern eines halben Dutzends von Sprachen; das aber doch ein Volk von einer ganz bestimmten und besonderen gemeinsamen Prägung war. Ich konnte ihm nicht leiblicher verbunden sein als durch Kassandra.*

> I loved the country and its beauty, the wide spaciousness and its unspoiled naturalness, I loved the people that lived there — the wide variety of different folks, not of one single nationality, but half a dozen nationalities; not one single, but half a dozen religious denominations; not one single but half a dozen different languages; but a people that still retained a very specific common character. I could not be more closely attached to that people than through the person of Cassandra (von Rezzori 1989: 42; unless otherwise noted all translations are mine).

The End of an Era

All the writers clearly define their ethnic origins and the ethno-derived social classifications: race also means class and vice versa. Gregor von Rezzori keeps emphasizing his Habsburg/Kakanian genealogy, his Italian grandfather (on his father's side) and the Moldavian grandmother (on his mother's side), a distinguished line of ancestors that set him apart from the nationalist Germans (Swabians or Saxons), who are Eginald Schlattner's ethnic group. Moses Rosenkranz reflects on his background as a rural Jew, born into a large family of seven children, barely surviving on his father's income as estate manager (to Polish landowners), small-scale farmer and pub owner, while Szvi Yavez displays the qualities of the 'educated' urban Jew — the *Maskilim* — with a leaning towards philosophy, Jewish history and classical Hebrew literature.

All the authors reveal an acute sense of ending and loss of home, but they articulate this sense of loss and closure differently depending on their ethnic background, their political orientation and their social status. Moses Rosenkranz paints an idyllic picture of the landscape — the mountains, the forests, the wide spaces of the valleys and the river Pruth — the quiet life on their farm and the excitement in the village pub which they ran throughout World War I. This is the romantic picture which he cast into an allegorical poem, a dirge that mourns the collapse of the Habsburg Empire.

Moses Rosenkranz and Gregor von Rezzori reveal a particularly strong awareness of closure, even while they still experience this process of decay and disintegration of 'the old order'. Rosenkranz ironically recalls how, in his adolescent confusion and uncertainty, and enamoured of a non-Jewish, upper-class girl, he wrote an allegorical epic poem in praise of the Habsburg past, including a heinously murdered mother Austria:

> Dort befand sich unter anderem auch, in jambischen Fünfheber mit kreuzweise männlichen und weiblichen Reimen, mein Klagegesang um das zerstörte Kaiserreich. Ich hatte es als ermordete Mutter dargestellt, deren verwaiste Kinder in die Sklaverei verschleppt werden. Am glühendsten hielt ich mich dabei beim zweitjüngsten Kronland, meiner Bukowina auf, die ich unter dem schlechten Gewahrsam einer kinderdiebischen Stiefmutter, von tartarischen Horden überfallen, in der sarmatischen Steppe verloren sah.

> I had written in iambic rhythm and alternating rhyme schemes a dirge to the defunct empire. I represented Austria as a mother who had been murdered, whose orphaned children were sold into slavery. Most attention I had paid to the old crown colony, my Bukovina, which I painted as maltreated by a mischievous stepmother, under attack by hordes of Tartars, lost in the Sarmatian steppes (Rosenkranz 2001: 168).

Although Moses Rosenkranz is not very specific about the style, form and content of his early attempt at creative literary expression, he obviously wants his readers to understand the extent and the quality of his loyalty to the Habsburg heritage, best captured in the untranslatable adjective 'kaisertreu'. Rosenkranz's *Kindheit* (ibid.) does not really end with the occupation of Bukovina by the Romanians in 1919, but with the various nomadic moves into the (formerly Habsburg) adjacent areas of Haliczina/Galicia, Bohemia and Moravia between 1920 and 1940, which only enhances the contrast between then and now. The Rosenkranzes first flee before the advancing Czarist Russian army in the winter of 1914–15. The Rosenkranz children move to neighbouring Galicia, get their schooling in Bohemia and eventually in Prague (another of the multicultural and multi-ethnic cities in central Europe). They finally return to Bukovina when Kakanian cosmopolitanism is being replaced by the provincial narrow-mindedness of Romanian nationalism and later by the Nazi-style ideologies of racial/genetic purity. Eventually they move from the expanses of the rural farm to a small flat in the city of Chernovicz. For Moses Rosenkranz — we have to understand from his writing — the period before 1918 ideally represented that ethnic, cultural, and linguistic multiplicity which Emperor Franz-Joseph last expressed in his famous war-time appeal 'An meine Völker (To All My Peoples)'. Everything that follows is degradation, or even a perversion, of the original status of Bukovina. Though clearly tinted by an ironic touch, this confession of adolescent feelings expresses Rosenkranz's sense of closure; and it figures as a testimony to the decidedly integrationist and assimilationist attitudes of (part of) the Jewish population within the Habsburg Empire.

After deportation to a concentration camp by Romanian fascists and 10-year imprisonment in the Stalinist Gulag (in the northernmost camp, Norilsk in Siberia), Rosenkranz returned to Bucharest from where he escaped before another Stalinist trial in 1961. He found refuge in the solitude of the Black Forest (in south-west Germany) which probably comes closest to the landscape of Bukovina (Huff 1994, 2001: 230–51).

Gregor von Rezzori, the offspring of the Austro-German administrative élite, cast his portrait of closure, his sense of loss and termination, into an episodic image that is the epitome of the social aspirations and life-style of the landed gentry. He was introduced to hunting by his father, an enthusiastic follower of Nimrod. He earned his initiation into the ranks of the adult gentry by killing a hare on a hunting excursion with his father as his tutor. From then on, he seems to have been respected by his father as almost an equal who could be spoken with, not only spoken to. And Rezzori repeats the same image 15 years later on the very eve of World War II on another hunting excursion with his father in the solitudes of the Carpathian forest. Again, young Rezzori proves his exceptional marksmanship by killing a hare. At this very moment when the hare topples and the hunting dog retrieves the booty, father and son experience this as a moment of ultimate closure: the last time that father and son went hunting together, the last time that they were together in the alluring mountain solitude of the Carpathians, the last time that they would hunt and shoot a hare, a moment of involuntary but definite farewell to the landscape of his youth. The image of the hunting expedition expresses perfectly the attitude of Rezzori's class. Hunting is a feudal privilege; it expresses control and command over people and nature, over life, flora and fauna. With a radically paternalistic mindset, Gregor von Rezzori also concentrates on the historical watershed of 1918, when universalism was replaced by provincialism. With Rezzori, the sense of loss is pervasive throughout his autobiographical account. He betrays his colonial mind — and thus inadvertently defines the post-colonial situ-ation in Bukovina — when he states that in the 1930s under Romanian rule they felt as '*Wir fassten uns als dereinstige Österreicher in einer hauptsächlich österreichisch geprägten Provinz auf wie nach dem Ende des Raj in Indien verbliebene Briten*' (erstwhile Austrians in an erstwhile Austrian cultural milieu like the British who had stayed on in India after the end of the Raj) (von Rezzori 1989: 42).

Eginald Schlattner, from the neighbouring province of Transylvania/ Siebenbürgen, with its solid 700 years of German cultural tradition, organizes his line of narration in his autobiographically inspired novel *Der geköpfte Hahn* (The beheaded Cock) (1998) around the apocalyptic closure of the multicultural experiment in the autumn of 1944. The protago-nist and first-person narrator intends to celebrate once more the good old days of company with his age-mates from Fogarasch after graduating from the German grammar school (Gymnasium). This is the summer of 1944, when the artillery of the Red Army can already be heard in the distance and the Romanian government changed sides from the alliance with fascist Italy and Germany to one with Russia, Great Britain and America. The protagonist plans to celebrate '*Unsere Klasse, die Quarta der Deutschen Schule in Fogarasch, feierte Exitus — so der tradi-erte Sprachgebrauch in Siebenbürgen: Abschied von der Schule, Abschied voneinander, Abschied von der Kindheit sowieso*' (Exitus — the trad-itional term in Transylvania: Farewell from school, farewell to all the age-mates, farewell to childhood and adolescence) (ibid.: 8). All the former school-mates way back from primary school are meant to gather once more for a final celebration. Already the intentionality of this gath-ering signals the strong awareness that this would be definitely the last gathering of its kind and also the last chance to organize it. However, the spirit of togetherness had already been destroyed by the different ethno-political factions. For quite some time, togetherness had existed only superficially, only in name. The Roma and Sinti children sat together with all the others in primary school, but the Roma who lived in a shanty town settlement on the banks of the river did not send their children to secondary school, certainly not their girls. From the mid-1930s, when Nazi racism had infected large sections of the German community, Sinti and Roma would not have been admitted into the German school system anyway. Due to the nationalist policies in Bucharest, the Romanian children had to attend the Romanian school; the children of the Hungarian élite (the narrator is very much in love with the daughter of a Hungarian estate owner) are sent by their parents to boarding schools; the Jewish children, though speaking German as their first language, were kicked out of the German school system when the impact of Nazi ideology increased. Thus, by 1944, when this last celebration of multiculturality was planned with the enthusiasm of a young, open-minded intellectual, the conditions for ethnic and cultural cohabitation and togetherness had long ceased to exist. They had been voluntarily destroyed by the political and ideological powers that there were at the time. Thus, the story that Eginald Schlattner tells is captured perfectly in the image he chose for his title: *Der geköpfte Hahn* — the beheaded cock; the lively and colourful community of Transylvania having already been beheaded, slaughtered. What remained in the summer of 1944 was the last wild flapping of wings and the headless running around before the ultimate demise that was coming with the advance of the Red Army.

Aharon Appelfeld's *Geschichte eines Lebens* (2005) occupies an intermediate position between the assimilationist position of Moses Rosenkranz and that of the Zionist Zvi Yavez. For Appelfeld, the good old days figure only as a vague remembrance, while the main emphasis of his account lies on the years of suppression and persecution and his attempts to install himself in a new life in Palestine/Israel. The family had for quite some time planned to escape the increasing anti-Semitism of the Romanian government.

> *Ich spürte, dass die nächsten Tage nichts Gutes bringen würden. Niemand ahnte, dass die Flut schon mit solcher macht auf uns zurollte . . . Manchmal hatte ich den Eindruck, Vater gräbt einen Tunnel, durch den er uns retten will. Doch das Graben geht so langsam voran, dass er vielleicht nicht rechtzeitig fertig wird.*

I felt, that the coming days would bring bad luck. But no one foresaw that the flood that rolled towards us, had already gathered such terrible strength . . . Sometimes I had the impression that my father was digging a tunnel through which all of us could escape, but the digging was too slow and would never be finished in time. (Appelfeld 2005: 42–43).

Appelfeld speaks about 'resettlement' in the ghetto of Chernovicz, deportation to a work camp, escape and survival in the forest, life as a child soldier with the partisans or as the houseboy of a prostitute, until he finally manages to reach the DP camps (Displaced Persons — survivors of concentration camps, prisoner of war camps and forced labour camps) near Naples in southern Italy from where he can catch a ship to take him to Haifa in the British Protectorate of Palestine. Again the essence of the narrative is built on the contrast between the 'Before' and 'After': the multi-ethnic haven, the ideal landscape of ethnic cohabitation and the following ruptures of multi-ethnicity, to the final collapse through Nazi extermination strategies (the *Endlösung* or Final Solution), to the Stalinist purges and deportation to the Gulag in Siberia.

Appelfeld associates the different periods of Bukovinian history with the succession of the generations. The old life is represented by the grandparents, the holidays on their farm, the excursions into the wide open landscape, roaming through the forest, the bath in the river, followed by a storytelling session beside his grandmother's spinning wheel, accompanying his grandfather to the evening prayers at the synagogue, or the visits and holidays at the estate of uncle Felix, who had established a worker's participation scheme on his farm and in his various other enterprises in the manner of Robert Owen. Uncle Felix represents the modern, socially responsible entrepreneur — the modernist and socialist — with a strong attachment to Jewish traditions, to Hebrew and Yiddish literature and philosophy. Appelfeld's mother, on the other hand, insists on speaking German and rather objects to his affiliation to the Yiddish lore which he encounters at his grandmother's, while the father is violently opposed to what he calls outdated Jewish ritualism. Only in the deportation camp, on the escape route from the joint Romanian and Nazi anti-Semites, does the father start to participate in basic religious practices and prayers again

Appelfeld kept diaries from a very early stage during the years of persecution and while living in the underground, through life in the preparation camps prior to immigration to Palestine until he started work in a Kibbuzim (he specializes in raising fruit trees). Contact with the Yiddish scholar Dov Sadan and the writer Lejb Rochman on the one hand, and the official policy of the resurrected *Erez Israel* — according to which the immigrants should shed their old victim identities, forget their past and start a new life as Israeli citizens on a clean slate — motivates Appelfeld to thematize the issue of memory and remembrance as well as the relation of personal life story to collective group history.

Zvi Yavetz, a historian teaching at the University of Tel Aviv, structures his account more in line with the concepts of social history rather than as a personal memoir. The first part is dedicated to the history of the Yavetz family, living in the *Ziegeleigasse* next to the town centre of Chernovicz. On the father's side, he descends from the Zucker family, an extended family with widespread business interests — from the local brewery to the textile factory and the department store in town. On the mother's side he can boast of a number of distinguished rabbis and Jewish scholars. Yavetz tells us very little about the business people of the Zucker family, but he keeps raving about the impressive figure of his grandfather, Moses Yavetz — his library, his taking him along to the synagogue and encouraging him for his first public reading of prayers during services. Thus, Zvi Yavetz concentrates on those events, on family and social structures, on role models that prioritize his Jewish identity before his Bukovinian identity. Yavetz is also the only author who hardly ever speaks about the beauty of the Bukovinian landscape.

The Natural Space of Bukovina

The sense of belonging and ultimate loss present in the work of all the authors owes much to the scenery, the landscape of Bukovina. They seem to follow an aesthetic created by romantic landscape painters like Moritz Schwind, Caspar David Friedrich or the 'painters' colony' at Schreiberhau in the western range of the Carpathian Mountains. They celebrate an archetypal type of landscape: high, blue mountains in the distance, deep forests, wide open valleys with smooth rivers, particularly the river Pruth. The type of landscape seems to radiate different types of beauty from season to season — from the fresh greens of spring to the yellow shades of summer to the red colouring of the beech trees in autumn. Winter, however, seems to be the best season to display the picturesque side of Bukovina. Even Zvi Yavetz, who apparently moves only within the town and within the social circles of the Jewish community, gives an enthusiastic description of winter in the countryside. Otherwise, he concentrates on cityscapes rather than landscapes, beginning with the moderate standard of his parent's house in the *Ziegeleigasse*, an unpaved street that is impassable with snow during the winter, soaked in an ankle-deep morass in spring or autumn, and buried under thick clouds of dust during the summer. Close to the city centre, this is a housing area without pipe-borne water or sewerage. Yavetz details the various social institutions in town, the ethnic organisation of the football teams (Maccabaeus for Jews, Dragos Voda for Romanians, Jahn for Germans, Dovbusch for Ukrainians). He mocks at the 'cheap entertainment' of the popular Yiddish theatre which he calls Krebbel Theatre. Besides the local entertainment at the Krebbel Theatre, Yavetz points to the tremendous popularity of American films. It seems that films produced in the big five Hollywood studios — from Goldwyn to Meyer, all owned and run by Jews recently immigrated to the US from Central Europe — appealed strongly to the aspirations and expectations of the Jewish community in Chernovicz.

Yavetz summarizes his personal indebtedness to Chernovicz in an image of family history, in a kind of genetic cultural inheritance:

> *Von meinem Großvater Moses Yavetz habe ich die Liebe zur hebräischen Sprache und zu Erez Israel geerbt. Bei meiner Mutter habe ich nicht nur Deutsch gelernt, sondern auch die Überzeugung, dass nichts schlimmer ist als Müßiggang. Von meiner Großmutter habe ich gelernt, dass man träumen darf . . . und dass man auf festen Füßen auf der Erde stehen muss.*

From my grandfather Moses Yavetz, I inherited the love for the Hebrew language and for Erez Israel. From my mother I learned not only German but also the firm conviction that there is nothing worse in the world than idleness, and my grandmother taught me that one may dream . . . but one still had to remain standing solidly on the ground (Yavetz 2007: 140).

Yavetz complements this observation with a general statement about the language attitude of Jewish intellectuals in the wider region of Bukovina, Galicia, Moldavia, and the attraction of Chernovicz.

> *Kein Wunder, dass die "Jiddischisten" wie Eliezer Steinbarg aus Lipcani und Itzig Manger aus Jassy sich in Czernowitz zu Hause fühlten. Kein Wunder ebenso, dass Dichter wie Iossel Lerner aus Briceni und Eliezer Podriatschik aus einer kleinen Stadt in Bessarabien es vorzogen, sich im deutschsprachigen Czernowitz niederzulassen statt im russischsprachigen Kischinew.*

No wonder that the "Yiddishists" like Eliezer Steinbarg from Licani and Itzig Manger from Jassy felt so much at home in Chernovicz. No wonder either, that poets like Jossel Lerner from Briceni and Eliezer

Podriatschik from a small town in Bessarabia [Moldavia] preferred to reside in German-speaking Chernovicz, rather than the Russian-speaking Kishinev. (ibid.: 176).

Zvi Yavetz's *Erinnerung an Czernowitz — Wo Menschen und Bücher lebten* (ibid.) (a quotation from the celebrated Jewish–German poet Paul Celan) gives the most distanced account of life in Chernovicz and Bukovina.

Language and Migration

Language seems to be the most significant marker in the definition of identity — of self-definition as well as identity ascriptions by other groups. Language usage and language attitudes, being determined by the social and cultural/ethnic environment, reflect the potential range of action within society. Moses Rosenkranz describes language use in his family as follows:

> *Wenn das Herz zum Ausdruck drängte, und miteinander, sprachen die Eltern jüdisch; mit uns Kindern, deutsch; mit der Dienstmagd, dem Gesinde auf der Pachtung und den Einwohnern des Dorfes, ruthenisch; mit den Gutsbesitzern der Umgebung polnisch; und mit den einkehrenden Reisenden, je nach Bedarf eine dieser Sprachen, deren keine sie wohl musterhaft beherrschen mochten, aber jede gefällig und phantasievoll zu verwenden schienen, denn es wurde ihnen immer mit Vergnügen und Interesse zugehört.*

To express what was in their hearts, talking among themselves, our parents spoke Yiddish; with us children they spoke German; with the maid, the servants on the farm and the villagers, Ruthenian; with the estate owners, Polish; with the travellers calling at our tavern any of these languages as the occasion might have demanded. They spoke none of these languages with perfection, but all of them with ease and imagination, so that everyone listened to them with interest and pleasure (Rosenkranz 2001: 10).

The Rosenkranz family have different languages for different purposes or emotional needs at their disposal: Yiddish for the soul, German for education, other languages for business and social interaction. Young Moses soon developed for his personal emotions and ideas 'a sphere of immaterial spirituality' beyond the shortcomings of imperfect language knowledge (ibid.: 11). Speaking about the education by private tutors,

Rosenkranz reveals another important aspect of language learning and language tuition: they were taught 'weltgerechtes Deutsch und Rechnen und gottgefälliges Hebräisch und Beten' (worldly German and Arithmetic and divine Hebrew and prayers) (Rosenkranz 2001: 31) — German to get on in the world and the sacred language Hebrew for religious practice and rituals.

Gregor von Rezzori finds himself in the same multilingual environment, yet as a sibling of the Austro-Kakanian élite, German unquestionably occupies first rank. Also due to his Habsburg elite status, he is brought up by a nanny, Cassandra, of undefined ethnic origin. She is illiterate and archaic, excessively pious and superstitious. The final guess is that she must be a *Huzulin*, a subgroup of the mountain *Goralen*, a tiny minority group of possibly pre-Slavonian population that withdrew into the remotest corners of the Carpathian mountains, i.e., the true indigenous 'first nation' people in the area. Young Gregor encounters the language mix as follows:

> *Zwar war zu Österreichs Zeiten Deutsch die offizielle Umgangssprache, aber je tiefer man ins Land kam, um so unverständlicher wurde es von den bunterlei Nationalitäten der Bukowina geradebrecht und unzulänglich verstanden. Kassandra hingegen, die keine einzige Sprache auch nur annähernd richtig sprach, drückte sich mit Brocken von Rumänisch, Ruthenisch, Polnisch, Ungarisch, auch Türkisch und Jiddisch aus, unterstützt von oft grotesk grimmassierender Mimik.*

> In the days of the Habsburgs, German was the official language. But the deeper you moved into the recesses of the mountains, the more incomprehensibly was it spoken or understood by the many nationalities in Bukovina. Cassandra, who could not speak any of the languages reasonably correctly, managed to express herself effectively with chunks of Romanian, Ruthenian, Polish, Hungarian but also Turkish and Yiddish, supported by a grotesque mimicry that was broadly laughed at, but well understood (von Rezzori 1989: 11).

In his contact with Cassandra, Gregor developed a language of their own which mixed all the languages of the area without attention to grammar. He calls it a 'quilt language', but when the family has to flee before the advance of the Czarist Russian army in winter 1914–15 it is Cassandra's hodgepodge language that saves the family. Madame von Rezzori's stylish German, Italian or French is useless to master the practicalities of life in wartime. Rezzori praises the artistic potential of this language mix in Bukovina in an almost Dadaistic programmatic tone:

*Während Straußerl meiner zwölfjährigen Schwester die Gedichte Michelangelos
and Vittoria Colonna vorlas, erzählte Kassandra mir, dem Achtjährigen, immer
noch Märchen — erzählte sie in ihrer Flickensprache, holte dazu Wörter von
überall her zu einem Decollagebild aus Sprachfetzen, zufälligen Wortfindungen,
skurrilen Wortschöpfungen, Wortwechselbälgen, Sprachhomunkuli . . . verlieh
ihnen dadurch eine Buntheit, Unmittelbarkeit und Lebendigkeit, die ich an ihnen
nirgends mehr wieder gefunden habe.*

While Strausserl (tutor of Gregor's twelve-year-old sister) recited
Michelangelo's poems to Vittoria Colonna, Cassandra was still telling me,
the eight-year-old, fairy tales — she spoke in her patchwork language; she
picked her words from everywhere and artfully arranged them into a col-
lage of language scraps, newly invented words, grotesque word formations,
verbal changelings or word homunculi . . . but she endowed her speech
with so much colour, immediacy and vitality, which I have never found
again (ibid.: 55).

This picture of the spoken language reminds us of the fantastic images
of Marc Chagall (a Bukovinian) with their collages of religious and ethnographic representations, or of Salman Rushdie's famous statement
that mélange, hybridization, bastardization, hodgepodge bring newness
to the world.

Zvi Yavetz, on the other hand, concentrates on the role of Yiddish and
Hebrew. Yavetz seems to move exclusively within the Chernovicz circles
of the educated Jewish community, but not among the Germanophiles.
He categorizes people according to their command of language, whether
they can speak decent Yiddish and read sufficient Hebrew. Someone who
cannot understand enough Hebrew to read the 'Hebrew Classics' meets
with Yavetz's disdain. His orientation clearly prioritizes Zionist ideals, the
supremacy of the Hebrew language and the longing for *Erez Israel*. He also
distances himself clearly from what he calls 'Bundists' and 'Yiddishists'.
The difference between the urban Jew Yavetz and the assimilationist
Rosenkranzes also becomes clear in their literary preferences. Yavetz
dedicates a full chapter to 'What do Jews read in Chernowicz?'. He lists
the popular authors, mainly Yiddish writers like Scholem Aleichem,
Ahron Lutzki, Eliezer Steinbarg, but also Paul Celan and Rose Ausländer
(who wrote in German). Yavetz gives a survey of the Chernovicz newspapers according to language (German, Yiddish and Hebrew) and their
political/cultural orientation. He comments on the cultural scene in the
town, particularly condemning the light entertainment of the Yiddish
theatre and film of the 1930s (Yavetz 2007: 171).

Moses Rosenkranz on the other hand, with his semi-literate father in the rural environment, could not easily access great literature. But he does speak enthusiastically about his experience reading a fairy tale by Clemens von Brentano — a German Romantic poet.

> *Clemens von Brentanos Märchen war der erste deutsche Text, den ich ohne lehrhafte Durchspeichelung zu lesen bekam . . . Ich begriff nicht den Sinn, den Inhalt, die Fabel, den Aufbau, den Stil, die Syntax des Märchens, aber ich habe es mit dem Herzen und durch das Blut in allen meinen Fibern aufgenommen . . . Hinter diesem Titelblatt erstreckte sich auf achtzig Seiten der dunkle Zauberwald der Sprache.*

> Clemens von Brentano's tale was the first German text which I read on my own without didactic interference. I did not grasp the meaning, the content, the structure . . . but I did absorb it with all the fibres of my heart and my blood . . . I entered the magic forest of language (Rosenkranz 2001: 135).

Moses Rosenkranz's reading preferences mark him out as a *Germanophile*: he admires the poetry of Mörike, Schiller and Goethe, but also 'the magicians of the German language Hofmannsthal, Rilke and Trakl, who breathed new strength into the waning Austrian empire' (ibid.: 33).

Linguistic Landscapes and Language Policies

Aharon Appelfeld introduces a new dimension concerning language attitudes, determined on the one hand by the pragmatics of language, ethnic identity, and racist oppression, and by the nation-building policies in the young state of Israel on the other. Appelfeld had been brought up essentially in German, but in spite of his mother's objections, he managed to gather a fair command of Yiddish on the farm of his grandparents and his uncle, and sufficient Hebrew for the basic prayers. While he was on the run from Nazi persecutors, he had to negate his Jewish identity in order to survive. He had to operate essentially in Ukrainian and Ruthenian, and once he reached the Refugee and Displaced Persons camp in preparation to go to Palestine, Hebrew gained preference.

Appelfeld's career, beginning with a well protected childhood in a German-speaking, assimilationist middle-class family, through his years in the underground with Ukrainian partisans, on the run and through the displaced persons camps, eventually ending in Palestine/Israel, started with a clear preference for German as the medium of expression and ends with Appelfeld becoming one of the most prolific and most prominent writers in Hebrew. In this context, where language becomes the decisive marker in the definition of personal or group identity, it is not really a surprise that Appelfeld centralizes language and language attitudes, and the socio-cultural contexts of language attitudes. He speaks about the languages that had been relevant in his life in terms of family relationships. He speaks not only about 'mother tongue' or other tongues; he also speaks about languages as twin sisters, as step-mothers and step-children. Thus, we perceive the languages of Central Europe, the loss of language and linguistic and literary traditions in the same categories of loss which he uses to describe the fate of his own family: the natural deaths of his grandmother and grandfather, his mother's murder at the beginning of World War II, the death of his father and the deaths of almost all his relatives in the Nazi death camps. For Appelfeld, all 'his' languages die a violent and inappropriate death just as the members of his family did.

Quite typical of the social aspirations of second and third generation, assimilationist families, Aharon Appelfeld's mother watches carefully over his language acquisition, which in her view must be 'pure' German, the urban medium (Corbea-Hoisie 2008: 67). But on the rural farm of his grandparents, he learned Yiddish, the language that links him to the Eastern European tradition of his people.

> *Die Sprache meiner Mutter war Deutsch. Meine Mutter liebte diese Sprache und pflegte sie. Die Wörter hatten in ihrem Mund eine Klarheit, als erklängen sie aus einem exotischen Glasglöcklein. Großmutter sprach Jiddisch, und das hatte einen anderen Klang, besser gesagt einen anderen Geschmack, denn es erinnerte mich immer an Kompott aus Trockenpflaumen.*

> The language of my mother was German. My mother loved that language and cared for it lovingly. In her mouth, the words carried a clarity like the sounds of a glass bell. Grandmother spoke Yiddish, and that had a different sound, or rather a different taste, because it always reminded me of a compote dish of dried plums (Appelfeld 2005: 113–14).

Outside the house, beyond the control of the family, Aharon encounters the usual language mix typical of the Bukovinian environment. Just as in the case of Gregor von Rezzori's housemaid and unofficial tutor Cassandra, it is again the Ukrainian maid servant who incorporates the language diversity and multiplicity of the place:

Unser Dienstmädchen sprach Ruthenisch, durchsetzt mit Worten von uns und von Großmutter . . . Eine Sprache, die wir zu Hause nicht verwendeten, die man aber dauernd auf der Strasse hörte, war Rumänisch. Nach dem Ersten Weltkrieg war die Bukowina . . . von Rumänien annektiert worden; die Sprache der Herrschenden war Rumänisch . . . Vier Sprachen umgaben uns, lebten in uns auf merkwürdige Weise zusammen und ergänzten sich. Wenn du deutsch sprachst und dir ein Wort, ein Ausdruck oder eine Redensart nicht einfiel, behalfst du dich mit Jiddisch oder Ruthenisch. Vergeblich versuchten meine Eltern, mein Deutsch rein zu halten. Die Wörter aus den uns umgebenden vier Sprachen flogen uns zu, ohne dass wir es merkten, und bildeten ein Sprachgemisch, das ungeheuer reich an Schattierungen, Gegensätzen, Humor und Ironie war. In dieser Sprache gab es viel Raum für Empfindungen, feinste Gefühlsnuancen, für Phantasie und Erinnerung.

Our maid spoke Ruthenian, sprinkled with words of my parents and my grandmother . . . A language which we did not use in the house, but which was omnipresent in the streets, was Romanian . . . Since Bukovina had been annexed by Romania, Romanian had become the language of political domination . . . The four languages surrounded us. In a curious way they lived in us side by side and complemented each other. If you spoke German and you were searching for an appropriate word, a term or a proverbial saying, you resorted to Yiddish or Ruthenian. My parents tried in vain to keep my German pure. The words of the four surrounding languages floated around us and without our noticing it, they formed a language mix that was immensely rich in shades of tone, in contradictions, in humour and irony. This language provided so much room for emotions, for the finest nuances in sensibility, for dreams, imagination and memories (Appelfeld 2005: 114).

While Rezzori underlined the absurdist or even modernist aspects of this language mix, Aharon Appelfeld points to the emotional richness, the directness and the exactitude of expression that corresponds so well to the Bukovinian mix of cultures and mentalities. These eulogies on multilingualism and multiculturalism however have met with strong objections from the side of Polish and particularly Ukrainian intellectuals and researchers. They have pointed to the fact that it is always the indigenous, lower-class servant who speaks this language mix, that there is always a note of condescension when German-language authors speak about the ingenuity of the language of the maids and servants, that it always conveys a sense of ethnic/racial superiority (Prochasko 2008: 140; Röskau-Radel 2008: 105–6). And it also seems significant to me, that the hodgepodge speakers always seem to be females.

This rich linguistic universe, however, vanished rapidly during Appelfeld's four years on the run and in the underground. At the end of World War II, when he had finally made his way from his hideouts in the Ukrainian forests to the DP camps in southern Italy, he realized that he had lost practically all the languages which he had formerly used so comfortably and competently. To survive in the underground, he had to hide his Jewish identity and therefore discard Yiddish and German. With the end of the war, Ukrainian and Ruthenian or Romanian would have equally betrayed him, associating him with either Red Army persecution or Romanian collaboration. In the end, Appelfeld finds himself without any language, without any system of (self-) expression, and particularly without any system with which he could intellectually negotiate his chaotic environment. The loss of language entails the loss of meaning and orientation.

Es ist das Jahr 1946, das Jahr meiner Einwanderung nach Palästina; das Tagebuch zeigt ein Mosaik aus deutschen, jiddischen, hebräischen und sogar rumänischen Wörtern. Ich sage "Wörter" und nicht "Sätze" . . . Diese Wörter waren zurückgehaltene Schreie eines Vierzehnjährigen, dem alle Sprachen, die er je gekonnt hatte, verloren gegangen waren, sodass er keine mehr hatte. Das Tagebuch diente ihm als geheimes Eckchen, in dem er die Reste der Muttersprache und gerade neu erworbene Wörter anhäufte . . . Wenn man keine Sprache hat, ist alles Chaos und Durcheinander, und man hat Angst vor Dingen, vor denen man sich nicht zu fürchten braucht . . . Ohne Muttersprache ist der Mensch verstümmelt.

[The year] 1946, the year of my arrival in Palestine, my diary reveals a mosaic of German, Yiddish, Hebrew and even Romanian words. "Words", not really "sentences" . . . These words were the silenced cries of a fourteen-year-old, who had lost all the languages which he had once spoken, so that he had no language at all. The diary served as a secret corner in which he could hide the remnants of his mother tongue and also gather the newly acquired words . . . If you have no language left to you, everything is chaos and confusion. You start being afraid of things . . . Without a mother tongue man is not only mute, but mutilated. (Appelfeld 2005: 113).

The importance that Appelfeld ascribes to language also becomes obvious from the parallelisms of language and the sense of belonging in geographical terms, from rootedness in terms of landscape and culture:

Ich war weder hier noch dort. Was ich gehabt hatte — Eltern, ein Zuhause und die Muttersprache — war für immer verloren, und die Sprache, die versprochen hatte, Muttersprache zu werden, erwies sich bestenfalls als Stiefmutter.

I was neither here nor there. What I had once owned — parents, a home, and a mother tongue — was for ever lost, and the language that should carry the promise of becoming a new mother tongue, proved to be barely more than a stepmother tongue (Appelfeld 2005: 117).

In this linguistic and emotional vacuum, Aharon Appelfeld finds himself exposed to the linguistic dictates of the preparation camps for Palestine. Hebrew is the only language that may be spoken in the camps. The use of mother tongues is strictly forbidden and heavily sanctioned. Appelfeld, however, does not respond favourably to this linguistic pressure of the Zionist functionaries:

Im Lager Atlit, wo die Briten uns internierten, lernten wir ein paar Wörter Hebräisch. Sie klangen exotisch und waren schwer auszusprechen. Sie besaßen keine Wärme. Ihr Klang weckte keinerlei Assoziationen, als seien sie aus dem Sand geboren, der uns von allen Seiten umgab. Schlimmer noch, sie klangen wie Befehle: Arbeiten! Essen! Aufräumen! Schlafen! Als sei es eine Sprache, in der man nicht leise reden kann, eine Soldatensprache.

In the Atlit camp, where the British interned us, we learned a few words of Hebrew. They sounded exotic and were hard to pronounce. They did not carry any warmth. Their sound did not ring any associations, as if they had been born from the sand that surrounded us on all sides. Even worse, they sounded like military commands: Work! Eat! Clean up! Sleep! As if it was a language you could not whisper in, a language of soldiers (ibid.: 115).

With the end of the war, the loss of his Bukovinian home, of his family, Aharon Appelfeld finds himself in a situation, where he has to reconfigure his social, cultural, linguistic identity from scratch. And he finds himself caught in the dilemma of highly problematic linguistic options: German, Yiddish, and Hebrew. Although German was his mother tongue, it was also his mother's murderers' tongue ('Die Sprache meiner Mutter war die Sprache ihrer Mörder' [ibid.: 117]). As such German can no longer be an option for self-articulation or artistic expression.

Wie konnte man weiter die Sprache sprechen, die mit dem Blut von Juden getränkt war? Dieses furchtbare Dilemma konnte dem Gefühl aber nichts anhaben, dass mein Deutsch nicht die Sprache der Deutschen war, sondern die meiner Mutter.

How could I possibly speak a language that was soaked with the blood of Jews? But this frightful dilemma could not erase the feeling that "my" German was not the language of the Germans, but it was the language of my mother (ibid.: 118).

Yiddish is associated with the past, with the East European Jewish tradition of the *shtetl*, and therefore in the eyes of the Zionists and the new settlers in Palestine, it is the language of the Jews as victims, undesirable and unacceptable in the construction of identity in the new nation. Following this confrontational argument, Yiddish stands for the ghetto mentality, while Hebrew stands for the future of the independent state of *Erez Israel*, reborn after 2,000 years of diaspora and dispersion. In the tumultuous intellectual and particularly emotional confusion of 1945, this confrontation between Yiddish and Hebrew also becomes a question of political orientation, of a psychological reorientation. In spite of the traumatic and sustainably traumatizing experiences, Aharon Appelfeld and many of his fellow sufferers feel that they cannot blindly accept the Zionist *tabula rasa* strategy: 'Forget where you come from, put down your roots in the land' (*Vergiss dein Zuhause, und schlag Wurzeln im Land*) (ibid.: 120). They feel that they still need the years of persecution, the experience of being victimized and of living under continuous death threats as an essential and constituent part of their life experience which they cannot simply erase or delete. Although this is an excessively painful experience — of total loss — the feeling that this loss cannot be compensated for or healed by another new and deliberate experience of loss, determined the debate in the camps between the Yiddishists and the Zionists.

Uns unterrichtete der Dichter Jasch, ein schmächtiger, glatzköpfiger Mann ohne jede Anmut, der aus der Nähe eher wie ein Kaufmann aussah, doch sobald er den Mund aufmachte, schlug dich seine Stimme in den Bann. Er brachte uns Gedichte und Lieder bei, und zwar auf Yiddisch. Er verstand sich als Gegner der Jugendleiter aus Palästina. Die vertraten das Hebräische, er das Jiddische. Die Gesandten aus Palästina waren größer als er, sahen besser aus; vor allem aber sprachen sie im Namen der Zukunft, im Namen einer Veränderung zum Guten, im Namen des Lebens, das uns in Palästina erwartete. Er aber sprach von dem, was vergangen war, sprach von Fortsetzung und dass es keine Fortsetzung geben werde, wenn wir nicht in der Sprache der Geschundenen redeten.

We were taught by the poet Jasch, a thin, bald-headed man without any grace, who looked at close range more like a shopkeeper. But once he opened his mouth, we all listened spell-bound. He taught us poems and songs (*Lieder*) in Yiddish. He saw himself as the opponent of the camp guides from Palestine. They stood for Hebrew, Jasch stood for Yiddish. These envoys from Palestine were taller than him, they looked better, above all they spoke in the name of the future, in the name of a change for the better, in the name of life, that was waiting for us in Palestine. But he spoke about that what had passed, he spoke of continuation and that there could be no continuation into the future if we refused to speak in the language of the downtrodden (Appelfeld 2005: 28).

On arrival in Palestine, during his service in the army, Appelfeld experiences Hebrew as a language superimposed on the sensibilities of the survivors. He slowly adapts to and adopts the new language. He is reconciled through the lectures of the renowned scholar Dov Sadan. He teaches the new Israeli citizens, who have just gone through their national service in the army, where they encountered Hebrew again as the language of military command — of order and discipline — not as the language of self-articulation. Being taught to see Yiddish and Hebrew, Yiddish literature and Hebrew literature as twin sisters rather than antagonists, changes Appelfeld's attitude to his new mother tongue.

> *Bei Dov Sadan lebten das Jiddische und das Hebräische wie Zwillings-schwestern zusammen . . . Das Hebräisch, das man uns neu eingewanderten Jugendlichen beibrachte, das Hebräisch des Militärs, war dagegen eine Sprache ohne jede Beziehung zu meiner früheren Sprache und Lebenserfahrung . . . Dov Sadan entwarf uns ein ganz anderes Bild: Hebräisch und Jiddisch, Volksdichtung und Poesie gehörten zusammen . . . Die jiddische und Chassidische Literatur erweisen sich als das Gegenteil von allem, was hier im Land geschah, und mir gefielen gerade diese beiden Welten sehr, als seien sie das Zuhause, das ich verloren hatte.*

> With Dov Sadan, Yiddish and Hebrew lived together like twin sisters . . . The Hebrew which we were taught as new immigrants or in the army was a language that had no connection with my previous languages or my previous life . . . Dov Sadan designed a completely different picture where Hebrew and Yiddish, folk literature and poetry constituted a whole . . . Yiddish and Chassidic literature seemed so different from everything that happened in this country, but for me, these miraculous worlds represented the home which I had sadly lost (ibid.: 119–21).

The memoirs of Bukovinian authors implicitly reflect the formation, the deformation and destruction of a multi-ethnic milieu. The historical processes of planned immigration (Germans, Saxons and Swabians from 1300 to 1800); the accidental settlement of the castaways of imperial inroads (Armenians and Bulgarians); or the poverty migration for greener pastures of Jews escaping anti-Semite, Czarist Russia lasted for centuries. The personal memoirs condense these historic processes into tales of family sagas, a single life span or even a single month of apocalyptic dimensions. The memoirs speak about nomadic existences, about the precarious experiences of immigration and integration, but even more about expulsion, expropriation or forced removals and ethnic cleansing. They recall the optimistic nomadic spirit of the incoming settlers and the disillusion and frustration of the outgoing expellees, refugees and displaced persons. And they speak about the importance of language for each and every group within these ebb-and-flow processes of nomadic migrations, the importance of language to ascertain the spirit of belonging to the region of migration, but also for the appropriation of a new home in a new geographical space.

References

Appelfeld, Aharon. 2005. Geschichte eines Lebens. Berlin: Rowohlt Verlag.

Braun, Helmut. 2005. 'Viersprachenlieder erfüllen die Luft — Die Stadt in der, Erinnerung der Dichterinnen und Dichter', in Helmut Braun (ed.), Czernowitz — die Geschichte einer untergegangenen Kulturmetropole. Berlin: Links Verlag.

Corbea-Hoisie, Andrei. 2008. 'Jüdisches und jiddisches Czernowitz', in Ariane Afsari and Deutsches Kulturforum östliches Europa (eds), Mythos Czernowitz: eine Stadt im Spiegel ihrer Nationalitaten, pp. 65–80. Potsdam: Deutsches Kulturforum östliches Europa.

Hausleitner, Marian. 2005. 'Eine wechselvolle Geschichte — Die Bukowina und die Stadt Czernowitz vom 18. zum 20. Jahrhundert', in Helmut Braun (ed.), Czernowitz — die Geschichte einer untergegangenen Kulturmetropole, pp. 31–81. Berlin: Links Verlag.

Huff, Matthias. 1994. 'Schönes Deutschland in der Ferne: Moses Rosenkranz, der Dichter aus der Bukowina', Deutschland Radio Berlin, 1 April.

———. 2001. '"Ich trug die Dörfer in mir": Gedanken zu Moses Rosenkranz' autobiographischem Fragment Kindheit' in Moses Rosenkranz, Kindheit — Fragment einer Autobiographie, pp. 230–51. Aachen: Rimbaud Verlag.

Mendelsohn, Daniel. 2006. The Lost — A Search for Six of Six Million. New York: Harper.

Osatschuk, Sergij. 2008. 'Tscherniwizi — das Czernowitz von heute', in Ariane Afsari and Deutsches Kulturforum östliches Europa (eds), Mythos Czernowitz: eine Stadt im Spiegel ihrer Nationalitaten, pp. 178–92. Potsdam: Deutsches Kulturforum östliches Europa.

Prochasko, Jurko. 2008. 'Das Czernowitz meiner Großtante — das ukrainische Czernowitz' in Ariane Afsari and Deutsches Kulturforum östliches Europa (eds), *Mythos Czernowitz: eine Stadt im Spiegel ihrer Nationalitaten*, pp. 137–49. Potsdam: Deutsches Kulturforum östliches Europa.

Rosenkranz, Moses. 2001. *Kindheit — Fragment einer Autobiographie*. Aachen: Rimbaud Verlag.

Röskau-Radel, Isabel 2008. 'Czerniowce — das polnische Czernowitz', in Ariane Afsari and Deutsches Kulturforum östliches Europa (eds), *Mythos Czernowitz: eine Stadt im Spiegel ihrer Nationalitaten*, pp. 104–36. Potsdam: Deutsches Kulturforum östliches Europa.

Roth, Joseph. 1932. *Radetzkymarsch*. Berlin: G. Kiepenheuer.

Rychlo, Peter. 2005. 'Czernowitz als geistige Lebensform — Die Stadt und ihre Kultur', in Helmut Braun (ed.), *Czernowitz — die Geschichte einer untergegangenen Kulturmetropole*, pp. 7–30. Berlin: Links Verlag.

Schlattner, Eginald. 1998. *Der geköpfte Hahn*. Vienna and Munich: Zsolnay Verlag.

von Rezzori, Gregor. 1989. *Blumen im Schnee — Portraitstudien zu einer Autobiographie, die ich nie schreiben werde*. Munich: Bertelsmann.

Yavetz, Zvi. 2007. *Erinnerung an Czernowitz — Wo Menschen und Bücher lebten*. Munich: C. H. Beck Verlag.

3

(Re-)configuring the Soloist as a 'Nomadic' Modernity Trickster

The Case of 'Composer' in Bukusu Circumcision Folklore

Chris J. C. Wasike

This chapter is a report of the findings of an investigation into the Babukusu circumcision song text as an object of masculine gaze. Using a case study of one prominent circumcision song soloist called Stargrant Wanyonyi Lusanya, whose performance I observed, I will point out how his peculiar mode of performance can be read using the theoretical tenets of 'nomadic tricksterism'. Of particular note from my findings is how circumcision songs as a seasonal and ritual-specific genre among the Babukusu, occupy an important place in the cultural construction and cosmology of the Bukusu community. Some of the songs I collected are sacred and cannot be sung outside the circumcision ritual space. For my analysis though, I only use excerpts and not complete texts to illustrate

---

* The term 'folklore' is used here advisedly taking cognizance of the intellectual polemics and contestations associated with it. In our current analysis it entails both the verbal and performative aspects of the circumcision genre. For a more cogent elaboration on this terminology, see also Oring (2006: 205–20); Roginsky (2007: 41–63); Smidchens (1999: 51–70).

my arguments. The chapter also engages with the general African (specifically the Bukusu) trickster motif as a 'nomadological' framing that can be used to read Bukusu circumcision songs as cultural discourses that gesture towards a male hegemonic instrumentality. By juxtaposing the Deleuzian view of 'nomadism', with the African conceptual understanding of the trickster as the interstitial and in-between character, I hope to reread the songs and the soloist's performance gimmicks as fluid concepts. The idea of nomadic thought as originally framed by Gilles Deleuze and Felix Guattari is based on the deconstruction of established and stable identities in favour of those that welcome fluidity and constant changes and states of 'becoming' (1988: 3–25). This view resonates with many scholarly readings of the African trickster as a character who constantly oscillates between the centre and margins of the social landscape (Pelton 1980; White 1999). He is a master of deception, ambivalence, ambiguity and liminal existence, as I shall illustrate further in the chapter.

Songs as cultural discourses are often sites of gender contests. Liz Gunner argues that the song genre often gets entangled in 'seamless masculinity with little place for gendered identities' (2009: 27). She emphasizes that 'song can be seen as unstable and unruly; a signifier with a power of its own not entirely beholden to its new owner' (ibid.: 29). The circumcision song, like many other sonic genres, is striking if not conspicuous because of its uncanny ability to invite anybody and everybody to join in. Its familiar and easy to learn call-and-response structure often gives it a likeable appeal and a wider social meaning. This genre is highly eroticized among the Babukusu and the lewd nuances and brash sexual imagery that punctuate its lyrics are sometimes discomfiting to the conservative and Christianized members of the society. Interestingly, it is this sexual objectification and the pointed metaphors of the song lyrics that have propelled the genre to renewed commercialized and nationwide appeal in Kenya. Aside from the embarrassing idioms that are sung by circumcision retinues in the rural spaces, advertising agencies, musicians and even politicians have appropriated the Bukusu circumcision song genre for commercial and political purposes, as we shall illustrate shortly. But before examining how the circumcision song soloist fits into the 'nomadic trickster' framing it is beneficial to delineate some of the nascent features of the Bukusu socio-cultural background from which he emerges.

Mythical Origin of Bukusu Circumcision and the Role of the Soloist

The Babukusu are one of the 17 or so sub-tribes[1] of the Luhya tribe, an ethnic Bantu-speaking group that predominantly occupy the western part of Kenya. They are neighbours to the Kalenjin on the northern and eastern sides, the Luo on the south and Teso and Bagisu[2] on the western border between Kenya and Uganda. The many other Luhya sub-groups include the Maragoli, Wanga, Banyala, Isukha and others. Administratively, the Bukusu occupy the larger Bungoma and parts of Trans-Nzoia districts. They speak the 'Lubukusu' language, a dialect that has marked similarities with other Luhya languages although it is distinctly different orthographically and phonetically. Economically, the Bukusu are known to practise both the rearing of livestock like cattle, sheep and goats, and small-scale agricultural farming. With the advent of modernity and the resultant decrease in the size of land available for such activities, more and more people are slowly migrating to urban areas or gradually adopting semi-urban lifestyles. Culturally, the Bukusu are significantly different from other Luhya sub-nationalities because of the elaborate manner in which they practice circumcision. Even for other groups that still practise the initiation rite, the Bukusu are conspicuous and recalcitrant by their persistent observance of this cultural practice.

Perhaps due to the cultural premium they accord this ritual, the symbolism of male circumcision is quite poignant in the cultural, gender and identity constructions within the community. The Babukusu men, for instance, pride themselves as the community of *basani* — 'the circumcised' — as opposed to 'others', who do not practise the rite. This ethnic exclusionism based on the rite, partly emanates from the mythical and larger-than-life narratives that are circulated to explain the genealogy of the practice among its people. Oral and written accounts confirm that this tradition has been carried out by its members for as long as

---

[1] For a more comprehensive discussion of the Babukusu genealogy and cultural history, see Makila (1976).

[2] The Bagisu of eastern Uganda are considered by the Babukusu as their genealogical cousins because they share linguistic similarities and the manner in which they both practice male circumcision. For more on the Bagisu and how their circumcision ritual relates to our analysis, see Heald (1989).

the community's memory can be stretched (Makila 1976, 2004; Wasike 2010). Bukusu cultural historians and oral artists contend that it was Mango, an elder from the eminent Bakhurarwa clan, who reformed and modelled the practice as it is known to this day. The story goes that Mango, the eponymous hero of circumcision, slew a big killer serpent called *khururwe yabebe* Trans-Nzoia — which literally translates as 'the massive fiery one' — that had been terrorizing Babukusu at a place called *Mwiala* (a sacred cave near Bwayi Hills in Bungoma District). As part of the community's heroic gesture of recognition for his unmatched valiance, he was circumcised and subsequently given a young beautiful maiden as a wife by the neighboring Sebei, a Kalenjin sub group. It is also believed that in his snake-slaying feat Mango used *embalu* (a sharp knife/sword), *wamachari* (a sharp, pointed spear used in close combat), *lisakha* (a long spear) and *sisindi* (a dry tree stump on which the snake laid its head before he chopped it off). Since then, the Bukusu have practised circumcision in the same elaborate way it was originally done on Mango. Mango is also the famed progenitor of the eight circumcision age-sets[3] of the Babukusu, namely *Kolongolo, Kikwameti, Kananachi, Kinyikeu, Nyange, Maina, Bachuma,* and *Sawa*. Each of these age-sets (*bibingilo*) has six sub-age-sets (*chibololi*) except the Bachuma sub-cluster which has eight. Mango was part of the first age-set of the Kolongolo cluster. In practice, each age-set except the Bachuma cluster takes a decade to complete.

The circumcision ritual as practised in the modern setting remains elaborate, although the influence of modernity by way of literacy, Christianity, modern medicine and the reality of HIV/AIDS has significantly attenuated the cultural attention to detail originally associated with it. But for those who practise it in its original undiluted fashion, care is taken to ensure that all its cultural processes are meticulously followed. Such extraordinary care is taken partly because the occasion of circumcision is an opportunity to demonstrate cultural valour and honour. Again, the collective and individual braggadocio associated with the successful undertaking of this ritual is manifested through the various word images that the Babukusu use to refer to it. These include *khukhebwa*

---

[3]. The eight circumcision age-sets of the Babukusu are very much linked to the Kalenjin circumcision age-sets. This explains why some cultural historians have claimed that the Bukusu circumcision was borrowed from their Kalenjin neighbours.

(being circumcised), *embalu* (the knife) or *khukhwingila* (which literally means 'to enter'). *Khukhebwa* alludes to the 'circular chopping' action in the removal of the prepuce during the operation, while *embalu* (the sharp knife like the one Mango used to kill the python) graphically symbolizes the 'fierce sharpness and fire' of the circumciser's knife that is reputed for the pain it unleashes on initiates during the operation. *Khukhwingila* points to the transitional process of the initiate moving from childhood and 'entering' the realm of adulthood. These terms are applied to different effect and affect by the soloist's lyricism during performances.

The actual preparation for the ceremony[4] usually begins with a boy (mostly an adolescent) declaring to his father or any other senior male relative (not a female relative or mother — which is 'cowardly') that he has 'the heart to be circumcised' (*kumwoyo kwe khukhebwa*). It is then at the discretion of the father to give the boy the green light. If the father is confident that the boy is 'old enough' (*kaangale*) to face the knife, he grants the boy's wish. But in cases where the father thinks the boy is too young, or suspects the youngster has been egged on by his peers or his mother without understanding the gravity of the ritual, he declines. After being given the go-ahead, the initiate acquires circumcision jingles (*chinyimba*), which he beats on metallic hand bangles (*birere*) as he stylishly dances to the accompaniment of songs sung by an entourage of singers (*baminya* — usually older cousins, brothers or even curious neighbours) in a process called *khulanga* — which literally means 'calling relatives' to witness the occasion. The exercise of the soon-to-be-initiated boy running around to invite his relatives is dramatic and could take between three days to a whole week depending on the number of relatives the family has.

On the eve of the day of circumcision, the initiate goes to his maternal uncles (*ebukhocha*) where an animal, preferably a bull, is slaughtered and a piece of the T-bone steak — otherwise called *luliki* or *likhoni* — is mounted on his neck and carried all the way to his father's compound. At his father's compound another bull is slaughtered and a piece of the animal's entrails (*khasombo*) is put round his neck as the undigested remains from the bull's innards (*buse*) are smeared on the boy's face. The purpose of this elaborate sacrifice is not just to invoke the spirits of the ancestors to guide the whole ritual, but to precipitate *lirima* (anger)

---

[4] For more on the circumcision songs and the preparation for the ceremony, see Makila (2004); Wanyama (2006).

and *bunyindafu* (bravado) which are considered important emotions in circumcision and the process of becoming a man. This section of the ritual is particularly brutalizing and is meant to test the patience and resilience of the boys in terms of their readiness to face trying moments like men. For a good part of the evening and the night before, the initiate is sung for, ridiculed and taunted by friends, relatives and neighbours who move round the dancing initiate in circular clockwise or anticlockwise motions. It is at this point that 'composer', the circumcision song soloist, literally budges onto the scene and totally appropriates the performance space. His mode of operation is nomadic, as I shall demonstrate later in this chapter.

However, on the specified day, the boy is taken to the river very early in the morning by a group of male relatives that sing to him a special encouragement song, *Oraho bachonga* which exhorts the boy to literally 'put his penis there to be carved'. At a secluded swamp pit (*esilongo*), he strips naked and bathes in the cold water as part of the traditional anaesthesia in the form of numbing the body to minimize pain during the operation. A male relative smears him with river mud (*khumana*) all over his body and a special piece of elephant grass called *kwa hututu* is mounted conspicuously on his head. On the way to the father's courtyard a sacred song *sioyaye*,[5] specifically meant for this occasion, is sung to urge on the boy to the final culmination of the operation. In the song he is taunted and dared to declare if he has second thoughts so that he can be left alone. The actual operation takes place in the father's or other senior male relative's courtyard (*khuluya*) — a spot in front of the house where grains are dried. It involves the surgical removal of the foreskin from around the *glans* by *omukhebi* — a specially trained and recognized traditional surgeon. The initiate is expected to display unwavering fortitude without betraying any signs of fear in this publicly-witnessed ceremony. Any slight signs of twitching, trembling, blinking of eyes or mumblings from the boy during the operation are immediately interpreted as *khuria embalu* (fearing the knife), which is an embarrassment to the family and clan at large.

---

[5] This is the most sacred circumcision song among the Babukusu. It is sung by senior members of the community on the final trip from the river to the homestead where the initiate will be circumcised. However, it is sometimes also sung when a piece of meat is being put on the initiate's neck, to remind him of the seriousness of the occasion. This song is rarely sung by the trickster soloist because of its sacredness.

As soon as the boy has successfully gone through the ritual, men roar their approval in unison to welcome the initiate into the male club and the women chime in with ululations and dances of triumph. The men celebrate this success with war songs that have conquest images like *khwera omurwa* (we have killed the Maasai enemy) and *khwahela ta!* (now we can breathe after winning). The boy who now moves on from being *omusinde* — uncircumcised — to *omusani* — circumcised — is congratulated with gifts such as clothes, money, special foods like dried meat (*enyama esike*) or even a live animal like a bullock. From then on, the initiate is allowed to enjoy the trappings of adulthood including marriage and ownership of property, partaking in cultural activities and ceremonies.

'Composer' Stargrant, Alias Staka Ngunyi, Sikuta Manyanga a.k.a. Papa Solo: The Man and His Art

Among the Bukusu, circumcision is a cultural instrument of performing power, and it acts as 'a symbolic message concerning personhood, gender, cosmology, status and community inscribed in the body' (Silverman 2004: 442). A closer analysis though, reveals that this is not achieved without the attendant contradictions that challenge and question the validity of using the ritual as a yardstick and symbol of calibrating masculinity in a society that is constantly responding to the ever-changing definitions of malehood. In the course of my interviews with circumcision soloist Stargrant Wanyonyi Lusanya, it emerged that these are some of the contradictions that he grapples with not just in his own life but throughout his live performances. Indeed, the composer's personal story is full of contradictions. Born almost 40 years ago and married with five children, Stargrant is not a professional circumcision song performer, but only does it because it is a calling or *kumusambwa*, a talent he inherited from his forefathers, he says.[6] In his element, people in the rural village of Wamunyiri, Bungoma call him pet names such as *Staka Ngunyi, Sikuta Manyanga*, 'Composer', and 'Papa Solo'. All these are honorific and praise platitudes that speak to his lyrical genius that is attested by many in the village during the season of circumcision. He is particularly fond of the

---

[6] Interview with Stargrant Wanyonyi Lusanya, 8 August 2008.

'composer' and 'Papa Solo' praise-names because they exalt his musical giftedness to the levels of renowned Congolese singers. The praise-names fundamentally attain greater significance within the performance space especially when they are woven into his song lyrics.

When he is not immersed in the month-long circumcision festivities, Stargrant runs and supervises a fleet of 10 bicycle taxis popularly known in Western Kenya as *boda boda*.[7] Because he also runs a small grocery shop at a nearby shopping centre, he has employed younger men who ride the bicycles picking up and dropping off passengers around the village, in exchange for a small cut in the fares that many rural passengers pay for this valuable service. Ironically he also confesses to the Catholic faith and occasionally volunteers as an usher at a local church during Sunday services. Ultimately for him, singing circumcision songs is a one-off seasonal affair. It is therefore interesting how aspects of his personal life dovetail, inform and sometimes subvert the compositions and lyrics of his performances.

From a literary perspective, I am keen to unravel how the soloist's techniques of creative execution are necessitated by contexts of the moment and the ambience of the ritual itself. The question to ask here is: to what extent does the circumcision song soloist assume the trickster's persona as a façade that helps him to sing what is ordinarily 'unsingable' and say what is morally unpalatable? Most of the songs analyzed here were recorded from live performances conducted by Stargrant as he moved from one homestead to another, on different nights and sometimes in one night, exhibiting his sonic prowess. The focus is on the performances on the night before the penultimate circumcision. Given the conviviality, licentiousness and celebratory mood that characterizes such nights, I will also tease out the extent to which the soloist/composer uses the cover of darkness to play out different foils and camouflages that are clearly nomadic and trickster-like. In a sense, I hope to unpack how the 'composer' as a nocturnal itinerant, a tactician of the nightly rural landscape, uses song to psych, ridicule and taunt the initiate, himself and the society at large.

---

[7] The term *boda boda* literally refers to the border-to-border bicycle taxis that were originally popular in transporting passengers across the Kenya–Uganda border at Busia town in western Kenya.

Theorizing Tricksterism and Nomadism in African Folklore

The figure of the trickster has been the subject of many scholarly works. From anthropologists, folklore analysts and literary critics the term 'trickster' has been variously examined, not just as a feature of human cosmology, but as a counterpoint that often helps us to appreciate the ironies and contradictions of life itself. Early folklore studies indicate that it was in fact Daniel Brinton in his seminal work entitled *The Myths of the New World* (Brinton 1868) who was among the first to directly use the term trickster in relation to the mesmerizing figure of North American Indian mythology and folklore; a character who often featured as a 'gross deceiver, a crude prankster, a creator of the earth, a shaper of culture and fool caught in his own lies' (ibid.: 161–62). This initial provenance and figuration of the trickster is echoed by Mac Linscott Ricketts (1965), when he summarizes the trickster's mannerisms thus:

> [He] is the teacher of cultural skills and customs, but he is also a prankster who is grossly erotic, insatiably hungry, inordinately vain, deceitful and cunning toward friends as well as foes; a restless wanderer upon the face of the earth, and a blunderer who is often the victim of his own tricks and follies (ibid.: 327–50).

This figuration of the trickster has been recast and persistently deployed in many interpretations of folklore texts. In the African literary canon, and particularly in oral folktales, this baffling figure has consistently been read as a trickster, transformer and cultural protagonist. From Ananse the Rabbit of the Ashanti in Ghana; Legba, the trickster god of the Fon in Benin; Ture of the Azande in central Africa; and Wanakhamuna, the Rabbit of the Babukusu in Kenya, the trickster image in folktales is often framed as a symbolic agency of the 'struggle to make the world human' (Pelton 1980: 9): a character who ceaselessly strives to oppose any kind of hegemony even as he hopes to become a 'master of the world' (ibid.).

Incidentally, most of the materials analyzed so far as relating to the trickster motif, have expectedly concentrated on the folktale. In an introduction to his collection of trickster narratives from the Azande people of central Africa, Edward Evan Evans-Pritchard makes fundamentally cogent remarks on the character of Ture, the trickster persona that is so beloved in the folktales. In his view, Ture is usually portrayed as 'a character of depravity; liar, cheat, lecher, murderer; vain, greedy, treacherous, ungrateful, poltroon and a braggart' (Evans-Pritchard 1967: 28). But what is most appealing about this selfish personality, who is incidentally the hero of most stories told to Azande children is 'his whimsical fooling, recklessness, impetuosity, puckish irresponsibility, his childish desire to show how clever he is, his total absorption in song and dance, his feathered hat and his flouting of every convention' (ibid.). 'In spite of his nefarious conduct', adds Evans-Pritchard, 'he is never really malicious . . . indeed he is an endearing innocence' (ibid.).

Evans-Pritchard's understanding of Ture of the Azande resonates with that of Ananse, Legba and Wanakhamuna despite the differentiated social contexts. In his study of the mythical and sacred features of the trickster among the Ashanti and Fon communities of west Africa, Robert Pelton (1980) critically examines Ananse and Legba respectively. He summarizes the salient characteristics of the trickster as being 'loutish, lustful, puffed up with boasts and lies, ravenous for foolery and food, yet managing always to draw order from ordure' (ibid.: 2). He adds that despite being featured as 'seemingly trivial and altogether lawless, he arouses affection and even esteem wherever his stories are told, as he defies mythic seriousness and social logic' (ibid.). He is the true embodiment of elusiveness and slipperiness, oscillating between the binaries of buffoonery and seriousness, the moral and obscene, licentiousness and conservativism.

Wanakhamuna the Rabbit, a trickster character that appears in Bukusu folktales, is configured in a similar way as Ananse and Legba. Boastful, capricious and an opportunist to boot, he appears in most situations as a brainy, clever but calculating character that easily outmanoeuvres other animals that are bigger in physique. Most trickster stories that have him as the hero often play out the trope of brain versus brawn, with Wanakhamuna always coming out on top. Being the braggart he is known for, after each of these conquests, he often boasts thus: *Ese Wanakhamuna makesi mangi, okhwa Wamukhayo, kamakesi kalinjira!* (I, Wanakhamuna the brainy one, son of the Indomitable, I am too clever for myself!). In such cases, self-praises are meant to taunt the bigger outsmarted character much to the chagrin or amusement of the audience in real society. However, Wanakhamuna does not win all the time. There are scenarios when he overreaches himself and his pranks fall flat. In such cases, his self-assuredness lands him in big trouble as he sheds tears of defeat much like what occasionally happens to Jerry in the popular *Tom and Jerry* television cartoons.

But perhaps the most succinct interpretation of the trickster that fits well into our current analysis is Bob W. White's (1999) engaging delineation of the animator in Congolese popular Lingala music. In his theoretically recuperative and insightful article entitled 'Modernity's Trickster: "Dipping" and "Throwing" in Congolese Popular Dance Music', White outlines the ambiguous position of this popular music animator referred to as the *atalaku* in Congolese dance music. He proceeds to elucidate how the animator is a 'social provocateur', who is part human and part a trickster, a 'live-time trickster' who amuses but also embarrasses his listeners because of his lewd imagery, obscene uglification and suggestively eroticized antics on stage (ibid.: 157). He goes on further to argue that *atalaku* is the archetypal embodiment of a character on the margins of society who is quite resourceful even in his helplessness (ibid.: 167) and his outrageous stage presence adds to the tension and pleasure of the live performances (ibid.: 157). His ability to integrate modern aspects of song composition into the traditional structures of folk music is particularly singled out as the mainstay of his creative genius and his constant dabbling as a praise-singer and buffoon reinforces and subverts social power hierarchies (ibid.: 168). My analysis will benefit a lot from the two configurations of the trickster as an *atalaku* and Wanakhamuna. Indeed both the *atalaku* and the circumcision 'composer' are ubiquitous Wanakhamuna-like characters that navigate between the centre and margins of society even as they appropriate and use their creative verbal skills to countermand their social marginalization. This, I argue, is only achieved because of their 'nomadic' propensities to appear and disappear both in temporal and spatial performative realities.

Before delineating how composer projects images of the 'nomadic trickster', it is imperative to briefly offer definitions and thoughts on nomadism as a theoretical constellation that informs my current analysis. Nomadic thought as first conceived by French philosophers Gilles Deleuze and Felix Guattari in *Nomadology: The War Machine* relates to the multiplicity of identities that grow from each other in what aims to be a never-ending process or what they call the 'principle of multiplicity' (1986: 5–6). In their view,

> [T]he nomad has a territory; he follows customary paths . . . the elements of his dwelling are concretized in terms of the trajectory that is forever mobilizing them . . . Whereas the migrant leaves behind a [hostile] milieu, the nomad is one who does not depart, [nor wants to] depart, who clings to the smooth space left by the receding forest . . . the nomad moves, but while seated, and he is only seated while moving . . . [and]

knows how to wait [with] infinite patience. Immobility and speed, cata-
tonia and rush, a "stationary process" [are nomadic] . . . He is a vec-
tor of deterritorialization . . . [adding] desert to desert (Deleuze and
Guattari 1986: 50–60).

The Deleuzian nomad is in fact a nascent, unstable and ambivalent manifestation that is constantly imagining and reimagining itself.
Rosi Braidotti adds that nomadism is a 'vertiginous progression towards
deconstructing identity; a molecularization of the self' (1994: 16). The
nomadic subject, argues Braidotti, is inspired by experience of people and
cultures that are literally nomadic (ibid.). But nomadism as an abstract
framework relates more to the kind of critical consciousness that resists
settling into socially-coded modes of thought and behaviour (ibid.: 5).
As an intellectual purchase, nomadism also speaks to the deconstruction
of established and apparently stable identities in favour of the tenuous,
fluctuating and constantly changing ones. These identities, or 'states of
becoming' in Deleuzian speak are part of a continuous process of constant
change and transformation of the individual based on dynamic interaction — a state of existence that moves beyond fixed categorizations.

Deleuze and Guattari further elaborate their theorization of nomadism by coining the term *rhizome*, a figuration that emanates from plant
roots that grow underground, sideways as opposed to the usual vertical
linear roots. The idea of a rhizome speaks well to our interpretation of
song as a discourse because, as they posit:

> [A song] is not an image of the world. It forms a rhizome with the world,
> there is an aparallel evolution of [song] and the world . . . Always fol-
> low the rhizome by rupture; [rhizomes] lengthen, prolong, and relay the
> line of flight; mak[ing] it vary . . . The rhizome is a map and not a trac-
> ing . . . open and connectable in all dimensions; it is detachable, revers-
> ible, susceptible to constant modification . . . conceived as a work of art,
> and constructed as a political action . . . The coordinates are determined
> . . . by pragmatics [of] composing multiplicities or aggregates of intensi-
> ties . . . The rhizome operates by variations, expansion, conquest, cap-
> ture, offshoots . . . [and contains] multiple entryways and exits and its
> own lines of flight (Deleuze and Guattari 1988: 1–13, 21).

The rhizome as so configured appears to be a metaphor for the movement between multiple ideas, without borders. Just like nomadism, rhizomatic thought has the uncanny affinity of engaging the world by crossing
boundaries and making interconnections with a multitude of various
ideas. The rhizome, in fact, stands for a restless political consciousness

and an espousal to subvert monolithic discourses. More importantly, in our case, the Deleuzian principle of multiplicity and the rhizome are essential iconicities understood in terms of how they iterate and underscore the 'fluidity' and 'an acute awareness of the non-fixity of boundaries' (Braidotti 1994: 12) for the circumcision song performer and his art. To a certain extent, we hope to critically examine how our soloist as a 'rhizomatic' and 'nomadic' trickster challenges the authority of hegemonic discourses both textually and performatively.

Mapping the Ruralscape and Symbolizing Nomadic Referents: Circumcision Song Rendition as a Site for Tricksterism and Rhizomatic Lyrical Images

The first time I encountered Stargrant in his performative element, I was completely swept off my feet not just by his imposing stage presence and dramatic poses, but more significantly by the unmistakable magic of his voice and magnetic personality. At every homestead he conducted his soloist duties he had a way of attracting attention to himself not because of his lean physical stature, but mostly through his superior lyricism. Such was the indomitable and ubiquitous role of the soloist at every ceremony of the night before circumcision that his audiences — both as listeners and the chorus that responds to his call phrases — were often left begging for more. 'Composer', as Stargrant was fondly christened, took charge of the circumcision folklore performance for a good part of the night, albeit with a sense of command and flair that left everyone at his bidding. The nature of the circumcision performance — *khuminya* in Lubukusu — consists of the soloist leading a retinue of chorus singers in a call-and-response song structure. As the initiate dances and knocks his jingles/metallophones to the rhythm of the song, the soloist conducts his chorus in circular clockwise or anticlockwise trots and excited jaunts around him. These stylish but light jogs around *omusinde* (initiate) are appropriately referred to in Lubukusu as *khusanya* (light running) or *khuracha* (an animated rhythmic trot).

Alongside the song, various people in the singing crowd chime in and intrude with wild screams, praises and hoots from all types of improvised wind instruments such as whistles, metal and plastic pipes, hollow pipes hewn from pawpaw or bamboo sticks, horns, gourds and even *vuvuzelas*. Notably, the wild chants and screams are taunts and praises that are intermittently directed at the initiate and his relatives or the soloist. Chants like '*Muchuli bwasiele!*' (Tomorrow is too near!), '*Bulanga!*' (Tell us the truth!), '*Ng'unyanga! Nyanga olifwa Papa Solo!*' (Sing! One day we will miss you when you die, Papa Solo!) repeatedly rend the air as an orchestra-like atmosphere is created and sustained by the mix of all these antiphonal acoustics of lyrics, shouts and instrumentations. Throughout this carnivalesque performance, 'composer' the song soloist leads through his verbal and performative antics.

As a performer, Stargrant is true to his various praise names and his personality clearly fits with what Deleuze and Guattari call the principle of multiplicity. According to him, 'composer' is a praise name his ardent song fans gave him as a recognition of his creative knack for improvising and playing around with words and sounds in his circumcision song renditions.[8] At one performance a member of the singing chorus shouted, 'Composer *Staka Ngunyi, Sikuta Manyanga, kutanga kumwenya papa!*', ("Composer" Staka Ngunyi, Sikuta Manyanga, animate the song daddy!) as a way of encouraging Stargrant to step up his performance. *Staka* is the Lubukusu orthographic short form of his Christian name Stargrant, while *Ngunyi* is a praise-name that emanates from the Lubukusu word *chingunyi*, meaning 'problems' or 'anxieties'. *Sikuta* is yet another praise-name constructed from the peculiar Bukusu circumcision singing mode of *khukuta kumwenya*, which literally means 'to swell the song' or sing with an animated tempo. But *Manyanga* is a clownish name that is derived from the percussive instrumentations made from stones, placed in used cans and shaken rhythmically to heighten the musicality of the song's performance. On various occasions Stargrant himself could be seen swinging the rhythmic shakers, hence his praise name *Manyanga*. In the performance arena of this genre, the use of different praise-names certainly conjures up images of a human 'nomadic trickster' in action. Like a character with multiple identities, the soloist oscillates between the centre and margins of the social and performative spaces, assuming different identities that are signified by the different praise names given to him.

The sense of 'composer' being and not being in the performance and social spaces as represented by the polyvalent significations that are associated with each praise-name is nomadic so to speak. Even in real life, Stargrant remains an elusive and slippery embodiment of different trades and vocations. From being an entrepreneur by virtue of his grocery shop and seemingly flourishing *boda boda* businesses to his frequent flirtations

---

[8] Interview with Stargrant Wanyonyi Lusanya, 8 August 2008.

with church matters as an usher, 'composer' Stargrant is a conundrum of many interests knotted into one. Like a 'nomad' in the literal sense, he seems to deftly navigate and move around making the best of his creative human proclivities and rapacious propensities. Yet like an archetypal trickster in African folklore he can, simultaneously, be and not be all the identities and categorizations associated with him, both in real life and within the performance space.

In my view though, 'composer' as a nomadic trickster best navigates the tenuous, interstitial and sometimes in-between spaces of performance and social realm by deploying various verbal and bodily pranks. His rapprochement with various identities and significations serves as agency of inscribing and prescribing the self and others in temporal and imaginary cultural spaces. Through his lead role in the songs' enactment, he often acts as a 'nomadic' social provocateur that deploys his linguistic prowess and idiomatic genius through song in order to articulate the contradictions of circumcision and life in general. In a popular song — Stargrant's favourite, actually — entitled *Amba mutalya* he best captures the genealogy, meaning and contradictions of male circumcision, even as he throws praises about himself and those who listen to him.

Amba Mutalya

Soloist	Chorus/Response
1. *Enje chelechenje kumumu kufwa Mulamwa wabira ne khamini!*	*Amba mutalya.*
2. *Mbukutu bali mbukutu, hututu bali hututu, chinyanga echo, omundu wecha bali Mango.*	*Amba mutalya.*
3. *Khwimbilisia bulayi mutalya kuno, khane Mango owakurera.*	*Amba mutalya.*
4. *Nacha khusiboti nanyolakho Maiko, papa ndi injinihia, khane mutalya naye aloba,*	*Amba mutalya.*
5. *Kuno musambwa kwa bakhale,*	*Aaah Webale oye Amba mutalya.*
6. *Khane Staka nase ngana*	*Aaah Webale oyee, Amba mutalya.*
7. *Khane ng'unya ne bung'ali*	*Aaah Webale oyee, Amba mutalya.*
8. *Khane Sikuta bali nduka*	*Aaah Webale oyee, Amba mutalya.*
9. *Oli nanyola khumadam kukhana kwemini, kwakhoma kuli fwakini, kuli situipiti khane mawe okubolele.*	*Amba mutalya.*

10. *Ali kumbafu, sitiupiti khane silimu eli munda*   *Amba mutalya.*
11. *Oli khwapima bifuki khwacha khutemperecha,*   *Amba mutalya.*
    bali mukhwasi kanja nekhwebuta.
12. *Nekhwimbilisia kalakha*   *Aaah, webale oyee,*
     Amba mutalya.
13. *Khane mutalya ne liloko*   *Aaah webale oyee*
     Amba mutalya.

English translation (unless otherwise noted all translations are mine):

	Soloist	*Chorus/Response*
1.	Very early, the sun is shining, my sister-in-law passed by dressed in a miniskirt	Catch the *mutalya.*
2.	*Mbukutu* then *mbukutu*, the horn bill is a hornbill, there once came a man called Mango	Catch the *mutalya.*
3.	We sing well about this *mutalya*, Because it is Mango who brought it.	Catch the *mutalya.*
4.	I went to Siboti, met Michael, the famous engineer, this is *mutalya* but he denies,	Catch the *mutalya.*
5.	This is the spirit of our forefathers	Aaah thank you oyee, Catch the *mutalya.*
6.	So Staka I can narrate	Aaah thank you oyee, Catch the *mutalya.*
7.	So I sing about the truth	Aaah thank you oyee, Catch the *mutalya.*
8.	So Sikuta I can rule	Aaah thank you oyee, Catch the *mutalya.*
9.	Then I found a madam, a woman with a good behind, she abused me 'fucking', 'stupid', so it's the mother who sent her,	Catch the *mutalya.*
10.	She persisted 'useless', 'stupid' but then she had HIV/AIDS in her stomach,	Catch the *mutalya.*
11.	When we tested his blood, and then the temperature, Our brother-in-law had started scratching himself	Catch the *mutalya*
12.	Let's sing slowly	Aaah thank you oyee, Catch the mutalya.
13.	So *mutalya* can also be witchcraft	Aaah thank you oyee Catch the *mutalya.*

In the above song, the soloist takes charge of the whole rendition through his call phrases. In fact, it is he who determines the tempo and rhythm of the song to which the initiate plays his metallophones. His wide repertoire of Bukusu idioms and imagery excites the audience and the chorus group as he ingeniously blends modern and traditional themes in his lyrics. For instance, when he upbraids and pokes fun at a 'sister-in-law passing by in a miniskirt' he is not just ridiculing the women folk in the rural context, but he is also satirizing modern Western-style dress codes that are embarrassing within the conservative ruralscape. In the subsequent line though, he describes how circumcision was founded by an eponymous hero called Mango.

Like a typical trickster and a nomadic one, he is a linguistic polyglot and wordsmith *par excellence* and true to his praise-name of 'composer', he commandeers the structure and content of all the songs. When he uses the conceited image of *mutalya* — loosely translating to 'something enigmatic' — he is deftly but deliberately enunciating the inherent contradictions associated with the male initiation ritual and the whole philosophy of life in general. The image of *mutalya* appears to capture the phallic symbolism and the concomitant contradictions that go with it. But the personal anecdote of how 'composer' tried to seduce a girl, who badly abused him, only for him to realize that she was infected with HIV/AIDS is an ironical comment on the sexuality of a circumcised male. Although the Babukusu circumcision is meant to reaffirm the sexual prowess of a dominant masculinity, the soloist appears to be sounding a warning that HIV/AIDS is a life-threatening reality that can't be ignored. His derisive but empathetic recounting of a brother-in-law's experience when he went for an HIV test and discovered that his blood was infected with the virus, his temperature was up and he had contracted a skin condition, is a stark confession that the AIDS pandemic is real even in the rural setting.

As he belts out sonic images and home truths Stargrant is always conscious of his infectious personality. In many of his lyrics, he draws attention to himself and to prominent personalities in attendance. Aware that his soloing magic can drive his audience into a frenzy, he proceeds to rub it in and sustain the tempo by throwing praise epithets about himself. In the above song extract for instance, he sings, 'So Staka I can narrate', 'I sing the truth' and 'Sikuta I can rule'. He even recognizes the presence of Michael, an engineer from a place called Siboti. Clearly, the soloist at such moments is beside himself as he relishes the delirious appreciation of his performative prominence. Just like Legba, the 'divine linguist' of the Fon, and Wanakhamuna, the Babukusu vain trickster, he is a polyglot with a bloated ego and immensely enjoys bragging, fooling and mesmerizing the crowd with his song antics. At his performative best, he is neither a conservative moralist nor a foul-mouthed lecher; he is both or none at all, literally 'nomadic' and preferring to remain at the interstices and in-between spaces. He is even in a trance himself, and can't believe how the whole audience is literally at his mercy, as they keep hollering and demanding for more from him. Interestingly, at some point the audience does not really care what he means or intends to communicate through his songs, but are more interested in his ability to arrest and sustain the musical tempo that he has created.

Yet 'composer' is at his vintage lyrical best when he engages in more graphic sexual symbolizations. Circumcision being a male domain, it is largely expected that most of the metaphors applied by the singers openly objectify the male organ and the sexual act. As Pierre Bourdieu (2001) has argued elsewhere, the sexual act has for a long time been used by men as an instrument of masculine domination. Among the Babukusu the male circumcision ceremony is one such occasion of affirming male dominance. But the attendant licentiousness, obscenities and moral permissiveness of such cultural forums is incidentally the trickster's territory. Robert Pelton (1980) observes that the trickster in the African world view is 'ravenous for foolery and food', embodying a moral grammar through which he 'links animality and ritual transformation . . . [and] shapes culture by means of sex and laughter' (ibid.: 2). Bob W. White (1999) adds that, '[w]hile he is not an animal', the trickster 'does display certain tendencies: bodily release through performance and voracious appetite and greed for food and sex' (ibid.: 157–75). Nowhere is this better illustrated than in the Bukusu circumcision song performance. In another popular song entitled *Tindo*, 'composer' sings thus:

Tindo

Soloist	Chorus/Response
1. *Tindooo we tindo*	*Ooooh mwana wefwe munyanye,*
2. *Tindooo wananga*	*Ooooh mwana wefwe munyanye,*
3. *Tindo wamwene wenyile*	*Munyanye,*
4. *Kumusinde ndi wenyile embalu,*	*Munyanye,*
5. *Tindo lukembe luluma*	*Munyanye,*
6. *Masewa muchuli bwasiele*	*Munyanye,*
7. *Tindoo bali khunyanyanga,*	*Munyanye,*
8. *Basani ndi khunyanyanga*	*Munyanye,*

9. *Nifwe Siniobi ndi khunyanyanga*   *Munyanye,*
10. *Staka ndi khanyanyanga*   *Munyanye,*
11. *Yaya ndi kongona, wee*   *Eeh kongona*
    nakhuwelekho ndi kongona,
12. *Kongona Mwalimu Teacher ndi kongona,*   *Eeh kongona,*
13. *Bali Composer, embalu ya musano oli*   *Eeh kongona,*
    kongona,
14. *Ali khwesa abele khalosi ndi khwesa,*   *Eeh kongona.*
15. *Kongona noli profesa, oli*   *Eeh kongona.*
    kongona

English Translation:

Soloist   **Chorus/Response**

1. *Tindo you Tindo*   *Ooooh our son you*
                                                    will be chewed,

2. *Tindo you called me*   *Ooooh our son you*
                                                    will be chewed,

3. *Tindo you wanted it yourself*   *You will be chewed,*
4. *You the uncircumcised want the knife*   *You will be chewed,*
5. *Tindo the circumciser's knife stings*   *You will be chewed*
6. *Masewa tomorrow you will see*   *You will be chewed,*
7. *Tindoo you know we chew,*   *Let's chew it,*
8. *We the circumcised men chew*   *Let's chew it,*
9. *Tindoo we are the copulators,*   *Let's chew it,*
10. *Staka also chews*   *Let's chew it,*
11. *I say empty it, when you are given always empty* *Eeh empty it,*
12. *Empty it Mwalimu Teacher, please empty it,*   *Eeh empty it,*
13. *It is composer, the knife is our tradition, please* *Eeh empty it,*
    empty it
14. *I say pull close even an old woman pull close,* *Eeh empty it,*
15. *Empty it even you professor, empty it*   *Eeh empty it.*

In the above particular song, the soloist doesn't hold back anything in terms of his glorification of the sexual act as a site of masculine signification. Intermittently referring to the initiate as *Tindo* and *Masewa* which are derogatory praise-names for those who are not circumcised, the soloist taunts and ridicules him to face the knife with bravado so that he can later reap the fruits by having sex. In a sense he plays around with the tonal variations of the word *munyanye* — which means both 'to eat' and 'to face a moment of reckoning' — to poke fun, scare and also psyche the initiate while entrancing the crowd with the polyvalent and humorous meanings of the same word. In actual performance, the first six lines are exhortations of the initiate to gather the courage of facing the knife the next morning. For instance when the soloist says, 'the circumciser knife stings', 'tomorrow you will see' he is blatantly warning the initiate not to imagine it will be easy. However from line 7, he proceeds to taunt, entice, psych and encourage the initiate to face the ritual with stoicism because afterwards he can also 'empty it' and enjoy sex like the soloist who is already an *omusani* — circumcised.

The last part of the song extract was even more graphic in actual performance as the soloist led the singing retinue in lewd dancing and gyrations of waists to simulate the sexual act. These dance formations are called *kamakari* (loosely meaning 'dance trains') with many people, especially the young, joining and holding each other's waists in the ecstatic circular movements around the dancing initiate. All this time, 'composer' weaves into and outside the performance circle, coaxing the initiate and sometimes even takes a seat and continues to shout his lyrics while seated as the rest of the singers continue dancing around the initiate in complete absorption. Like the *atalaku* trickster in Bob W. White's analysis of popular Congolese dance music, 'composer' becomes the typical master of buffoonery and clownish behaviour. Sometimes he could be dressed in weird clothes and a fitting cap or head gear to camouflage himself. Because of his greed for not just food and sex, but power and attention, he raises the tempo of the song and praises key personalities in attendance in order to solicit for money, food and drink. In the above song performance for instance, he ostensibly sang the lines, '*Mwalimu* Teacher, empty it', 'even you professor empty it' to entice money from me which I had to gladly give. But in extreme cases he may commandeer the initiate and the whole singing entourage to go and dance for relatives seated in the main house just to get recognition for his services.

Because of what he does, the soloist has a joking relationship with the elderly and he can easily bully and cajole them to give him alcohol, food or money as tokens of appreciation for his services. Like a character in Rabelais he eschews good manners, overindulges and is obsessed with orifices and faecal humour, gouging himself with lots of food and alcohol and hardly hesitates if an opportunity for copulation arises. He generally makes the best out of his situation, 'chewing' away food, alcohol and sex, 'emptying' himself and expiating his personality through his lyrics. His offensive lyrics might be a threat to social order outside the circumcision space, but he also affirms and sustains the social equilibrium by using the cover of darkness and his costumes while borrowing from the traditional ritual to fit into modern exigencies. Surprisingly, he remains aware, like a nomad, that at the end of the transient celebratory period he will go back to his subaltern self.

The circumcision soloist is, however, not just a village wag who is all jokes with no sense of knowledge about the outside world. Like the Deleuzian nomad he fully understands the need to always change to fit into different circumstances according to social contexts; he embraces any movements between multiple ideas. His lyrics and verbal antics are as 'rhizomatic' as they are humorous, revealing an ever evolving social order in which as an artist he engages with the world by crossing boundaries and making interconnections with the reality of modernity. This is best captured in the following song:

Mulongo

Soloist/Call	Chorus/Response
1. Ee Mulooongo	Hahoo
2. Mulongo elavu ndila	Hahoo
3. Mwana wa maayi ndila ndie	Hahoo
4. Newenya sina khuwa	Hahoo
5. Yakhaba mobaili khuwa	Hahoo
6. Ebele Landani khucha	Hahoo
7. Yakhaba Narobi khuche	Hahoo
8. Yaya Muloongo	Tila omwana mukhana Mulongo
9. Samwene ndi Papa Solo	Tila omwana mukhana Mulongo
10. Switi ndi landa kewa	Landa ekewa khunyole musili
11. Sikuta nalila ndi	Landa ekewa khunyole musili
12. Haho ndi papa Jemsi	Hahooo Mulongo
13. Wamwene wenyile	Hahooo Mulongo
14. Newenya khwingila	Hahooo Mulongo
15. Yaya mbalu echunanga ndoma	Hahooo Mulongo
16. Rayoni khinanga sikisu	Hahooo Mulongo
17. Masewa muchuli bwasiele	Hahooo Mulongo
18. Yaya khukhwese ndombolo ndi	Tila omwana omukhana Mulongo.

English translation:

Soloist/Call	Chorus/Response
1. Mulooongo	Hahoo
2. Mulongo my love, I am crying	Hahoo
3. Daughter of the beautiful one How do you want me to cry?	Hahoo
4. Whatever you want I will give you	Hahoo
5. Be it a mobile phone I will give	Hahoo

6. Even London we will go	Hahoo
7. Be it Nairobi let's go	Hahoo
8. My dear Muloongo	Hold a young damsel, Mulongo
9. As Papa Solo I say	Hold a young damsel, Mulongo
10. Sweetie, go round the meadows	Go round to the meadows
	I meet you in the bush
11. Sikuta sings	Go round to the meadows
	I meet you in the bush
12. Hahoo you my son James	Hahooo Mulongo
13. You wanted it yourself	Hahooo Mulongo
14. You want to be initiated	Hahooo Mulongo
15. Remember the knife pains bitterly	Hahooo Mulongo
16. Rayoni dance like the Bagishu initiates	Hahooo Mulongo
17. Masewa tomorrow is already here	Hahooo Mulongo
18. So let's dance ndombolo[9]	Hold a young damsel, Mulongo.

In the above song, 'composer' lyrically oscillates between urban and rural spaces; modernity and the traditional so to speak. He clearly maps out the social landscape based on the binaries of tradition/modernity, rural/urban, conservative/permissive and so on. But as a folklore trickster, he acts as a 'nomadic' social provocateur that is more at ease with the rural environment but desires the city life. Although he rules the nocturnal village setting and the meadows which he sings fervently about, he is remotely aware of the promise of a consumerist and techno-savvy city life which appears to have even better prospects. Like a trickster in his element, he sings about his sexual anxieties and conquests in the ruralscape, but the spectre of using the allure of suburban bliss to make even bigger conquests beckons even more.

For example, in the same song above he bemoans his ineptitude and inability to convince a damsel named Mulongo to be his love. In a desperate attempt to get her attention, composer hoodwinks and promises the impossible, including buying for her a cell phone (a gadget of romantic fascination in the village) and flying to far-away cities like London and Nairobi. When he sings, 'Whatever you want I will give you, Be it a mobile phone, I will give', he is not just an embodiment of a desperate naïve man smitten by love, but a true trickster who knows his way with deception and pranks. His desperate overtures gesture towards the

---

[9] The term *ndombolo* is directly borrowed from the popular Congolese dance style which is very much liked and imitated in Kenya.

Deleuzian nomad, who often 'resists settling into socially coded modes of thought and behaviour' (Braidotti 1994: 5). But reading the same lines differently, the sheer fact that the soloist's life horizons stretch beyond the rural context speaks to tricksterism and what Braidotti calls a 'nomad who resists settling into one sovereign vision of identity' (ibid.: 14). He is a man who lives in the village but he frequently transports himself momentarily and spiritually into the urban space. His ability to conjure, and configure the city space through his songs is trickster-like. Even more dramatic is how he ambiguously takes on the persona of a jilted lover who has to keep on pleading with his sweet heart to come back to him. He captures this well when he infuses English romantic expletives such as 'love' (pronounced as *elavu*) and 'sweetie' (articulated as *switi*) in his song.

'Composer' apparently deploys his linguistic prowess and idioms better through singing, in order to articulate the contradictions of living in the palimpsest of modernity. He draws attention to the anxieties and contradictions of the Bukusu circumcision ritual, against a backdrop of social and personal inadequacies and the stark reality of the ever changing definitions and benchmarks of cultural belonging — the reality of modernity which constantly redefines what it means to be a man. Like Deleuze and Guattari's rhizome, the song performances are 'lines of creative escape' from the statist apparatus of capture and regulation (1986: 6–7). For instance, in *Mulongo* 'composer' juxtaposes the realities of rural and urban life. In the first lines, the theme of the song is about unrequited love. The spurned man represented by the soloist promises to offer the most adored modern gifts such as the cell phone (*mobaili*)[10] in order to win the love of a reluctant damsel. But in the same song he urges the initiate to develop a thick skin and go for the knife because 'he wanted it himself'. This interconnectedness between the urban imaginary and the rural circumcision reality is further underscored when 'composer' coaxes his audience to dance the *ndombolo* dance. Suffice it to add that, this deliberate connection between tradition and modernity is deployed through the soloist's singing skills in order to entice the initiate.

'Composer' also appears to both affirm and subvert the significance of circumcision in the modern context. While the initiate is encouraged to stoically face the knife because good sex and the trappings of modernity

---

[10] This is actually the Lubukusu language orthography and corruption for 'mobile' phone — a word that is commonly used in Kenya in reference to the cellular phone.

are beckoning, the frustrations of the jilted persona in the song are a sad reminder of what he also has to expect as a man. Overall, he uses the song lyrics to project his masculine anxieties and his ideal imaginary and yearning for places beyond the village. The circumcision song appears to have a rhizomatic relationship with, not just the performance and social space, but with the rural and urban space; local and global so to speak. It is a political and cultural entity that is appropriated by the soloist, connected to all dimensions of life through structural variations, expansions and 'specific lines of flight' (Deleuze and Guattari 1988: 11–13, 21).

Conclusion

This chapter set out to examine how the nature of the Babukusu circumcision song performance invites a trickster-like and nomadic reading. Using songs by Stargrant Wanyonyi Lusanya, I examined how his livetime performance endears him to the public because of his personality. The soloist's personality was the focus of our analysis. By juxtaposing it within the trickster and nomadic mode, we sought to understand how his slippery, tenuous, and indeterminate identities play out in his performance. Our figuration of tricksterism as an intellectual paradigm for our analysis was informed by the concepts of the trickster in the African context and nomadism, as formulated through the ideas of Deleuze, Guattari and Rosi Braidotti.

The preliminary analysis noted that the soloist is referred to using various pseudonyms and praise-names. These names, speak to his tricksterism and nomadic behaviour. The chapter has also illustrated how the soloist's extemporaneous composition and improvisation of lyrics marks him out as a linguistic polyglot and nomadic trickster. From his ability to expand, vary and infuse new and strange words in his lyrics, the soloist is a wizard with word coinages and rhythmical concatenations. His real power and genius, resides in how he configures an entirely new sonic grammar, which is not just peculiar to the circumcision occasion but to him in particular. Apparently, he succeeds in navigating the contradictions between his ordinary life and performative persona by using the cover of darkness and his weird costumes. Although the circumcision space is licentious and permissive, 'composer' wittingly seeks recourse to tricksterism and nomadism in order to get away with his vulgar and obscene demeanour while at the same time succeeding in passing across social messages and attaining temporary visibility. Stargrant is a devout Catholic man who in ordinary life is extremely shy when associated with what he does during circumcision nights. But as he confesses, his singing prowess is like a spirit that engulfs him seasonally and he has to exorcise it within that space and period. Outside the performance arena, he is an entirely different character.

Ultimately, our affable but trickster-like circumcision song soloist uses his lyrics to stir life into the rural landscape. His tunes have certainly become, in Gunner's words (2009), too 'unruly' and 'unstable' to be confined to the village and the 'nomadic' tunes of the Babukusu circumcision song have finally been appropriated for commercial and political purposes in urban settings. For instance, the song *Mulongo* has certainly become popular after being redone by a musical group called Kayamba Fiesta.[11] In the run up to the 2007 General Elections in Kenya, the song was sung at many public functions during political campaigns. Since then, the song has become a regular airplay favourite on FM radio stations and can be heard blaring in *matatus*, bars, coffee shops and popular night spots in the country's capital Nairobi and other major towns.

References

Brinton, Daniel. 1868. *The Myths of the New World*. Philadephia: David McKay & Co.

Bourdieu, Pierre. 2001. *Masculine Domination*, trans. Richard Nice. Cambridge: Polity Press.

Braidotti, Rosi. 1994. *Nomadic Subjects: Embodiment and Sexual Difference in Contemporary Feminist Theory*. New York: Columbia University Press.

Deleuze, Gilles and Felix Guattari. 1986. *Nomadology: The War Machine*, trans. Brian Massumi. Cambridge, MA: The MIT Press.

———. 1988. *A Thousand Plateaus: Capitalism and Schizophrenia*, trans. Brian Massumi. London: The Athlone Press.

Evans-Pritchard, Edward Evan. 1967. *The Zande Trickster*. Oxford: Clarendon Press.

Gunner, Liz. 2009. 'Jacob Zuma, the Social Body and the Unruly Power of Song', *African Affairs*, 108(430): 27–48.

Heald, Suzette. 1989. *Controlling Anger: The Sociology of Gisu Violence*. Manchester: Manchester University Press.

---

[11] Kayamba Fiesta is a splinter group from the original Kayamba Africa, a popular acapella group in Kenya. These two different groups are commercial bands that play almost similar genres of music although they have specialized in remixing and reworking traditional music tunes from different ethnic backgrounds in Kenya.

Makila, Fred E. 1976. *An Outline History of the Babukusu of Western Kenya*. Nairobi: Kenya Literature Bureau.

———. 2004. *Bukusu Cultural Traditions*. Nairobi: Kenya Literature Bureau.

Oring, Ellen. 2006. 'Folk or Lore? The Stake in Dichotomies', *Journal of Folklore Research*, 43(3): 205–20.

Pelton, Robert. 1980. *The Trickster in West Africa: A Study of Mythic Irony and Sacred Delight*. Berkeley: University of California Press.

Ricketts, Mac Linscott. 1965. 'The North American Indian Trickster', *History of Religions*, 5(2): 327–50.

Roginsky, Dina. 2007. 'Folklore, Folklorism and Synchronization: Preserved-created Folklore in Israel', *Journal of Folklore Research*, 44(1): 41–63.

Silverman, Eric K. 2004. 'Anthropology and Circumcision', *Annual Review of Anthropology*, 33: 419–45.

Smidchens, Guntis. 1999. 'Folklorism Revisited', *Journal of Folklore Research*, 36(1): 51–70.

Wanyama Melitus N. 2006. 'Form and Content of African Music: A Case Study of Bukusu Circumcision Music'. Unpublished PhD Thesis, University of Pretoria.

Wasike, Chris J. C. 2010. 'Textualizing Masculinity: Power Discourses and Anxieties in the Babukusu After-Burial Oratory Performance'. Unpublished PhD Dissertation, University of the Witwatersrand.

White, W. Bob. 1999. 'Modernity's Trickster: "Dipping" and Throwing in Congolese Popular Dance Music', *Research in African Literatures*, 30(4): 156–75.

4

Rabbit-Proof Fence
Surviving Loss and Trauma
through Testimony and Narration

Dolores Herrero

During the last three decades, the testimony and writing of indigenous peoples in white settler colonies has emerged and developed as a potentially powerful catalyst in the rewriting and revisiting of the official past. *Follow the Rabbit-Proof Fence* (Pilkington 2003) is about one of the darkest chapters of Australian history: the Stolen Generations. The 'Aboriginal Protection and Restriction of the Sale of Opium Act (Queensland)', which was passed in 1897, allowed the authorities 'to cause every Aboriginal within any district . . . to be removed to, and kept within, the limits of, any reserve' (Legislative Assembly of Queensland 1897). Furthermore, Article 31 allowed them to provide 'for the care, custody, and education of the children of Aboriginals' and prescribed 'the conditions on which any Aboriginal or half-caste children may be apprenticed to, or placed in service with, suitable persons' (ibid.; for more information, see Legislative Assembly of Queensland 1897).

This is the socio-political background which must be acknowledged so that the tragedy and trauma that *Follow the Rabbit-Proof Fence* (Pilkington 2003) denounces can be fully understood. Three girls — Molly, Gracie and Daisy — are half-caste Aboriginal children living together with their family of the Mardu people at Jigalong, Western Australia. One day a Constable — a 'Protector' in the sense of the aforementioned Act — comes to take the three girls with him and far away from their homeland and relatives. They are placed in the Moore River Native Settlement north of Perth, some 1,600 kilometres away. The great majority of children who underwent this ordeal never saw their families again. Many of them are still trying to find them.

The book is the true account of Doris Pilkington/Nugi Garimara's mother Molly, who led her two sisters on this extraordinary trek across remote Western Australia. The three girls managed to escape from the authoritarian and castrating rule of the settlement's Head. Following the rabbit-proof fence, which at that time ran from north to south through Western Australia, they trekked the long distance back to their family. These Aboriginal girls' journey was longer than many of the celebrated walks of the Australian explorer heroes, and reveals a past more cruel than the average reader (and spectator) could possibly imagine.

Most non-Australians, however, came to know about this story and the undercover genocide that it reprobates thanks to Phillip Noyce's film, *Rabbit-Proof Fence* (2002), which soon became a breakthrough production, for many *the* film of the Stolen Generations. It was the tremendous impact that this film made on many spectators that eventually led them to read the biographical novel on which it is based. Although both novel and film apparently tell the same story, they are very different indeed, and it is this difference that I want to focus on and discuss.

It is undeniable that the film offers a powerful image of Aboriginal survival of colonial violence and subjugation, of indigenous resilience and resistance. However, as Felicity Collins and Therese Davis assert (2004: 133), it is also true that the film clearly draws on 'narrative techniques and visual devices from Hollywood genres to create a compelling adventure story', a universal story of individual heroism: a very young heroine decides to escape and eventually manages to do it, thus baffling the repressive established authorities. When the film was first shown in a remote East Pilbara schoolyard in Western Australia, the mechanisms of a global industry and the specificities of a local community were brought together to deliberate effect. Although Noyce's decision to stage its world premiere in Jigalong brought to the fore the film's attempt to pay tribute to local and lived indigenous experience, it is also clear that, once the film was distributed globally, many spectators felt attracted to the film's universal elements of a successful story of escape and courage. To put it differently, they framed the meaning of the story within their own mythologies and discourses of nation, thus playing down the specificity of the plight undergone by Australian Aborigines.

The mixed reactions that the film provoked in the Aboriginal communities speak for themselves. For many critics, Aborigines and non-Aborigines alike, this film reveals itself as yet another Hollywood commodity. The main reasons why *Rabbit-Proof Fence* became a box office success were, to quote Greg McCarthy's words, 'Noyce's marketing of the film and his established international reputation' (2004: 11), together with 'the wedding of the Aboriginal narrative to a Hollywood aesthetic style — a simple story line, a recognisable closure, an emphasis on heroic endeavour and a stress on an emotional response from the audience' (ibid.: 12). The film clearly appeals to the senses, and could be said to be a convenient mixture of popular genres such as political history, maternal melodrama, the romance-quest and the action film — for the film's cinematographer, Chris Doyle, it could be labelled as 'a road movie on foot' (Collins and Davis 2004: 138). Consequently, the film safely packages difference as a collectivized universal experience for the ultimate goal of commercial success. 'Whitefella's cry is cheap', many Aboriginal critics expressed. As they saw it, since the film ignores and degrades specificities, and places material events and cultural artefacts on the same level, it perpetrates the same assimilationist tendencies that it apparently tries to do away with.

Unlike Noyce's film, the book is not a sheer account of individual heroism. Readers who delve into the book after having seen the film find it shocking that it takes the narrator *four* full chapters to start telling the story of the three girls (the one and only story in the film!). Significantly enough, the first four chapters describe the arrival of the whites in Australia, the setting of their first military outposts and colonies, and the lethal consequences that this had for the different Aboriginal communities, which were forcibly removed from their homelands and made to gather in government depots such as Jigalong — the birthplace of the three protagonists of the trek. Although at first many Aborigines did not want to see the jobs that the whites made them do 'as exploitation but as a form of kindness shown to them' (Pilkington 2003: 19), they soon realized 'what the arrival of the European settlers meant for them: it was the destruction of their traditional society and the dispossession of their lands. . . . the Aboriginal social structure was not only crumbling, but it was being totally destroyed' (ibid.: 13–15). They became aware that their whole world was coming to an end.

However, as Doris Pilkington's novel reveals, they showed no open defiance. Mudrooroo Narogin, a most polemical Aboriginal author, provides us with the only plausible explanation for this shockingly passive attitude: the Aborigines, like most indigenous peoples, are 'minorities submerged in a surrounding majority and governed by them' (Narogin 1985: 33). In other words, they cannot help seeing themselves as militarily inferior, still-defeated, always-invaded, never free of a history of white occupation. Therefore, they confess to complicity with the occupying white culture, because it is only within the domain of this dominant culture that they can possibly reclaim and partly preserve their own — the lesser of two evils. It is this apparent contradiction that explains why indigenous writers like Mudrooroo have often labelled their contemporary works as 'alienated'. They inevitably — and bitterly — comply with white dominance: their works are 'white' in style, genre and language, and they therefore lack the complexities and subtleties of specifically Aboriginal genres and dialect oral forms. Furthermore, most Aboriginal works, *Follow the Rabbit-Proof Fence* being no exception, constantly emphasize the need to surrender in order to survive.[1]

> Soon, Aboriginal people all over the state learned to acknowledge the white man's brutal strength and their cruel use of superior weapons and were forced to accept the white system of justice and punishment. . . . they understood that they must conform to these changes in their lifestyle, obey their new bosses and try not to offend them (Pilkington 2003: 15, 27).

Yet, the fact that the Aborigines do not openly rebel against this cultural genocide does not mean that it does not affect them. As is stated in Doris Pilkington's novel, 'their pain and suffering remained hidden and repressed, silent and deep' (ibid.: 16). Silences and ellipses are worth a million words: their ordeal was so brutal that it is simply unutterable; language cannot possibly contain and express their plight. By briefly narrating the extermination of a whole group before focusing on the three girls' adventure, the book makes it clear from the very beginning that the tragic fate that awaited these three girls was not an isolated phenomenon. Their story was that of all the other members of the group. As is well known, the certainty of belonging in a community is of fundamental importance for indigenous peoples, for it is the community and the spirits

---

[1] Mudrooroo's well-known novel *Doctor Wooreddy's Prescription for Enduring the Ending of the World* (1996), as its very title suggests, also shows a similar philosophy of stoic resignation. For more information on this, see Herrero (2001).

of its ancestors that ultimately matters, that provides individuals' lives with meaning and purpose. On the other hand, what at first might seem to deprive the three girls' story of pathos and importance only contributes to endowing their plight with a rather more traumatic dimension: theirs was not an isolated story, but the story of a whole massacred race on the verge of extinction.

Like the film, Doris Pilkington's novel is a hybrid text, but its hybridity is endowed with a rather more problematic nature. It does not entail the combination of several popular and highly commercial genres, but rather the difficult integration of reality and fiction: of a transcribed testimony on the one hand, and a biographical novel on the other. At once autobiography, biography, novel, and oral story, the narrative is also none of these; it is a generic anomaly. It is Molly, Doris's mother, who underwent this ordeal, but it is Doris who listens to Molly's oral narration of the events and who finally reports the story by turning it into a coherent written text. The implications of this double process should not be underestimated. As John Frow argues, 'to report is to carry a story back from one place to another' (1998: 3). A report fuses a double set of enunciative relations: that which relates to the witness (Molly), splitting her between an 'I' who speaks in the present and an 'I' who suffered in the past; and that which relates to the listener and transcriber of the story (Doris), split between a present order of exposition and a past order of enquiry. In this twofold division between a present of speaking and writing and a past of reality, the past functions as the 'other' to the time of writing, and is made intelligible by this relation. Moreover, reports and transcriptions of somebody else's accounts are bound to deploy, at least to a certain extent, the citational strategy that produces, according to Michel de Certeau, the characteristically laminated text of historiography, split between a singular, coherent, continuous writing and a plural and disseminated set of languages which are quoted, interrogated and judged as if they were the primary matter of the real itself (1988: 94). It is from the citation of this language of otherness (the archive, the document, the testimony, etc.) that knowledge of historical reality can be partially achieved. To quote de Certeau's words, history is constituted by a play of languages in which

> the role of quoted language is . . . one of accrediting discourse. With its referential function, it introduces into the text an effect of reality; and through its crumbling, it discreetly refers to a locus of authority. From this angle, the split structure of discourse functions like a machinery that

extracts from the citation a verisimilitude of narrative and a validation of knowledge. It produces a sense of reliability (de Certeau 1988: 94).

And yet, however strong the readers' demands of verisimilitude and reliability may be, it is fiction's truth that most of them mainly seek and accept. When Doris Pilkington sent her first manuscript of *Rabbit-Proof Fence* to the publisher Magabala Books — the straightforward transcription she had written after hearing the story from her Aunty Daisy — they sent it back on the grounds that it was 'more like a university critique', and asked her to 'write it as a fiction or in a narrative form' because 'the reader wants to believe that it's a true story' (Brewster 2007: 153). The reason for the human preference to cling to this 'willing suspension of disbelief', to use the well-known Coleridgean expression, can be no other than the fact that we need to believe that, contrary to what everyday experience tells us, life can be made intelligible, ordered, accounted for and explained. Doris Pilkington's book wonderfully encapsulates this contradiction. On the one hand, it strives to commit itself to knowledge grounded on facts, precise records and citational references. On the other hand, it must rely on the imagination so as to be able to produce a coherent and ordered narrative that supersedes and effaces any possible incongruities and ellipses in the original sources. As Doris, the narrator, puts it:

> The task of reconstructing the trek home from the settlement has been both an exhausting and an interesting experience. One needed to have a vivid imagination, the patience of many saints and the determination to succeed despite the odds . . . By combining my imagination and the information from records of geographical and botanical explorations undertaken in the area during the early 1900s and later, I was able to build a clearer picture of the vegetation and landscape through which the girls trekked (Pilkington 2003: xi–xii).

Yet, no matter how attractive and appealing to the reader the final outcome may be, it is also clear that its paradoxical nature renders the final text rather contradictory and problematic. This novel does not show the fragmented and disrupted structure that is so characteristic of most experimental trauma narratives, nor does it contain the temporal discontinuities and obsessive hallucinations that are so recurrent in this kind of texts. Instead, *Follow the Rabbit-Proof Fence* offers quite a simple and linear story, which is, more often than not, told in a most straightforward and apparently detached way, and which sometimes even acknowledges, much to the reader's amazement, the kindness which few white people, such as the stewardess Gwen Campbell and the crew member George Johnson, showed them during their transportation to the Moore River settlement:

> As the days wore on Gwen Campbell tried gently to gain their trust . . . George Johnson, a crew member, told them of the exciting and fascinating places he had visited . . . Sometimes he and Gwen encouraged the three youngsters to go for a stroll on deck in the evening, while it was pleasant and warm. They were good sailors, George told them (ibid.: 53–54).

Although the novel does contain scenes which clearly disclose the whites' brutality towards the Aborigines, and the traumatic effect that this inhuman treatment has on these indigenous communities, it is also true that the narration on the whole lacks detailed descriptions of the feelings of extreme anguish and humiliation experienced by these girls and their relatives. The reader is informed of facts — of very harsh and unpalatable facts — it is true, but the narration is concise and unadorned; it refuses to delve into the psychologically devastating effects that this traumatic experience has on the Aborigines' minds. As a result, the reader abhors this savage kidnapping, but on the other hand finds it difficult to feel the shock and profound empathetic unsettlement that s/he automatically expects to feel as part of the process of reading the narration of somebody else's traumatic past. The scene in which the girls are wrenched from their mothers could be given as an example.

> The cries of agonised mothers and the women, and the deep sobs of grandfathers, uncles and cousins filled the air. Molly and Gracie looked back just once before they disappeared through the river gums. Behind them, those remaining in the camp found strong sharp objects and gashed themselves and inflicted wounds to their heads and bodies as an expression of their sorrow.
>
> The two frightened and miserable girls began to cry, silently at first, then uncontrollably; their grief made worse by the lamentations of their loved ones and the visions of them sitting on the ground in their camp letting their tears mix with the red blood that flowed from the cuts on their heads. This reaction to their children's abduction showed that the family were now in mourning. They were grieving for their abducted children and their relief would come only when the tears ceased to fall, and that will be a long time yet (ibid.: 44–45).

Similarly, once the three girls reach the settlement and are taken to their dormitory, Molly soon realises the fate that awaits them, but describes the place in a most cool and dispassionate way: 'Molly saw that the uninviting weatherboard and latticed dormitory had bars on the windows . . . Just like a gaol, she thought, and she didn't like it one bit' (Pilkington 2003: 63);

> It looked more like a concentration camp than a residential school for Aboriginal children . . . Molly lay staring at the ceiling, pondering their fate and the kind of lifestyle they could expect at this strange place and she didn't like it one bit (ibid.: 72–73).

Molly has the courage to face up to trouble, refuses to surrender and, being the step-daughter of a former nomad from the desert, she makes the most of the bushcraft skills and survival techniques that she learnt from him, and soon decides to escape. It is not the bush that can annihilate her, but the confinement that the white authorities want to impose on her: 'Molly, this fourteen-year-old girl, had no fear because the wilderness was her kin. It always provided shelter, food and sustenance' (ibid.: 82). It is Molly who will guide the other two girls, who can do nothing but surrender to her strong will and determination.

> "We're not going to school, so grab your bags. We're not staying here."
> Daisy and Gracie were stunned and stood staring at her.
>
> "What did you say?" asked Gracie.
>
> "I said, we're not staying here at the settlement, because we're going home to Jigalong" (ibid.: 77).

Molly's courage and purpose clearly contrast with the blockage felt by most trauma victims, who are totally unable to react against, even acknowledge, what is actually happening to them. As well-known trauma critics like Cathy Caruth have explained (1995: 4–10), it is the very unassimilated nature of trauma, the fact that the event was not acknowledged or experienced fully at the time, that later on returns to haunt the survivor.[2] At first sight, the case of Molly seems to be different.

---

[2] Although the study of trauma began as early as the 19th century, this field of analysis reached its climax in the 20th century, an era saturated with unprecedented violent and wounding events, and mainly in the works of theorists such as Cathy Caruth, Shoshana Felman, Geoffrey Harpham and Dominick

As is stated in the novel, Molly soon realizes what is happening to them and decides to act, to do something to oppose the government's decision. '[S]he decided that she wanted to have a part in planning her own destiny' (Pilkington 2003: 129). Here lies the main difference: it was this courageous decision that allowed her to preserve her dignity, and it is this dignity that eventually enables her to revisit the traumatic past and tell her daughter about her long trek. However, the fact that it is only many years later that Molly actually manages to verbalize what happened, and that it is her daughter that finally turns her disconnected oral story into a coherent and chronologically-ordered written narrative account, also suggests that Molly might also have eventually fallen prey to the numbness that affects many trauma survivors in the first place. As regards the detached and straightforward nature of the narration, it should not be ignored that the book was initially addressed to the other members of the Aboriginal community who, like Doris herself, also suffered the same kind of traumatic kidnapping. There is no need to describe in crude detail what everybody knows; they have all suffered the same kind of plight in their flesh. Moreover, to reduce their accounts to their bare essentials and play down the most heart-breaking particulars is, over and above everything, a strategy for survival. It is only by smoothing their most traumatic memories that they can pretend that they can forge ahead and lead 'normal' lives.

To bring this analysis to an end, it should be stated that *Follow the Rabbit-Proof Fence* raises some important questions: what does it mean when Aboriginal writers denounce the traumatic experience undergone by other Aborigines? What is the connection between individual and

---

LaCapra, to name but a few. It was in 1980 that the American Psychiatric Association officially acknowledged the phenomenon of trauma under the title 'Post-Traumatic Stress Disorder' (PTSD). In her seminal work *Trauma: Explorations in Memory* (1995), Cathy Caruth explains what the PTSD is all about: 'There is a response, sometimes delayed, to an overwhelming event or events, which takes the form of repeated, intrusive hallucinations, dreams, thoughts or behaviours stemming from the event, along with numbing that may have begun during or after the experience, and possibly also increased arousal to (and avoidance of) stimuli recalling the event' (ibid.: 4). Caruth makes it clear that the pathology in question cannot be defined by the event itself, nor in terms of a distortion of the event. It consists, rather, in the way in which this event is *not* experienced or received. The force of the *non*-experience, Caruth goes on to explain, is registered in 'the collapse of its understanding' (ibid.: 7).

collective trauma and cultural representations of it? Is it possible to offer a textual/literary representation of trauma? And to do away with the destructive patterns that rule racist post-colonial societies? It is clear that an accurate representation of trauma can never be achieved since, as Kalí Tal argues, 'by its very definition, trauma lies beyond the bounds of "normal" conception. Textual representations . . . are mediated by language and do not have the impact of the traumatic experience' (1996: 15). As is well known, the combination of the compulsive need to verbalize and the impossibility of recreating the traumatic experience for the reader is one of the defining characteristics of trauma literature. However, it is only by striving to bear witness to these traumas that some kind of change can be enforced. Bearing witness is a highly politicized act. As Kalí Tal goes on to argue, it is born out of a refusal to surrender to outside pressure to revise or to repress experience (ibid.: 7). It is a decision to advocate conflict rather than submission. Its ultimate aim is change. The battle over the meaning of a traumatic event is fought in the arena of political discourse, popular culture, and scholarly debate, and the outcome of this battle inexorably affects the rhetoric of the dominant culture, and by extension influences political action.

Furthermore, trauma narratives become a speaking and listening practice with a clear ethical agenda. Trauma urges us to get involved in each other's stories. Caruth insists on this in her book *Unclaimed Experience: Trauma, Narrative and History*, when she affirms that it is the 'plea by an other who is asking to be seen and heard' that 'constitutes the new mode of reading and listening that both the language of trauma and the silence of its mute repetition of suffering, profoundly and imperatively demand' (1996: 9). Both Molly (the primary teller of the story) and Doris (the transcriber and secondary narrator of the story) manage to survive loss by acting out the other/hidden side of official Australian history. Finally, by working through personal, communal and national trauma, not only do they disclose and make amends for the atrocities of the past, but also strive to pave the way for reconciliation in a better and rather more hybridized future.

References

Brewster, Anne. 2007. 'The Stolen Generations: Rites of Passage — Doris Pilkington Interviewed by Anne Brewster', *Journal of Commonwealth Literature*, 42 (1): 143–59.

Caruth, Cathy (ed.). 1995. *Trauma: Explorations in Memory*. Baltimore, MD and London: Johns Hopkins University Press.

Caruth, Cathy. 1996. *Unclaimed Experience: Trauma, Narrative and History.* Baltimore, MD and London: Johns Hopkins University Press.

Collins, Felicity and Therese Davis. 2004. *Australian Cinema after Mabo.* Cambridge: Cambridge University Press.

de Certeau, Michel. 1988. *The Writing of History*, trans. Tom Conley. New York: Columbia University Press.

Frow, John. 1998. 'A Politics of Stolen Time', *Australian Humanities Review*, 9, http://www.australianhumanitiesreview.org/archive/Issue-February-1998/frow1.html (accessed 12 December 2008).

Herrero, Dolores. 2001. 'Mudrooroo's *Doctor Wooreddy's Prescription for Enduring the Ending of the World*: Appropriating and Undermining White/Official Culture from the Aboriginal/(Un)Official Fringe', *Cuadernos de Filología Inglesa*, 9(2): 23–44.

Legislative Assembly of Queensland. 1897. 'Anno Sexagesimo: Primo Victoriae Regiae — Aboriginals Protection and Restriction of the Sale of Opium Bill', Bill no. [17], Museum of Australian Democracy, Canberra, http://www.foundingdocs.gov.au/resources/transcripts/qld5_doc_1897.pdf (accessed 17 December 2008).

McCarthy, Greg. 2004. 'Australian Cinema and the Spectres of Post-Coloniality: *Rabbit-Proof Fence, Australian Rules, The Tracker* and *Beneath Clouds*', *London Papers in Australian Studies*, no. 8, Menzies Centre for Australian Studies, London.

Narogin, Mudrooroo. 1985. 'White Forms, Aboriginal Content', in Jack Davis and Bob Hodge (eds), *Aboriginal Writing Today*, pp. 21–33. Canberra: Australian Institute of Aboriginal Studies.

———. 1996 [1983]. *Doctor Wooreddy's Prescription for Enduring the Ending of the World*. Melbourne: Hyland House.

Pilkington, Doris (Nugi Garimara). 2003 [1996]. *Follow the Rabbit-Proof Fence.* St Lucia: University of Queensland Press.

Tal, Kalí. 1996. *Worlds of Hurt: Reading the Literatures of Trauma.* Cambridge: Cambridge University Press.

Film:

Rabbit-Proof Fence, dir. Phillip Noyce, 2002.

5

Collective Chronicles

(Fictional) Life Histories of Australia's Stolen Generations

Birte Heidemann

♋

The concept of the 'Stolen Generations' is often used to describe those children of Australian Aboriginal and Torres Strait Islander descent who were removed from their families by white institutions such as government agencies, church missions and welfare bodies. This policy was managed by the Aboriginal Protection Board (APB), a government board established in 1909 with the power to take Aboriginal children from their families without parental consent or court order and place them either in white institutions such as missions and children's homes or in foster families. From 1909 to 1969, this forced removal of children from their families was official government policy, though unofficially the practice took place both before and after this period. For more than three generations, the white Australian society had assumed political and legal rights over the indigenous peoples by euphemistically claiming that their main motivation for the removal was only 'child protection'. Taught to reject their Aboriginal heritage, indigenous children were taken from their parents in order to be educated 'white'. In that sense, they were stolen in literal terms — not only from their families but simultaneously from their culture, their language and their history. In other words, the Stolen Generations have been deprived of almost everything that constitutes one's identity. Dominated by child abuse, racism, violence, rape or unemployment, such silenced (hi)stories have resulted in alcohol and other drug addictions, depression, mental illness, and frequently in suicides.

However, a slow but significant sea change has occurred off Australia's literary landscape. Drawing upon a transformation of *mental* territories, Graham Huggan contends that '[t]he Stolen Generations, long peripheral to the Australian national imaginary, have in the last couple of decades become central to it' (Huggan 2007: 97) making themselves heard by means of a literary genre which allows them to both document a dispossessed past and articulate a disrupted present. Though generically defined by a selective subjectivity, indigenous life histories espouse the idea of cultural collectivity, thereby voicing the shared past of a dispossessed people. A proxy for a cohesive cultural heritage, Aboriginal autobiographies represent, as it were, a repository of silenced life stories reflected in Toni Morrison's concept of re-memory. Invoking the significance of a poetics of memory, Anne Brewster characterizes the process of (life) writing 'as a technology of memory' (2005: 397) purporting the reversibility of memory which simultaneously enacts a poetics of forgetting (ibid.: 398). In her essay on Aboriginal women's writing, Brewster discusses the writer's role to counter a deliberate form of forgetting arguing that there is 'a driving urge on the part of these writers to break the silence, the *cultural amnesia*, of white Australia' (Brewster 1997: 125; emphasis in original) to reclaim the stolen history of generations of indigenous Australians.[1]

Taking up the idea of writing oneself into existence, this chapter provides a close reading of Doris Kartinyeri's autobiography *Kick the Tin* (2000) and Jane Harrison's drama *Stolen* (1998). While both writers are of Aboriginal descent, it is only Kartinyeri who has been removed from her family by the APB; all the same, the two texts equally engage with the effects of being stolen. Due to its dramatic form, I would like to term Harrison's play a *fictional* life history with the notion of performativity adding an additional angle to the genre of life writing. In the process of raising white Australia's awareness of the Aboriginals' dispossessed past, the chapter argues that the mediated immediacy implied in this inflected form of life history makes it the most political art form.

---

[1] Since the 1970s, through increased Aboriginal activism, more and more about Australia's black history had been revealed. Aboriginal women's autobiography had first made an impact with Sally Morgan's *My Place* (1987), an account of Morgan's search for the truth about her Aboriginality and her family's history (see Webby 2000: 17).

Given that the two texts represent fact and fiction, the chapter suggests that this generic division allows for (re)configuring the self-representation of the Stolen Generations thereby echoing what Paul John Eakin defines as 'making selves' (1999). A writing strategy of both tracing and placing the self within a collective history, the subsequent analysis will detail the forms and functions of (fictional) life histories by exploring (*a*) whether writing one's life initiates a healing process for the individual, and (*b*) to what extent drama's double project of (re)writing *and* performing opens a political space for unveiling the hidden histories of the Stolen Generations. Focusing on the thematics of fracture and fusion, the chapter will reveal how these two forms of life writing aesthetically realize the process of identity formation and, correspondingly, whether the two texts can be read, or even represented, as a literary realm of fusion.

Writing as Healing: Doris E. Kartinyeri's Autobiography *Kick the Tin*

My healing began when I decided to write my autobiography . . .
With lots of coffee, cigarettes and frustration, with laughter and medication, the journey began (Kartinyeri 2000: 1).

Kick the Tin is the autobiographical account of Doris Kartinyeri on the Stolen Generations telling 'the story of one woman's journey. It is a painful passage which progresses from beautiful childhood innocence . . . to a terrifying world where sexual abuse, confusion and alienation are a backdrop to an emerging adolescence' (ibid.: xvii). Kartinyeri was born in 1945 at Raukkan, a Ngarrindjeri community, and stolen from the hospital on the day before the funeral of her mother, who had died of complications one month after her birth. Without her father knowing, officers of the APB removed her from the hospital and placed her in a children's home where she stayed until the age of 14. Forced to lead a life far away from her family, Kartinyeri comments on the emotional effects of being stolen as follows:

> It was an unnatural act for any Aboriginal child to be separated from their family. I didn't receive any parental nurturing or have the privilege of growing up with my brothers and sisters. I never experienced any emotions involving the loss of my mother. I lost my family ties and heritage. I know this has affected my whole family (ibid.: 10).

In the case of Kartinyeri, the textual technique of life writing proffers a literary space for creatively coping with this uprooting act separating Kartinyeri from her 'natural' bonding, that is, her family, her heritage, her identity. On the other hand, Kartinyeri gradually comes to re-connect with what had been stolen, as she was '. . . searching for [her] people and [her] inner self for spiritual healing' (ibid.: 120). Putting her fragmented past down on paper primarily presents, as it were, Kartinyeri's personal process of healing; this hopeful notion simultaneously sets the predominantly positive tone permeating her tragic tale.

Espousing the thematics of fracture and fusion, the book's layout is characterized by a collage-like composition of family photographs and poems which complements the written text. Kartinyeri even annexes the document that was unwittingly signed by her father, which allowed the United Aborigines Mission to put his daughter into the care of the children's home. By lining the layers of her palimpsest-like life, she reconstructs her scattered story by re-tracing what has been taken away from her. Though not overtly discussed in the text, Kartinyeri connects her life story with other stolen children through a series of photographs that tell their own tale(s) next to their pictures and names. The captions in the photographs conspicuously indicate that most of the male children are deceased; whereas Kartinyeri conceals their cause of death, which was probably that they died in their attempts to escape from Colebrook. While these childhood friends are part of her personal past, Kartinyeri's life history constitutes a collective text giving as much voice to the silenced stories of the Stolen Generations as to her own. Drawing on this polyphony of voices, Kartinyeri creates a bilingual book which blends (even 'abrogates') two languages as she constantly interweaves her 'standard' English writing with indigenous words and expressions either translated in footnotes or compiled in a separate glossary. In the sense of (linguistically) negotiating what she calls 'living in two worlds' (ibid.: 135), her autobiography reads as a gradual reclaiming of her native origin.

In line with this textual tapestry, the book's formal fabric follows Kartinyeri's fragmented road of life. In other words, the chronologically organized chapters correspond to her various life phases with each heading hinting at the continual process of Kartinyeri's spiritual healing. With each passing moment and experience or event, the book brings her closer to finally finding emotional closure. Whereas the autobiography begins with her being 'Stolen' from the hospital, the second chapter's title, 'The

Beginning of Grief', unambiguously underlines the end of Kartinyeri's carefree early childhood days, as the second stage of her stay in Colebrook Home was disfigured by what she calls 'Bible-bashing' and 'brainwashing' (Kartinyeri 2000: 42). Inversely, the notion of religion brought about a double standard dramatically subverting the taboo subject of sexuality when several staff members, either men or women, sexually harassed or abused both boys and girls at the home. Dominated by distrust and deceit, Kartinyeri's description of Colebrook reveals the loss of her sense of security.

Leading a heteronomous life in the confines of the AFB, Kartinyeri was treated like a commodity traded among white foster families who (ab)used her both as a domestic servant and a sex slave. Echoed in the chapter's title 'Shunted About', her teenage years were marked by uncertainty, and the constant removals and rapes had a traumatizing effect on her later life: 'I felt these terrible experiences had ruined my life. I had lost all my dignity, self respect and, most importantly, my identity and sanity. I was isolated in a valley which swallowed me up' (ibid.: 62–63).

As all her actions have so far been controlled by others, Kartinyeri finds it difficult to lead a self-determined life and organize a family of her own. After the divorce from the father of her two eldest children, she begins to search for her mutual family, finally ending up at their community Raukkan. In 'Need to Belong', Kartinyeri remembers their first encounter as an alienating act defined by heterostereotyping tendencies. Having been educated 'white', Kartinyeri is initially denied access to their community, subject to a similar feeling of unbelonging which has so far characterized her life among white people. In other words, she has to face an inverted form of 'othering' decisively displayed on a linguistic level:

> It was difficult for me to fit in with the Aboriginal community . . .
> I needed to familiarise myself with the local Nunga language . . . I was
> treated like an outsider . . . At this time I drank quite excessively to over-
> come my frustration within the town (ibid.: 78–79).

As a consequence of her communal exclusion, Kartinyeri develops strategies to escape this dilemma of dislocation. When drowning her pain in alcohol proves ineffective, she sets forth on a 'Journey from Reality'. What is officially diagnosed as bi-polar disorder is her way to break out of the confines of a world she was not able to cope with any longer. Trapped in-between two mental spaces, Kartinyeri attempts but fails to kill herself on several occasions. By the same token, the emotional heteronomy experienced at the hands of the APB continues to haunt her threading its way through her life's path:

> I have experienced emotional manipulation . . . As a child in Colebrook
> Home, there were authority figures who took advantage of me emo-
> tionally. My whole life has been moulded into a statue without liberty.
> My movements were restricted as a child and they feel restricted now
> (ibid.: 96–97).

During one of her stays in a mental hospital, Kartinyeri decides to run
a reverse route which counters those restrictions. Writing down her life
history as much requires a re-discovery of her own past as the discovery
of a new language — English. To that end, Kartinyeri attends college
classes before she can actually begin the writing process. In the course
of completing her autobiography, Kartinyeri meets other members of the
Stolen Generations with whom she collectively re-constructs their fic-
tionally shared lives after the enforced removal. By espousing the poetics
of memory, she prods the healing properties of sharing life (hi)stories:
'We will never forget . . . when we share the pain we begin to heal' (ibid.:
114). Resonating hope and healing, the final chapters 'Finding my Voice'
and 'Ngarrindjeri Mimini' conclude, but also complement Kartinyeri's
autobiography as they reveal a nebulous fusion of her fractured history.
Both by writing her life history and repeatedly representing the Stolen
Generations at conferences and public events, Kartinyeri revokes her
own voice and identity.

> I am a fifty-four year old Ngarrindjeri *mimini*. I am proud to be a Nunga.
> The battles and struggles of living in two worlds that I endured throughout
> my life have proven my aboriginality . . . I believe that my illness resulted
> from the combination of deception and despair throughout my life. I
> believe that I am only now coming to terms with all that I endured in the
> past. The healing has just begun (ibid.: 135; emphasis in original).

By means of a linguistic de-coding of her cultural heritage, Kartinyeri
connects with her community by rightfully reclaiming herself as
Ngarrindjeri *mimini*, a woman belonging to the Ngarrindjeri people.
While the writing process has engendered a sense of (self-)acceptance,
it simultaneously produced a therapeutic text about and for the Stolen
Generations. In other words, beyond the personal lies a collective story
which privileges polyphony over singularity and silence. As Brewster
rightly remarks, 'the construction of the self in minority autobiography
is seen as a social act which relates to and represents the experience of
the community rather than that of the individual' (Brewster 1997: 127).
Drawing upon the generic fusion within *fictional* life histories, the analysis

in the next section reveals that drama's pluralized performativity serves this very purpose, i.e., providing a polyphonic platform to stage several stories.

Staging Life Stories: Jane Harrison's Drama *Stolen*

> *Stolen* is not about blame, it is about understanding and acceptance (Harrison 2000: vii).

Seen through the prism of intersecting lives, Jane Harrison's play *Stolen* (re)presents a plural profile of various (fictional) life histories of the Stolen Generations in an attempt to stage what has been stolen from Australia's indigenous communities. *Stolen* is Harrison's first play and premiered in 1998; an abridged version was first presented as a reading to a predominantly Koori audience in 1993.[2] In the playwright's note, Harrison underlines the play's authentic approach by recounting the reaction of the indigenous audience: 'After the reading, a number of Koori people told us that they strongly identified with a particular scene — many were in tears at seeing their lives revisited in dramatic form. We knew then that we were on the right track' (ibid.). A descendant of the Muruwari people of New South Wales, Harrison grew up with her mother and sister admitting that she had not been familiar with the notion of the Stolen Generations before she started working on *Stolen*. To that end, she artistically engages in revealing the ramifications of the hidden histories of Australia's indigenes: '[i]n 1992, when the project was begun, there was very little knowledge or understanding about the plight of the Stolen Generations outside the Aboriginal community itself. Despite my Aboriginal heritage, I knew nothing about it' (ibid.).

A kaleidoscope of characters, *Stolen* tells the fictional life histories of five Aboriginal children — three girls and two boys — who were forcibly removed from their families and brought up in a children's home. Having been segregated from society at an early age, the adult characters struggle to deal with their disrupted lives in different ways. By focusing

---

[2] *Stolen* premiered at the CUB Malthouse, Melbourne, on 21 October 1998 and has had productions every year since. It was first produced by Ilbijerri Aboriginal and Torres Strait Islander Theatre Co-operative and Playbox Theatre Centre, in association with the Melbourne Festival.

on every life history individually, the plotline follows no obvious chronological order as it leaps backwards and forwards through time. Yet, the play opens with the characters as children and closes with them as adults. These constant shifts in time result in radical changes of location; that is a scene in a prison cell might follow one in the children's home. As *Stolen* was written for the stage, distinct dramatic devices such as the stage décor complement the characters' stories.[3] To that end, the play's sparse setting is minimized to five old institutional beds representing the respective 'homes' of the characters. In other words, this sterile space evokes a cold and clinical quality which in fact counters any sense of home thereby emphasizing the miserable living conditions of the five characters. Due to the shifts in time and space, the setting's dominant devices are adapted to the characters' respective stages in life. Accordingly, the beds are either transformed into such diverse places as a children's home, a prison cell, a mental institution or a girl's bedroom. As much as the changes of scene are characterized by an improvised interdependency of dramatic décor, they equally illustrate the interchangeability of the characters' life histories.

By the same token, Harrison's play chronicles a collective story shared by the Stolen Generations at different times and in various spaces — each character embodying (stereo)typical elements such as abuse, racism, mental illness and suicide.

The characters in the play are represented as fragmented, having been tainted by the notion of unbelonging in their sustained search for identity. This notion of fragmentation is virtually verbalized, as the characters increasingly speak in a 'stream of consciousness' style defying any linear lineaments in the plotline. Although they seem to interact with each other in some scenes, the characters' monologues are marked by what I would like to call counter-communication. All the same, they are mutually connected through the content of their monologues which revolve around an eventual reunion with their relatives.

One of the central characters, Sandy, is always on the run haunted by a hunt for a place called 'home'. His constant companion is a suitcase

---

[3] Taking up the notion of performativity, Terry Goldie argues: 'It is a commonplace in the study of dramatic literature that the play on the page is only a partial outline. In fiction, the reader who lifts the words from the page is controlled only by the interaction between imagination and text. The reader of the drama must also posit limitations to the imagination, the limitations of stage and actors' (1993: 170).

symbolizing both rootedness and restlessness. Born to an Aboriginal mother who was abused by a white man, he tries to find the way back to his roots. Sandy's quest for identity is thus driven by his bi-racial background and yet, being stolen. When Sandy reached the end of his sojourn, he finds himself inadvertently, on the right track leading home: 'Been everywhere. Except one place. Home . . . I'm going back. Home. . . . I don't have to run anymore . . . I don't have to hide. I'm going — home' (Harrison 2000: 35–36).

The life history of Shirley is defined by a sense of double(d) loss: not only that she had been stolen from her parents as a child, her own children were being stolen from her as well. Shirley relates to the moment of removal as a haunting image, an indelible memory which repeats itself unrelentingly:

Rain rain go away
I'm looking out of the back of the car
The car's big and black
Mummy's face is getting smaller and smaller
She's so little I can hardly see her
She's all blurry
Raindrops, tears, raindrops, tears (ibid.: 4).

Whilst talking about her children's removal, Shirley tells a strikingly similar story which echoes the elements of rain, a black big car and diminishing facial features. This parallel pattern of memory as much alludes to the interchangeability of (hi)stories as it counters a poetics of forgetting:

It rained the day they took my son. I stood there getting soaked to the skin and watched the back of that big black car and his little face, so little . . . I stood there in the rain and I couldn't talk (ibid.: 9).

Shirley never gives up searching for her children and eventually manages to meet not only her daughter Kate but also her newborn granddaughter. As a nurse wants to hold the baby, she (over)reacts defensively because of the fear that the story of removal might repeat itself in the third generation of her family: '[t]he nurse must have thought I lost the plot. I nearly did lose the plot so many times in my life. But I didn't, and I'm glad' (ibid.: 35). While Shirley realizes how much she still suffers from separation anxiety, her life finally comes full circle, manifested in the reunion with her long-lost family.

Instead of spending her formative years in a children's home, Anne has been raised by a wealthy white family enjoying a privileged and protected childhood. Informed by the socio-cultural context of white Australia, she has never identified herself with being 'black'. Only when her birth mother wants to meet her, is Anne caught in-between two cultures, and, for the first time, loses her sense of self:

> What about me? What do I want? I don't know. I don't know where to belong anymore… But hey, it's Mother's Day and I've got to make tracks. [*She pulls out a box of gift-wrapped chocolates.*] I got Mum some milk chocolates. [*She pauses, then pulls out another box.*] And I got my *mother* some dark chocolates. [*She laughs and pops one in her mouth*] Either way, I love them both (ibid.: 34; emphasis in original).

By means of a symbolic enunciation of racial differentiation, Anne is finally able to reconfigure her relatives; yet, her diction still demarcates along familiarity instead of family. Though biologically related to each other, she is not quite ready to bond with the woman she was stolen from.

The two most tragic figures of the play are made up of mischievous Jimmy and little Ruby who gradually give up on themselves. Ruby has been forced to work as a domestic servant from a very young age and has been repeatedly raped by her white master. On stage, she mostly mumbles to herself or cries like a baby after her mother. Yet, their reunion comes too late as Ruby has sought refuge in an alternative reality. When her family has finally located her in a mental hospital, she has already grown amnesic and is unable to recognize her relatives. Whereas Jimmy is portrayed as an aggressive boy who is involved in criminal acts as an adult, he seems to be the most vulnerable character in the play. He was separated from his family at a very young age, while his mother spent her entire life writing letters to welfare officers. However, her attempts to establish contacts with her son are in vain as the welfare officers withhold the letters from Jimmy and keep telling him that his mother is dead, forcing him to '[j]ust forget her' (ibid.: 12). The day Jimmy is released from prison he is informed about his mother's life-long search. Yet, both their life histories find a dramatic ending as his mother dies just when they are about to meet. Before he takes his life, Jimmy both continues and concludes the correspondence by writing a first and final letter to his now deceased mother:

> Dear Mum, forgive me. I have sinned. I've been a thug and a thief — but I've never stolen anyone's soul … Oh, Mum, why couldn't you have lived

a bit longer just so I could meet you? I waited so long. Brothers, don't give up fighting. Don't let it happen again. Don't let them take babies from their mother's arms. Someone's gotta fight. I just can't no more. They stuck a knife into me heart and twisted it so hard. Prison don't make you tough, it makes ya weak, ya spirit just shrivels up inside. I'm going now, to be with my mother. I can't fight. I'm punched out. My only wish is that we go to the same place. Willy Wajurri (Harrison 2000: 33–34).

Forging the idea of life after death, he puts into words what he has been dying to tell his mother all his life. In the sense of summarizing his story, the letter reads primarily as a tragic testimony of his personal struggle. Between the lines, however, his words raise hope for a happy ending yet again — in another life. By signing the letter with his birth name, *Willy* symbolically erases his past and, in so doing, reclaims what has been stolen from him.

Re-Memory of the Forgotten Other

While representing fact versus fiction, both forms of life histories constitute collective chronicles of the Stolen Generations as they reveal, record and remember lost lives. Encompassing the poetics of memory and forgetting, Toni Morrison's essay 'The Site of Memory' (1987) introduces the concept of 're-memory' which enables the writer to re-memorize stories of human beings which would otherwise be forgotten. Based on her work on African-American slave narratives, Morrison contends that the (re)writing process allows for subverting a partial representation of history by providing 'route[s] to a reconstruction of a world, to an exploration of an interior life that was not written and to the revelation of a kind of truth' (ibid.: 115). Conversely, the contemporary case of Australia's Stolen Generations is predominantly characterized by a proxy narrative, i.e., individuals voicing versions of people's life stories who might still be alive.[4]

Invoking this idea of historical and cultural collectivity, Morrison proposes a dual approach to writing one's autobiography which affects both the role of the writer and the reader: 'One: "This is my historical life — my singular, special example that is personal, but that also represents the race." Two: "I write this text to persuade other people — you, the

---

[4] I owe the conceptual exponents of the discussion on Toni Morrison's 're-memory' to Cecile Sandten (2009: 306–18).

reader, who is probably not black . . .'" (Morrison 1987: 104–5). Due to drama's mediated immediacy, fictional life histories play a major part in this process of persuasion by (in)directly addressing a white Australian audience to at least acknowledge the hidden histories of the Aboriginal communities. Whereas an autobiographical account articulates a healing process for the 'collective self', the performativity implied in fictional life writing empowers a stolen (hi)story to be seen *and* heard.

References

Brewster, Anne 1997. 'Aboriginal Women's Autobiography: Alice Nannup's *When The Pelican Laughed*', in Dieter Riemenschneider and Geoffrey V. Davis (eds), *Aratjara: Aboriginal Culture and Literature in Australia*, pp. 121–27. Amsterdam and Atlanta: Rodopi.

———. 2005. 'The Poetics of Memory', *Continuum*, 19(3): 397–402.

Eakin, Paul John. 1999. *How our Lives Become Stories: Making Selves*. Ithaca, NY: Cornell University Press.

Goldie, Terry. 1993 [1989]. *Fear and Temptation: The Image of the Indigene in Canadian, Australian, and New Zealand Literatures*. Montreal: McGill-Queen's University Press.

Harrison, Jane. 2000 [1998]. *Stolen*. Strawberry Hills, NSW: Currency Press.

Huggan, Graham. 2007. *Australian Literature: Postcolonialism, Racism, Transnationalism*. Oxford: Oxford University Press.

Kartinyeri, Doris E. 2000. *Kick the Tin*. Melbourne: Spinifex Press.

Morgan, Sally. 1987. *My Place*. Fremantle, WA: Fremantle Arts Centre Press.

Morrison, Toni. 1987. 'The Site of Memory', in William Zinsser (ed.), *Inventing the Truth: The Art and Craft of Memoir*, pp. 102–24. Boston: Houghton Mifflin.

Sandten, Cecile. 2009. 'Ethnic Life Writing: The Work of Beatrice Culleton Mosionier and Yvonne Johnson', in G. N. Devy, Geoffrey V. Davis, and K. K. Chakravarty (eds), *Indigeneity: Culture and Representation*, pp. 306–18. New Delhi: Orient BlackSwan.

Webby, Elizabeth. 2000. 'Introduction', in Elizabeth Webby (ed.), *The Cambridge Companion to Australian Literature*, pp. 1–18. Cambridge: Cambridge University Press.

6

Enforced Migration and Other Journeys in Aboriginal Experience

Sally Morgan's Stories of Becoming Disinherited and Dispossessed

Britta Olinder

Originally the Australian Aborigines were nomads freely moving around on the continent, 'following the logic of unending travel' (Blainey 1982: 185) until the white colonizers severely restricted their movements and forced them to unwanted migration, an 'experience of becoming disinherited and dispossessed'.[1] Instead of historically or anthropologically exploring the nomadic behaviour of the Aborigines, I have chosen the literary investigation of Sally Morgan's *My Place* (1988b), primarily for its demonstrating so clearly the effects on several generations of the enforced migration of children, taken from their mothers to be brought up far away in boarding schools or as servants in white families. The book is known as an autobiographical account of the writer's growing up and — not until she was 15 — becoming aware that she was actually aboriginal, a revelation followed by her mental journey towards a full sense of Aboriginal identity. That journey is undertaken partly by research in libraries or listening to, recording and taking down the life stories of, in turn, her great-uncle, her mother and her grandmother, partly by going

---

[1] Quoted from the Call for Papers for Chotro 2.

back to the place her family came from. The writer declares that she wants to fill a vacuum: 'there's almost nothing written from a personal point of view about Aboriginal people. All our history is about the white man. No one knows what it was like for us' (Morgan 1988b: 163). This is not the place to give an account of the growing Aboriginal literature, often of an autobiographical nature. To mention two random examples suggesting the centrality of migration in one form or another: first, Kath Walker or Oodgeroo Noonuccal's collection of poetry entitled *We Are Going* (1964; the first volume of Aboriginal poetry to be published); and second, *An Aboriginal Mother Tells of the Old and the New* (1984) by Elsie Roughsey or Labumore by her Aboriginal name. It was published in 1984, three years before *My Place*, and has chapters like 'Going Back for the Old Life', 'Going Out for the New Life' and 'Going Into the Life of Civilization' reflecting a migratory pattern of its own (for an early survey of Aboriginal writing, see Horton 1988).

The concept of migration/nomadic patterns of behaviour, i.e., moving from one place to another is one aspect to be explored, here closely connected with the concept of being disinherited and dispossessed, but I will also deal with other journeys undertaken — or not undertaken — by Aborigines as well as the genre or form of the book in question, its life stories, what it tells us about the language you are brought up with and languages learnt later, notably a language enforced on you, and how the language issue affects your identity. There are many other aspects to investigate concerning this book and its author, such as her paintings — another and possibly more important artistic expression of her Aboriginal identity — but something outside my scope here.

Migration

Migration is usually about leaving difficulties behind and heading for better living conditions, e.g., when food is getting scarce people move to more fertile areas. In a chapter entitled 'The Logic of Unending Travel' Geoffrey Blainey indicates the conditions of Aboriginal nomads: 'the frequency with which they moved camp — and the exact timing of their movements — reflected their understanding of climate, winds, marine life, insect life, the maturing of plants and the habits of wild animals' (Blainey 1982: 185). He gives a picture of a positive, promising migration. Examples in Sally Morgan's book refer to 'English people, who migrated out here in the hope of a better life' (1988b: 282). In *My Place* there are, however, mainly other kinds of migration or nomadic behaviour described. Of particular interest are, as mentioned previously, the stories of colonial slavery, or more precisely, the continual reminders of how half-caste children were taken from their mothers and placed in institutions or as servants in white homes, the stories of 'the stolen generations' (see Rudd 2008). In the case of Aboriginal children taken from their families, it might have been planned from the beginning to be to the advantage of these children, the background being the custom in the English upper classes to send their children, especially boys, to boarding school. The issue of children growing up away from their family, especially their mothers, is hotly debated in many countries in connection with adoptions or evacuated war children. As far as Aboriginal children in Australia are concerned, this undoubtedly grew out of racial prejudice and, while presented as a measure of protection of children having some white blood in them, developed into the exploitation of child labour, thus with negative, even tragic effects, in short, a perverted migration.

Another kind of migration consists of children running away from those conditions, like Sally Morgan's great-uncle Arthur, who hated the unbearably violent conditions of the school he had been forced into to the extent that he ran away never to return. There are many stories of this kind — a well-known one is Doris Pilkington's *Follow the Rabbit-Proof Fence* (1996), also made into a film. Arthur's moving on from one place, one job to another until he acquires his own farm can also be seen as a kind of nomadism.

In addition, Arthur tells us of a third variation of migration natural to his people, talked of as 'going walkabout'. 'We would go for weeks at a time, from one station to another, visiting people that belonged to us' (Morgan 1988b: 175). He mentions that his Aboriginal father, i.e., his stepfather, would sometimes 'go walkabout, right down to Fremantle, then up through Leonora, Ethel Creek and back to Corunna Downs' (ibid.: 176). This is the closest we get to what is normally understood as nomadic behaviour, this habit of walkabout or going 'pink-eye', explained in a note as a 'period of wandering as a nomad, often as undertaken by Aborigines who feel the need to leave the place where they are in contact with white society, and return for spiritual replenishment to their habitual way of life' (ibid.: 325).

What Kind of Book?

My *Place* could be called a multiple autobiography, i.e., one autobiography embracing three other autobiographies, to be compared with

Shakespeare's play-within-the-play or, perhaps, Homeric episodes branching out from the main narrative line. Gradually, Sally Morgan thus traces her own, her mother's, her grandmother's and her great-uncle's lives back to the place and conditions they originally belonged to. In an interview she speaks about it as '"our book". It's a true family autobiography' (Morgan 1988a: 94). On the back cover it is seen in different ways: '[t]he sort of Australian history which hasn't been written before, and which we desperately need' (*Weekend Australian*), emphasizing the factual side and '[a] moving and quite remarkable account of personal discovery' (*Sydney Morning Herald*) where the individual perspective comes to the fore (ibid., jacket cover). In addition the veracity of the story has been called into question by the white family responsible for the separation of the writer's grandmother and later her mother from their biological family ties and natural surroundings. Through these allegations of fabrication the basic autobiographical issue of 'fact or fiction' was brought into the public discussion on the web. Another view of the work as not genuinely Aboriginal started the heated discussion in *Australian Historical Studies* between contributors reading Morgan's book as an inaccurate psychological, social and historical account while others point out that the critical task is to assess the book, not the person and certainly not to think they know that person better than herself. Here, however, I am not going to discuss questions of reality or truth, personal or historical, but to investigate the motif of nomadism in the four stories.

Sally's Story

The first memory recounted is when she was five and on her way to see her father in hospital. That is where he spent most of his time. There were occasions when he was well and happy, but he never got over the war and the family obviously suffered from his depressions, irresponsibility and threatening violence. When Sally was nine he died. Along with the sorrow there was relief: 'Fear had suddenly vanished from our lives' (Morgan 1988b: 51). Rebellious as her father she developed 'an active dislike of school' early (ibid.: 19). The other kids kept asking her what country she came from; they could not believe her parents were Aussies. Her mother told her to say she was Indian but refused to talk more about it. She observed that her paternal grandmother treated her and her brothers and sisters differently from their cousins, allowing the latter inside while Sally and her siblings had to stay outside when they visited. The other grandmother, Nan, on the contrary, was always present at home looking after the children when their mother was away working, but, she reflected, there 'was so much about Nan I didn't understand' (Morgan 1988b: 67).

One day Sally found Nan crying, something she had never seen before and when she asked what had happened her grandmother burst out: 'You bloody kids don't want me, you want a bloody white grandmother, I'm black. Do you hear, black, black, black!' (ibid.: 97). It was only then that, with a shock, Sally became conscious of the fact that her grandmother was not white and consequently neither was she herself nor her sisters and brothers. The problem was that neither her mother nor her grandmother was willing to answer any questions about their past. Gradually, however, Sally took in the fact that she was not Indian as her mother had let her believe (ibid.: 38), but Aboriginal. This opened a new field of vision and she realized that she 'knew nothing about Aboriginal people' (ibid.: 100), except that there was a social stigma attached to them. She observed her grandmother behaving as if she were afraid and ashamed, comparing 'people like us' to 'those Jews' adding 'we better look out for ourselves' (ibid.: 105). It was only after several years that, in a surprise attack, she made her mother admit that they were really Aboriginal. That was seen as a beginning of further explorations into her mother's past, any information about which was only very reluctantly conceded. The next step forward was when Sally's great-uncle Arthur, her grandmother's brother, began visiting and on one occasion she overheard sister and brother 'jabbering away in what sounded to me like a foreign language' (ibid.: 148–49). Sally had now reached a point where she decided to write a book about her family history and first went to see her Aunty Judy, whom her grandmother as nursemaid had looked after, to hear what she could contribute. Then Arthur, who had been entertaining them with all sorts of yarns about himself, asked if she could put his story in the book, something that was, of course, warmly welcomed. Hearing about Arthur's life Sally realized that she had to find out more of her family's history and thought of the former station-owner's second, younger wife, now over 90. That was why she travelled to Sydney and on to Wollongong to meet her and gather more information.

When Sally had finished transcribing the cassettes recording Arthur's life and other family members read it, it was decided that some of them were going to explore his and his sister's birthplace, Corunna Downs. It was talked about as going North, going bush. They did not know what to expect and were warned it would only be dirt and danger, but once there they only explained who they and their connections were and they found relatives and people who knew or knew about both Arthur and Daisy, as

Sally's grandmother was called here. It was like 'we'd suddenly come home
. . . we had a sense of place now' (Morgan 1988b: 230). One meeting after
another added to their 'sense of belonging' (ibid.: 232). The result was:
'We were different people, now. What had begun as a tentative search
for knowledge had grown into a spiritual and emotional pilgrimage. We
had an Aboriginal consciousness now, and were proud of it' (ibid.: 233).
In many respects this trip sounds like an old-time walk-about. It also
resulted in her mother now being prepared to tell her part of the family's
history, what she had been so reticent about earlier. Sally's grandmother
had always been, not only reluctant but afraid to say anything about the
past but when she heard Arthur's stories she enjoyed them so much and
gradually agreed to share some of her memories on condition that she
could keep her secrets. In this ambivalent mood she encouraged herself
by thinking: 'Time to tell what it's been like in this country' (ibid.: 349).
Not long after she had finished there was 'the bird call' for her and she
died. This marks the end of the journey Sally had undertaken, to a large
extent with the help of the other three life stories.

Arthur Corunna's Story

Arthur Corunna's story begins on the Corunna Downs Station in the
north of Western Australia. His mother was Aboriginal and his father
the white station-owner, who shared with Arthur's Aboriginal father
the latter's two wives before marrying an Englishwoman. When Arthur
heard that they were to take him to the big house to be educated, he
tried to run away but was rounded up. From then on he was not allowed
to use his own language. Even so he was among his own people: 'All the
people round there, we all belonged to each other. We were the tribe
that made the station . . . I always wish I'd never left there. It was my
home' (ibid.: 181). But then he and his half-brother were to be taken
away. They promised that he would be back soon but even so the departure was quite traumatic:

> 'I clung to my mother . . . I cried and cried, calling to my mother "I don't
> want to go . . ." She was my favourite. I loved her. I called, "I want to stop
> with you. I want to stop with you!" I never saw her again' (ibid.: 182).

After a few years at the mission, which he remembered as 'just like a
prison' (ibid.: 183) and when he had been beaten so hard he could not
walk for a while — in his old age he could still show the scars — he managed to run away. His story details the adventures of his flight and then

the different jobs he got on farms. After hard labour for others he managed to share a farm with a white man and finally had saved enough to
get one of his own. In his life he thus illustrated 'two of the most important male Australian legends, nomadic bushworker and pioneer settler'
(Attwood 1992: 311), legends normally applied to men of European origin while Arthur was on his own, 'a black man with no one to help him'
(Morgan 1988b: 207). His experience is summed up in: 'It's hard for the
black man to get ahead' (ibid.: 209). Several times he was cheated of his
money, even of his first farm but succeeded in acquiring another one, got
married and had children and grandchildren. 'I look back on my life and
think how lucky I am. I'm an old fella now and I got one of my granddaughters lookin' after me' (ibid.: 213). He concludes his story:

> I got no desires for myself any more. I want to get my land fixed up so my
> children can get it and I want my story finished. I want everyone to read it.
> Arthur Corunna's story! . . . You see, it's important, because then maybe
> they'll understand how hard it's been for the blackfella to live the way he
> wants. I'm part of history, that's how I look on it. Some people read his-
> tory, don't they?' (ibid.).

Arthur's life story, thus, takes the shape of migration, moving geographically and socially, a class journey — in Western terms.

Gladys Corunna's Story

What stands out particularly in Sally's mother's story is, at the beginning,
the separation from her mother as she was taken to a Children's Home
at the age of three and, later, the tragic fate of her white husband who
never got over his experience of World War II.[2] Gladys, who had all the
time let her children believe that she spent a happy childhood in the former station owner's house, playing with his white children, had in reality
been taken from her mother and sent away by the lady of the house to a
children's home for orphans and was only allowed to be with her mother
during holidays three times a year — that is if the white family did not
have visitors, because in that case she had to stay at school. What she
wanted more than anything as a child was a family to belong to, but she

---

[2] To what extent travelling to other continents to fight a war should be
regarded as migration is not really relevant here since I am dealing with the
movements of indigenous people.

knew from harsh experience: 'Even when I was sick, I belonged to the Native Welfare Department. I wasn't even allowed to have the comfort of my own mother' (ibid.: 250). The way people treated her was not only hurtful but made her 'suddenly very unsure of [her] place in the world'. She felt like an outsider with the people she was expected to regard as her family (ibid.: 270). On two occasions this white family sent her mother away to get a job and a place to stay for herself, but they soon pleaded with her to come back when they needed her again. Meanwhile Gladys, who had moved from the Babyland Nursery to the older children's home and then on to be taken in by a reliable family and enrolled in a High School, was then, at last, allowed to live with her mother. After school she got a job, met her future husband and got married. Part of her story is actually her husband's, as she retells how he was transported as a prisoner-of-war and fleeing through Africa, Italy and Germany. In some respects this seems a reflection or counterpart of Arthur's flight, although a more sinister story and with a tragic outcome, not least due to the repercussions of his war experiences on their marriage. After Bill's death Gladys's life became a struggle to keep the family together without letting on that they were partly Aboriginal, 'a welfare lady[3] came out to visit us. I was really frightened because I thought, if she realised we were Aboriginal, she might have the children taken away' (ibid.: 304). From her mother she knew that 'Aboriginal people like her weren't allowed to have families' (ibid.: 275), the women 'weren't allowed to keep children fathered by white men' (ibid.: 301).

> In those days, it was considered a privilege for a white man to want you, but if you had children, you weren't allowed to keep them. You was only allowed to keep the black ones. They took the white ones off you, 'cause you weren't considered fit to raise a child with white blood (ibid.: 336).

There were thus good reasons to fear the government and Gladys says that she 'was really scared of authority. I wasn't sure what could happen to me' (ibid.: 279). She remembered an incident from her childhood when she had been called to her mother's sickbed from the orphanage to learn from her that '"Auntie Helen died. The doctor didn't care. You see, Gladdie, we're nothing, just nothing." I felt very sad, and sort of hopeless. I didn't want to be just nothing' (ibid.: 259).

---

[3] It is not emphasized but the reader can also see the ironies of hypocrisy in words such as 'welfare'.

The issue of identity is crucial. At the Children's Home they were taught never to talk openly about being Aboriginal. 'It was something we were made to feel ashamed of' (Morgan 1988b: 264). She also remem-bered an occasion when a lady waiting at a bus station asked about her national-ity, could she be Indian? And when she answered that she was Aboriginal, the woman was shocked, compassionately pitying her. She could not but wonder what was wrong with being Aboriginal: 'I won-dered what she expected me to do about it. I suddenly felt like a criminal' (ibid.: 279). Thus, even at a later stage she confessed: 'I'm still a coward, when a stranger asks me what nationality I am, I sometimes say a Heinz variety. I feel bad when I do that. It's because there are still times when I'm scared to say who I really am' (ibid.: 306). Even so she feels embar-rassed to think that once she wanted to be white. At this later stage in her life she declares:

> All I want my children to do is to pass their Aboriginal heritage on.
> I suppose, in hundreds of years' time, there won't be any black Aboriginals left. Our colour dies out; as we mix with other races, we'll lose some of the physical characteristics that distinguish us now. I like to think that, no matter what we become, our spiritual tie with the land and the other unique qualities we possess will somehow weave their way through to future generations of Australians. I mean, this is our land, after all, surely we've got something to offer (ibid.).

Gladys's enforced migration from the security near her mother to a tough life at the children's home can be seen as a milder treatment than her mother had experienced as a child, especially since Gladys received an education and could in her late teens move about with much less restrictions than her mother. And she was free to marry and have a family.

Daisy Corunna's Story

In the book she is mostly called Nan, sometimes, particularly by her brother, Daisy. But her tribal name, she declares, was Talahue. Her life had been such that even to think about what had happened was painful. The sorest points were the identity of her father and of the father of her daughter Gladys. She will not answer any questions about that but says at one point that 'the trouble with us blackfellas, we don't know who we belong to, no one'll own up' (ibid.: 325), reflecting the fact that so often they were let down by white fathers and their families. Meanwhile it has become obvious, particularly from her brother, Arthur's story that in both cases it was the white station owner at Corunna Downs, father in the family she was to work for as a servant — or shall we call it slave? She recalls a happy life at her birthplace up north with her mother, grandmother, sisters and brothers. Quite early, however, she had to start working up in the main house of the station and then 'I wasn't allowed down in the camp. If I had've known that, I'd have stayed where I was. I couldn't sleep with my mother now and I wasn't allowed to play with all my old friends' (Morgan 1988b: 331). She observed that the latter were 'camp natives' while she herself had become 'house native'.

That separation was, however, only the first step. Soon they took her away from the station, telling her mother that she was to be educated, to go to school so as to be able to come back and teach her mother. Nothing came of these promises and it soon became clear that it was not for school or education that she had to leave the station but for hard work. Her departure is described in heart-rending terms and once away from them she missed her own people back home, crying herself to sleep every night.

It is Daisy's story that makes the abuse of human and cultural rights appear most clearly. 'The blackfella couldn't live his own life then' (ibid.: 334) and they were not allowed to be out after dark. She tells her granddaughter that 'in those days, we was owned, like a cow or a horse' (ibid.: 336) and when Gladys was born, her brother Arthur wanted them to come and live with him, but she was not allowed to go anywhere. She had to have permission to travel and the white family she served would not let her go. Later when Gladys was three, she was taken from Daisy who wanted to keep her child but was too frightened to say anything.

The story about her being ill is now told from Daisy's point of view. When her cousin fell seriously ill, she was asked to give blood for her. 'I said yes. She belonged to me, I had to give blood, but I was real scared' (ibid.: 341). But the doctor made mistakes and lost the blood she had given, so they took more, more than they should. The cousin died anyway and Daisy heard the doctor saying: '"Doesn't matter, she was only a native". Then they looked at me and the nurse said, "I think this one's going, too"' (ibid.). Daisy was, however, taken from hospital and nursed back to health by her white mistress who is thus praised as 'a good bush nurse' (ibid.). All the same she did not pay Daisy her wages and kicked her out several times, all for the good in the end, since Daisy could then get a good job bringing in money. Later when her daughter fell ill, Daisy moved in with the younger family to look after the children and that was where she stayed making it possible after her son-in-law's death for Gladys to go out working. At the same time, when they had visitors, she took care to stay out of the way since 'you only had to look at me to see I was native' and they 'didn't like people like us rearin' kids with white blood in them'. This was again the fear that 'the government might come and get you' (Morgan 1988b: 348). The effect was a very real impediment to her freedom of movement.

Daisy was the one most deeply hurt by the enforced migration early in her life but still concluded her story by hoping that things would change for the better:

> At least, we not owned any more. I was owned by the Drake-Brockmans and the government and anyone who wanted to pay five shillings a year to Mr Neville to have me . . . I been scared all my life, too scared to speak out . . . Do you think we'll get some respect? I like to think the black man will get treated same as the white man one day (ibid.: 350).

The Language Issue

Language is often related to movement, geographically and culturally and could thus be seen as one aspect of migration to be taken into account. What surprised Sally when recording Nan's story was that her

> voice had changed as she reminisced. She could speak perfect English when she wanted to, and usually did, only occasionally dropping the beginning or ending of a word. But in talking about the past, her language had changed. It was like she was back *there*, reliving everything. It made me realise that at one stage in her life it must have been difficult for her to speak English, and therefore to express herself (ibid.: 351).

Another surprise for Sally was when she happened to overhear Arthur and Daisy speaking a language she did not understand — it was their mother tongue, closely connected with their early childhood when they lived with their mother and the rest of the tribe. When Arthur was at school to be educated he was, however, not allowed to 'talk blackfella' and he adds: 'I liked my language, but I got a good hiding if I spoke it. I had to talk English' (ibid.: 178). It is a language policy to be recognized

---

[4] A note in *My Place* gives the information that Mr A. O. Neville was Chief Protector of Natives, Western Australia, 1915–40. The legal removal of 'half-caste' Aboriginal children from their mothers was part of his policy (Morgan 1988b: 211).

from colonized areas in other parts of the world. Whole generations were cut off from this aspect of the culture they belonged to. In this case, however, Sally's youngest child was learning a little from his great-grandmother:

> One afternoon, after his usual session with Nan, he strolled into the kitchen and garbled out a set of instructions in what, to me, sounded like a foreign language:
>
> 'What was that?'
>
> 'That's what Nan taught me', he said, smiling. He was obviously very proud of himself. 'You know how we speak English, well she doesn't. That's what she speaks.'
>
> 'I see. And what does it mean?'
>
> 'It means get me a drink! I'm still waiting, you know' (ibid.: 318–19).

Learning his great-grandmother's mother tongue became a sign of the attempted migration in return that the whole family are taking part in.

Conclusion

The mental migration towards full recognition of the identity of the main characters is reflected in Sally's development, from her ignorance or innocence, via curiosity, her wish to know more, to know the truth, fighting against the reluctance and fear on the part of her mother and grandmother, through stages like overhearing her great-uncle and grandmother speaking a different language, listening to and taking down Arthur's story which revealed a lot to her, through the pilgrimage to Arthur's and Daisy's birthplace, recording her mother Gladys's story and finally hearing also that of her grandmother. This is a journey to be compared to the great epics, which were often about travelling and often had — just as here — stories within the main story. It is an exploration mapping the infringements of the human rights of Aborigines, the damage done to their sense of identity, but also showing the direction from shame and fear towards pride and confidence. This journey towards the knowledge, acceptance and dignity in being Aboriginal is summed up by Sally Morgan's sister saying as their grandmother Daisy is dying:

> Well, we're only just coming to terms with everything, finding ourselves, what we really are. And now, she's dying, she's our link with the past and

she's going . . . With her gone, we could pass for anything. Greek, Italian, Indian . . . We wouldn't want to, now. It's too important (Morgan 1988b: 354).

Throughout the whole book the consequences of enforced migrations are evident in making people disinherited and dispossessed. It has also been demonstrated that there is a way back to knowing who you really are, to knowing your identity and being able to speak with confidence about what you can call 'My Place'.

References

Attwood, Bain. 1992. 'Portrait of an Aboriginal as an Artist: Sally Morgan and the Construction of Aboriginality', *Australian Historical Studies*, 25(99): 302–18.

Blainey, Geoffrey. 1982 [1975]. *Triumph of the Nomads: A History of Ancient Australia*. Melbourne: Sun Books.

Horton, Wesley. 1988. 'Australian Aboriginal Writers', in Anna Rutherford (ed.), *Aboriginal Culture Today*, pp. 275–304. Sydney: Dangaroo Press.

Morgan, Sally. 1988a. '"A Fundamental Question of Identity": Interview with Mary Wright', in Anna Rutherford (ed.), *Aboriginal Culture Today*, pp. 92–109. Sydney: Dangaroo Press.

———. 1988b [1987]. *My Place*. London: Virago Press.

Pilkington, Doris (Nugi Garimara). 1996. *Follow the Rabbit-Proof Fence*. St Lucia: University of Queensland Press.

Roughsey, Elsie (Labumore). 1984. *An Aboriginal Mother Tells of the Old and the New*, ed. Paul Memmott and Robyn Horsman. Fitzroy, Victoria: McPhee Gribble.

Rudd, Kevin. 2008. 'Apology to the Stolen Generations', 13 February, http://www.dfat.gov.au/indigenous/apology-to-stolen-generations/national_apology.html (accessed 22 March 2012).

Walker, Kath [Oodgeroo Noonuccal]. 1964. *We Are Going: Poems*. Brisbane: Jacaranda Press.

7

Contemporary Nomads, or Can the Slum-Dweller Speak?

Cecile Sandten

♋

Human dignity is violable: slums neither have a face nor do they have a voice.
We live in the age of the city: The city is everything to us — it consumes us, and for that reason we glorify it.

Onookome Okome (2002: 316)

New Metropolises, Post-Colonialism, 'Diffuse Urbanism' and 'Slumification'

The relationship between colonialism and urbanism or, more especially, between post-colonialism and the metropolis has, as Anthony D. King rightly remarked, been 'woefully neglected' (King 2006: 320). Hence, it is necessary, arguing along the lines of cultural theorist Rüdiger Kunow, that after the 'cultural turn' we now have to engage with the 'spatial turn' (Kunow 2003: 186). The analysis of space in relation to post-colonialism is even more necessary, as according to urban theorist Mike Davis '[f]or the first time the urban population of the earth will outnumber the rural' (Davis 2006: 1). And 'the scale and velocity of Third World urbanization . . . utterly dwarfs that of Victorian Europe (ibid.: 2). Therefore, he justly goes on to assert, 'the exploding cities of the developing world are also weaving extraordinary new urban networks, corridors, and hierarchies'" (ibid.: 5). In addition, the world agrarian crisis is leading to an '"overurbanization" [of the new metropolises which] is driven by the reproduction of poverty, not by the supply of jobs'" (ibid.: 16). Life in the so-called new metropolises is, therefore, for many 'contemporary nomads' a life in devastating living conditions.[1] It is a struggle within the jungle of metropolicization, as Davis appallingly outlines:

> the cities of the future, rather than being made out of glass and steel as envisioned by earlier generations of urbanists, are instead largely constructed out of crude brick, straw, recycled plastic, cement blocks, and scrap wood. Instead of cities of light soaring toward heaven, much of the twenty-first-century urban world squats in squalor, surrounded by pollution, excrement, and decay (Davis 2006: 19).

In his diasporic journal and travelogue, *Maximum City: Bombay Lost and Found* (2004), Suketu Mehta states: 'Bombay is the future of urban civilization on the planet. God help us'" (ibid.: 15). With this prediction, Mehta not only hints at the growing (economic) importance of Bombay but also ironically complains about its poor or even degenerate forms of life outside, or 'downside' the proudly monumental spaces of the prosperous post-colonial, 'new metropolis'. Central to this development is also the fact that the social, territorial, and cultural reproduction of group identity has dramatically changed. As Arjun Appadurai rightly asserts, ethnoscapes have changed because groups are no longer based on the same territory and/or in the same history due to displacement (Appadurai 1991: 191–210) in spite of the fact, as Sheela Patel argues, that 'communities migrating to cities often congregate on the traditional basis of ethnic language, kinship, religion or caste, among others. Sometimes evictions, displacements and relocations (formal or informal) modify this communal structure' (Patel 2001).[2] Thus, for defining a coherent group identity the old concepts of 'diaspora' or 'cultural identity' have become

---

[1] In colonial and imperial Eurocentric ways of thinking, the metropolis was seen as the seat of political, economic and cultural power — a perception that has not changed much until today. In particular, London, Paris and Moscow are being regarded as centres of European and East European expansion. London and Paris were, in fact, the centres of the two largest colonial empires of the world and still are appropriate examples of world cities that have been described and depicted in literature, films and academic writing to a great extent. In contemporary (postmodern times they are forced to share their status as world cities with one older metropolis — New York City — and more recently with new metropolises such as Mumbai, Kolkata, Cape Town, Delhi, Hong Kong, Lagos, Mexico City or Tokyo, which contradict almost every defining feature of the 'modern' city.

[2] 'However, these traditional ties usually remain the preferred means of linkage that form primary communities. This inevitably leads to types of authority

obsolete. These aspects also hold true for various other megacities, such as Bangalore, Kolkata, Chennai, or Delhi. Taking Mehta's statement as a cue, and looking at medial and textual representations and negotiations of what German architect and urban theorist Thomas Sieverts calls 'diffuse urbanism' (2003: 3), I will in this chapter explore representations of the radically unequal and explosively unstable situation of the metropolitan *under*world with particular focus on what I have termed the 'contemporary nomad'. This term encompasses, for example, the slum-dweller in various literary and medial guises: as voiceless urban squatter, repressed political or economic migrant, or (rather more positively) 'post-colonial *flâneur*'. I will discuss how the 'contemporary nomad', that is, the slum-dweller, has been excluded from speaking, which means from articulating him- or herself, from taking action, from being acknowledged as a human being, in spite of the fact that over the last three decades many organizations for the urban poor have come into existence.[3]

---

based on caste, race, tribe, religion and ethnic identity. The leaders of such communities often have interests and priorities that differ from the needs and aspirations of their very poor constituencies. Therefore, the poor are often forced to participate in an agenda that does not necessarily benefit them. In many ways, the slum dweller federations empower the poor by giving them a more "modern" identity and they allow people to form associations other than those based on traditional ties . . . Instead of relying on religion and kinship alone, their need for association and community would find expression in these new voluntary arrangements. They would then not need to continue to seek protection from eviction or demolition through an informal allegiance to a communal identity' (Patel 2001).

[3] Realizing the potential of cities as geographic, political, social, cultural and economic spaces conducive to individual development, the urban poor have begun to explore a range of associations through which they are able to have an impact on the decision-making processes of their cities. The National Slum Dwellers Federation (NSDF) in India is, for instance, one of the largest 'urban poor' organizations and social movements in the world. It formed an alliance with Mahila Milan, savings cooperatives run by women slum and pavement dwellers, and with a Mumbai-based NGO, Society for the Promotion of Area Resource Centres (SPARC) in 1985. Another organization is the Slum/Shack Dwellers International (SDI), an umbrella group formed by urban poor and homeless federations from many different nations. The National Alliance of People's Movement is another, which is an umbrella organization of different social movements. And there is the NGO, Proud, a Christian organization.

Can the Slum-Dweller Speak?

Mike Davis acknowledges that 'not all urban poor, to be sure, live in slums, nor are all slum-dwellers poor' (2006: 25). In addition, as Jeremy Seabrook suggests, '[i]t would be foolish to pass from one distortion — that the slums are places of crime, disease and despair — to the opposite: that they can be safely left to look after themselves' (1996: 197). Yet, slum-dwellers are most frequently repressed by corrupt authorities, the police or the economy, they are without rights to land, water, electricity or other basic human needs, or as Davis puts it:

> There are probably more than 20,000 slums on earth, ranging in population from a few hundred to more than a million people. The five great metropolises of South Asia (Karachi, Mumbai, Delhi, Kolkata, and Dhaka) alone contain about 15,000 distinct slum communities whose total population exceeds 20 million. 'Megaslums' arise when shanty-towns and squatter communities merge in continuous belts of informal housing and poverty, usually on the urban periphery (2006: 26).

Davis further explains that 'today squatting, *stricto sensu*, continues primarily in low-value urban land, usually in hazardous or extremely marginal locations such as floodplains, hillsides, swamps, or contaminated brownfields' (ibid.: 39). So, the urban theorist outlines disturbingly, 'millions of temporary workers and desperate peasants also hover around the edges of . . . world capitals of super-exploitation' (ibid.: 46).

Thus, I argue that the 'contemporary nomad' can often be equated with the urban squatter, the voiceless slum-dweller, the anonymous masses of people who live without rights in in-between spaces and within fluid borders between legality and illegality, or, as Sieverts suggests, in the *Zwischenstadt* ('in-between city') (Sieverts 2003: 3). In his study about slums across the globe, Robert Neuwirth also analyzes Mumbai's largest squatter community, Dharavi, which is 'home to between five hundred thousand and 1 million people (estimates vary depending on who's doing the counting)' (2006: 120). Neuwirth further writes that 'each day, an estimated 300 people flee their homes in the hinterland and move to Bombay' (ibid.). Therefore, the question whether the slum-dweller is able to speak seems a most promising one in relation to my current research topic on 'Postcolonialism in the Metropolis', especially when it is analyzed with Gayatri Spivak's seminal text, 'Can the Subaltern Speak?' (1994). In this provocative essay, Spivak addresses the way the 'subaltern' woman as subject is positioned, represented, spoken for or constructed as absent or silent or not listened to in a variety of discourses. Her speech is represented as non-speech: mis-characterized, ignored, distorted, erased. In my analysis of a representative number of medial and literary texts, I will therefore apply this idea to the situation of the contemporary slum-dweller in today's megacities. With this strategic move, I aim to dismantle the hegemonic and capitalist discourse, which was brought into the so-called 'Third World' by European colonialism, and which, for instance with special regard to the occupation of space, 'denied native populations the rights of urban land ownership and permanent residence' (Davis 2006: 51). As Davis again puts it: 'in the subcontinent, the British also segregated and policed the influx from the countryside' (ibid.: 52). According to him,

> the new-fangled Town Improvement Trusts, in particular, were highly effective in clearing slums and removing so-called 'plague spots' from the interstices of better residential and commercial areas, and preserving spatial zoning around colonial and native middle-class areas (ibid.: 52).

This trend to 'outcaste' the rural poor, migrants and slum-dwellers, has continued in contemporary India and other emerging nations. Today, 'the lion's share of the budget [for municipal housing and rehousing the poor] is used to meet the needs of the middle- and upper-income [people]' (ibid.: 66) instead of those of the urban poor. The following examples will show that the 'untouchables', 'outcastes', tribal migrants, and/or slum-dwellers have, over the decades, seemingly experienced the same fate, which accordingly is represented in literary and medial texts.

Mulk Raj Anand's Novel Untouchable

Mulk Raj Anand is with the poor and the downtrodden, voicing the concerns and predicaments of the lower classes in Indian society and siding with the lost and the sufferers. The writer has a most critical view on caste which he expressed on numerous occasions and translated into fictional terms in all his narratives. As the first modern Indian writer in English, Anand draws a very moving picture of the life of an 'untouchable'. His story is told chronologically without pathos and sentimentality. *Untouchable* (Anand 1940) can be subdivided into two parts the first of which depicts the morning and the second the afternoon of a day in Bakha's life. The casteless people live, expelled from society, on the fringes of the town under inhuman hygienic and social living conditions, as Anand displays in his novel:

The outcastes' colony was a group of mud-walled houses that clustered together in two rows, under the shadow both of the town and the cantonment, but outside their boundaries and separate from them. There lived the scavengers, the leather-workers, the washermen, the barbers, the water-carriers, the grass-cutters and other outcastes from Hindu society (Anand 1940: 9).

They live in huts, surrounded by dirt and bad smells:

The absence of a drainage system had, through the rains of various seasons, made of the quarter a marsh which gave out the most offensive stink. And altogether the ramparts of human and animal refuse that lay on the outskirts of this little colony, and the ugliness, the squalor and the misery which lay within it, made it an 'uncongenial' place to live in (ibid.: 9).

Anand places his protagonist, a latrine sweeper by the name of Bakha, in contrast to this world by depicting him as a young man who is seeking cleanliness, nice clothes and education. Right in the first scene we see the depiction of the dramatic conflict between Bakha and his society, which dominates the whole novel. Bakha's will to live and his desire to find fulfilment as a sensitive, hard-working and responsible young man continually encounters opposition from and rejection by the caste Indians in particular, but also that of his own family and friends, who have long put up with their own fate as outcastes. In subsequent episodes which underline the dramatic structure of the narrative, Anand illustrates the inhuman living conditions of the 'untouchables', who in a most literal sense are not granted any space to live in.

Further, Anand uses many different events in order to openly show the problems of the 'untouchables'. He introduces inner monologues and omniscient commentary as well as the description of Bakha's dreams and memories; he thus provides the reader with a very authentic picture of societal circumstances. In addition, he offers the reader a psychologically-differentiated presentation of a human being who becomes vivid only through the very documentary character of its author's narration.

Anand uses the second part of his novel in order to envision concrete possibilities which will help Bakha and his fellow 'untouchables' to abandon the burden of their outcaste position. In spite of the fact that there is solidarity among the 'untouchables', the question remains whether solidarity and friendship help them to console themselves? Or whether humanity lies in single individuals? Another question that arises is whether any particular ideologies will offer a solution? An English missionary, Colonel Hutchinson, wants Bakha to convert to Christianity.

Gandhi speaks of the equality of all men and argues for the revolution of the heart; finally, the poet Iqbal Nath Rarashar, after having listened to Gandhi's speech, discusses the technical progress of building a flush-toilet system as an alternative to latrine sweeping.

As in the first part of the novel, neither Bakha's youth nor his position in society allow him to actively take part in the events. He is emotionally only able to absorb fragmentary aspects of Christianity and Gandhi, human behaviour and the idea of technical progress. However, in his very inability to actively take part in the events lies the authenticity of his character, so that the hopeful outlook of the novel seems to be appropriate: maybe there will be a revolution of the heart — and toilets with a flush system (see Riemenschneider 1988).[4] Moreover, the powerful critique of the Indian caste system suggested that British colonial domination of India had not helped to decrease but had actually increased the suffering of outcastes such as Bakha. After 19 rejection slips Anand's novel was published in England with a preface by E. M. Forster:

> *Untouchable* could only have been written by an Indian, and by an Indian who observed from the outside. No European, however sympathetic, could have created the character of Bakha, because he would not have known enough about his troubles. And no Untouchable could have written the book, because he would have been involved in indignation and self-pity (1940: vi–vii).

With this statement, Forster suggests that 'untouchables' need a voice that speaks for them in order to address their problems adequately.

Salaam Bombay! (1988)

This is also the case in the movie *Salaam Bombay!* (1988) directed by Mira Nair. Nair studied sociology and theatre at Delhi University and earned a graduate degree in sociology from Harvard University. *Salaam Bombay!* is set in Bombay and depicts the 'underworld' by drawing the viewer's attention to issues such as (child) prostitution, juvenile delinquency, child abuse, and street life. The protagonist Krishna, a boy of

---

[4] Dieter Riemenschneider has published several essays and book chapters on Anand's work. For a full account of his and other readings by international and Indian critics over a period of six decades, that is, from the beginnings of a critical discourse in the 1930s to 2004, see Riemenschneider (2005). See also Gandhi (2003: 178).

about 12 years of age, supposedly sets fire to his brother's motor-bike. His mother takes him to the nearby Apollo Circus and tells him that he can only come back home after he earns ₹500 which he needs to pay back for the damaged bike. When the circus, where he is working, moves on they accidentally leave him behind. Thus, with the money he has left, Krishna is forced to move to the nearest city, which is Bombay, all by himself. Becoming a street boy, working at a local tea shop that services a neighbourhood brothel and befriended by a street-adolescent, Chillum, who sells drugs, Krishna encounters the underworld of a 'Third World' metropolis. Krishna is re-named 'Chaipau', which is the term for tea boy. Jyotika Virdi writes about the movie:

> Several parallel stories are woven into the plot: one revolves around "Sweet Sixteen," a young girl from Nepal kept hostage at the brothel, a victim of the traffic in women; a second story deals with another prostitute in the brothel, a single mother, in love with a local drug pusher and struggling to raise her five year old daughter, Manju; a third story is about Krishna's friend Chillum and his addiction to "brown sugar" (Virdi 1992).

Krishna falls in love with Sweet Sixteen. He gets beaten up for trying to help her escape her fate as a prostitute. Thus, he loses his job as a tea boy, and together with other children robs an old man of his belongings in broad daylight. He is arrested by the police and is sent to a juvenile home from which he escapes only to find out that the world of prostitution, drugs and street life, which he left behind, is no longer the same. Chillum is dead and another person has taken his place as a kind of new Chillum. However, Krishna is never able to earn the ₹500 and go back to his family. According to Virdi, '*Salaam Bombay!* marks a departure from the powerful and one-sided flow of media texts from the "First" to the "Third World". As a film from "Other Worlds", to borrow a term from Gayatri Spivak, *Salaam Bombay!* is made by Mira Nair, an Indian film-maker, a woman of color' (ibid.).

Thus, the movie interpellates precisely the question of self-representation from the 'Other World' regarding life in the metropolis. It shows the displacement of the children from their rural homes to the back alleys of Bombay. These children try to make a living through child labour, being exploited by adults. They are, thus, unsuccessful, unheard of, always at the brink of crime and death. In this 'docudrama', it can be argued that Nair speaks for these children and young adults, especially for Krishna, in order to make the children's fate in a 'Third-World'-metropolis seen and heard.

Urban Reportage — *Maximum City*: *Bombay Lost and Found*

In Suketu Mehta's travelogue, autobiography, reportage, urban portrait and diasporic journal, the issues outlined so far are also addressed, yet in a different mode, as Mehta, after 21 years of absence from his home city, Bombay, plunges into it in order to find it.

Throughout the book, the aspect of juxtaposition in the metropolis Bombay is highlighted: 'Bombay is where worlds collide' (Mehta 2004: 223). Investigating the city's bloody 1992–93 riots, Mehta meets Hindus who massacred Muslims, and their leader, the notorious Godfather-like founder of the Hindu nationalist Shiv Sena party, Bal Thackeray. He also dares to explore the violent world of warring Hindu and Muslim gangs. Travelling into the city's labyrinthine criminal underworld with tough top cop Ajay Lal, he develops an uneasy familiarity with hit men who display no remorse for their crimes. Mehta also deploys a documentary style when he investigates Bombay's sex industry, with the depiction of a dancing girl called Monalisa, with whom he nearly falls in love, and a cross-dressing male dancer, Honey, who leads a strange double life. Moreover, Mehta includes 'Bollywood' in his account of Bombay's subcultures.

Throughout the book Mehta describes crowds and great masses of people and, thus, density and lack of solitude and privacy. Accordingly he writes: '[t]he battle of Bombay is the battle of the self against the crowd' (ibid.: 589), and he continues: 'Bombay itself is reaching its own extremity: twenty-three million people by 2015. A city, in which the population should halve, actually doubles' (ibid.: 588). He further explains that 'it is a crowded city, used to living with crowds' (ibid.: 537). All these quotes underline Mehta's intention of depicting Bombay as a phantasmagorical representation of a post-colonial cityscape, on the one hand, but also as a city, as he puts it, 'of possibilities': 'Once you leave Bombay, the rest of the world is a village' (ibid.: 225).

Bombay is so crowded that even for the most profane chores, such as going to the toilet, people have to queue. Mehta constantly plays with figures in order to underline the issue of the crowds, the lack of space, and the contrast between rich and poor. He compares India's desires for modernity with the daily insufficiencies that Bombayites have to face: 'there is no guarantee of a constant supply of electricity in most places in the country. In this as in every other area, the country is convinced it can pole-vault over the basics' (ibid.: 25). According to Mehta, Bombay has to face illiteracy, childhood diseases, a non-existent water-supply, an absence of power-units and telephone networks, of proper roads, and a proper toilet system. Women are worse-off because there is no privacy; there is heat and there are rains and floods. In addition, the criminal justice system is collapsing; there is a parallel economy (Mehta 2004: 195) with hit-men, gang-war (ibid.: 179), and corruption; there is no urban planning, no infrastructure, and a high migration rate.

Mehta does not report about 'untouchables' as such, as do Anand and, to a certain extent Nair, but his report reveals a lot about the living conditions of slum-dwellers as anonymous masses: 'Mumbai's estimated annual housing deficit of 45,000 formal-sector units translates into a corresponding increase in informal slum dwellings' (ibid.: 117). By underlining Bombay's 'internal diversity' (Hannerz 1996: 315), Mehta, with the reader in complicity, plunges into the masses like Walter Benjamin's *flâneur* who neither has to go to work, nor resembles a tourist, but who walks the streets seemingly without purpose.

In his book, Mehta puts forward the dialectics of Bombay as a city that he lost and found, a city now swollen to 18 million inhabitants and choked by pollution, a city which, as the author puts it, 'survives on the scam' (Mehta 2004: 28). The semantics of the uncanny are utilized when going into and studying the underground, or as Mehta's thesis goes: 'In Bombay, the underworld is an overworld' (ibid.: 147); and 'the heart of Bombay is the heart of the gangwar' (ibid.: 158); or 'in Bombay, to be a capable businessman, you have to be in touch with the underworld' (ibid.: 40, 250). The underworld is often equated with slum-life, the wasteland of non-existent architecture, the naked *flâneur* of lowest social status who is walking across the (architectural) dirt for lack of choice: '"Bombay is a bird of gold". A man living in a slum, without water, without toilets, was telling me why he came here, why people continue to come here . . . "Nobody starves to death in Mumbai"' (ibid.: 18). Mehta further writes: 'In daytime I had been walking around the Bihari slums of Madanpura, scenes of fantastic deprivation' (ibid.: 40).[5] In *Maximum City*, Bombay is depicted by means of a juxtaposition of different people and a kind

---

[5] There are 57,000 families living in one of Mumbai's biggest slums, Dharavi, for instance. They have established their own economic system with pottery, tannery and recycling. Thus, Dharavi resembles a kind of 'middle-class' slum. According to government figures, 600,000 people live in this slum, undeveloped real estate of just under two square kilometres — right in the middle of the city. Yet, 20 square metres are worth €22,000.

of experimentation with form. There is, on the one hand, Mehta's own (auto)biographical account in terms of the presentation of the home-town aspects or of the depiction of food. There is also, on the other hand, Mehta's schizophrenic view of Bombay, showing the corruption of institutions and organizations in which he is seemingly complicit. The book is characterized by a whole web of stories of people and the battle between the self and the crowd, the underworld *vs* the apparently normal (New York-based) people and the contradictory views and the attitudes towards Bombay. In this respect, the slum-dwellers take the form of anonymous masses that are depicted as crowds or criminals. Thus, the 'subaltern', to use Spivak's term, that is, in this case the slum-dweller, cannot speak but is, once again, spoken for, yet in terms of a rather general problem: as 'diffuse urbanism', 'slumification' and overpopulation. This is juxtaposed with the former gleaming city of Mehta's memory, which has turned into a teeming, frustrating, but frequently glorious mess.

Born into Brothels: *Calcutta's Red-Light Kids* (2004) — Seeing the World Through their Eyes

> It's almost impossible to photograph in the red light district. It's a whole separate society within itself, and when you walk down that lane it's just another world. And of course as soon as I entered the brothels I met the children. They were all over me, and I would play with them and take their photographs and they would take mine (Briski and Kauffman 2004).

Eight children from the red-light district, the Sonagachi area, of Kolkata were invited to use a camera and make their environment theirs. They were, thus, able to interact, perceive, structure, appropriate and make sense of the world and the city for themselves. With this, the children felt that they were seen by others that they photographed, too. Usually, the disadvantaged children lead a life in the slums and streets of India's cities where they do not have any security. Many people come from the villages to seek a better life in the cities. There is a high infant mortality rate in the slums; relationships do not last; everything is reduced to its monetary value; children are often beaten up by policemen and sexually and physically abused. They frequently find a refuge in drugs, and often, parents, in order to make a living, make their children work at a very early age. Their main profession is begging. To add to this list: 40 per cent of India's children live in poverty; they have less than ₹10 (= €0.17) per day to buy food and water; in addition, they have only a limited access to education and medical facilities. This commonplace knowledge is taken up in the documentary *Born into Brothels*, too. Accordingly, Michel Frann writes about the film:

> *Born Into Brothels* may be an ideal test case for certain questions about the state of documentary: an independent movie that won an Academy Award, a narrative crowd-pleaser with a real-world agenda, a work shot on video about the uses of film — it embodies and engages a range of contradictions and paradoxes. Directed by British photojournalist Zana Briski and US film editor Ross Kauffman, the film follows Briski's project of teaching photography to a group of children who live in Sonagachi — Calcutta, India's red-light district — as well as Briski's efforts to get these children of sex workers admitted into boarding schools. Perhaps the film's central paradox is its reliance on the children for access to the exotic world of Sonagachi, even as it attempts to distance and remove them from that world. The structure of the film — and particularly its omissions — helps position the children as both the victims of the red[-]light district and the vehicles of an aestheticizing vision of it (Frann 2007: 53–61).

In spite of the rather critical message which Frann conveys, the children who take photographs are, to a certain extent, able to become what I have termed 'postcolonial *flâneurs*'. They are able to leave the chaos and hard times behind, at least for a while. For instance, 13-year-old Gour says: 'When a camera is in my hands, I can take a picture of someone who has gone away, died or been lost and have something that I will be able to look at . . . We don't have the money to live, let alone for studies'. The ten-year-old Kochi says: 'If my sister wouldn't have come to get me, my father would have sold me'. And the 11-year-old girl Shanti says: 'We like taking photographs so much, we forget our work'. And the 15-year-old girl Suchitra says: 'When I have a camera in my hands, I feel happy. I feel like I am learning something . . . I can be someone' (Briski and Kauffman 2004). These quotations show that through the camera the children were able to establish an identity of their own.

In addition,

> the children's work has been auctioned at Sotheby's, and is featured in a book documenting the project as well. Proceeds from these ventures are returned to the children through the Kids With Camera foundation, which Briski set up to support similar projects around the world (Frann 2007: 53).

Yet, only two out of the eight children were able to make photography their goal in life. But these two who were able to 'get out' found themselves in the position of understanding/speaking the 'other', the object they photographed, and were thus creating themselves perhaps also as a 'native informer' class. However critical the viewer of this documentary might be, also with regard to the fact that Briski and Kauffman are white 'Western' photographers/filmmakers, it is nonetheless important to point out that the children were able to gain a voice, i.e., agency, at least for some time. They were able to actively depict the topography of their usual Calcutta 'non-places' but also of places which were of beauty and meaning to them.

Conclusion

The question 'Who can write as Other?' (Fee 1995: 242–45) in terms of 'can majority group members speak as minority members, whites as people of colour, men as women, intellectuals as working people' (ibid.: 242), or is it permissible to 'produce' Third World subjects for First World consumption, is a most problematic question when addressing the issue of the 'subaltern', the contemporary nomad, the voiceless slum-dweller. In the 'new' metropolises people often live in *favelas* and slums, sometimes as illegal squatters, under unbearable living conditions: without any possibility of achieving basic literacy, without adequate health care (especially for children), without adequate sanitary facilities (especially for women), without basic water or electricity supply, and human rights. Though many slum-dwellers have been living in their respective slum for several generations, it is still possible to regard them as (contemporary) nomads: they have been moving in and out of their poor hutments due to evictions ordered by the city council and have frequently been perceived as 'urban pirates'. Often considered 'outcastes' within the still valid Hindu caste system, they do the lowest jobs, work as prostitutes, beggars, cleaners, scavengers — just in order to survive.

Through having had a look at the different (media) texts that depict 'slum-dwellers', 'untouchables' — or in other terms the 'othered', that is, societal outsiders, who are constantly on the move or who are being moved — it has become obvious that these people are most often exploited and silenced within the anonymity of the metropolis and forced to live as contemporary nomads — without human rights, home, voice and tradition. Thus, the question of power becomes a central one when focusing on the issue of representations of the 'othered' 'other'. It seems as if he or she has to be spoken for in order to gain agency. In spite of what I have outlined, and especially with respect to a whole range of associations through which slum-dwellers and street-dwellers are depicted, they are increasingly able to have an impact on the decision-making processes of their cities. More frequently, the urban poor are beginning to envisage for themselves a new role as part of the citizenry, as active agents participating in municipal agenda-setting and helping administrations solve the city's infrastructure problems (see Patel 2001). This is a far cry from the stereotypical image of the poor as anonymous and passive recipients of aid which is often shown in the media. Yet, writing, filming, and photographing must nonetheless promote the societal 'othered' access to power. It is perhaps a way to self-representation of the 'othered (under)world', in contemporary 'new' metropolises. Anand's (to a lesser extent in terms of a current view on contemporary metropolises), Briski's, Mehta's and Nair's explorations in recent media/texts have offered two important aspects in an environment struggling with the economic and social inequalities of a more and more globalized market — firstly, the different representations of post-colonial cityscapes as topographies of 'non-places', or rather dystopian spaces, and secondly the need of the 'underworld nomadic othered' to speak.

References

Anand, Mulk Raj. 1940 [1935]. *Untouchable*. London: Penguin.

Appadurai, Arjun. 1991. 'Global Ethnoscapes: Notes and Queries for a Transnational Anthropology', in Richard G. Fox (ed.), *Recapturing Anthropology: Working in the Present*, pp. 191–210. Santa Fe NM: School of American Research.

Davis, Mike. 2006. *Planet of Slums*. London: Verso.

Fee, Margery. 1995 [1989]. 'Who Can Write as Other?', in Bill Ashcroft, Gareth Griffiths and Helen Tiffin (eds), *The Post-Colonial Studies Reader*, pp. 242–45. London and New York: Routledge.

Forster, E. M. 1940 [1935]. 'Preface', in Mulk Raj Anand, *Untouchable*, pp. v–viii. London: Penguin.

Frann, Michel. 2007. 'From "Their Eyes" to "New Eyes": Suffering Victims and Cultivated Aesthetics in *Born into Brothels*', *Post Script: Essays in Film and Humanities*, 26(3): 53–61.

Gandhi, Leela. 2003. 'Novelists of the 1930s and 1940s', in Arvind Krishna Mehrotra (ed.), *An Illustrated History of Indian Literature in English*, pp. 168–92. New Delhi: Permanent Black.

Hannerz, Ulf. 1996. *Transnational Connections: Culture, People, Places*. London and New York: Routledge.

King, Anthony D. 2006. 'World Cities: Global? Postcolonial? Postimperial? Or Just the Result of Happenstance? Some Cultural Comments', in Neil Brenner and Roger Keil (eds), *The Global Cities Reader*, pp. 319–24. London and New York: Routledge.

Kunow, Rüdiger. 2003. 'Spaces Grown too Large for the Self: Arriving in the Global City', in Günter Lenz and Utz Riese (eds), *Postmodern New York City: Transfiguring Spaces — Raum-Transformationen*, pp. 181–201. Heidelberg: Winter.

Mehta, Suketu. 2004. *Maximum City: Bombay Lost and Found*. London: Headline.

Neuwirth, Robert. 2006. *Shadow Cities: A Billion Squatters. A New Urban World*. London: Routledge.

Okome, Onookome. 2002. 'Writing the Anxious City: Images of Lagos in Nigerian Home Video Film', in Okwui Enwezor (ed.), *Under Siege: Four African Cities — Freetown, Johannesburg, Kinshasa, Lagos*, pp. 315–34. Ostfildern-Ruit: Hatje Cantz Verlag.

Patel, Sheela. 2001. 'Partnerships with the Urban Poor: The Indian Experience', *United Nations Chronicle*, 38(1), http://www.un.org/Pubs/chronicle/2001/issue1/0101p48.html (accessed 30 April 2009).

Riemenschneider, Dieter. 1988. 'Untouchable', in Walter Jens (ed.), *Kindlers Neues Literatur Lexikon*, 1: 410–11. Munich: Kindler.

———. 2005. *The Indian Novel in English: Its Critical Discourse 1934–2004*. Jaipur and Delhi: Rawat Publications.

Seabrook, Jeremy. 1996. *In the Cities of the South: Scenes from a Developing World*. London: Verso.

Sieverts, Thomas. 2003. *Cities without Cities: An Interpretation of the Zwischenstadt*. London: Routledge.

Spivak, Gayatri Chakravorty. 1994 [1988]. 'Can the Subaltern Speak?', in Laura Chrisman and Patrick Williams (eds), *Colonial Discourse and Post-Colonial Theory: A Reader*, pp. 66–111. London: Harvester Wheatsheaf.

Virdi, Jyotika. 1992. '*Salaam Bombay!* (Mis-)representing Child Labor', in *Jump Cut*, 37: 29–36, http://www.ejumpcut.org/archive/onlinessays/JC37folder/SalaamBombay.html (accessed 23 December 2008).

Films:

Born into Brothels: Calcutta's Red-Light Kids, dir. Zana Briski and Ross Kauffman, 2004.

Salaam Bombay!, dir. Mira Nair, 1988.

8

Understanding the Narratives of Peripatetic Communities

The Kinnari Jogi Version of the *Mahabharata*

T. S. *Satyanath*

♋

On the Representation of Indigenous Communities

Most of our understanding of mediaeval Indian culture is based on the study of agrarian communities. Such an inherent agrarian bias has not only marginalized the representational systems of the hunters, pastoralists and nomads who did not form a part of the settled agrarian community, but has also excluded the artisan and servicing communities who did form a part of settled agrarian communities. Apart from this, we also need to remember that many of the non-agrarian communities, despite living amidst agrarian communities for several centuries, have been able

*An earlier version of the chapter was presented at the international conference 'Chotro 2: Nomadic Communities in the Post-Colonial World: Culture-Expression-Rights', 4–7 January 2009, Bhasha Centre, Baroda and Adivasi Academy, Tejgadh, Gujarat, organized jointly by the Bhasha Research and Publication Centre, Baroda, and the Association for Commonwealth Literature and Language Studies. The author wishes to acknowledge Professor G. N. Devy and Professor Geoffrey V. Davis for providing an opportunity to present this paper at the conference, and the comments and observations made by the participants during the paper presentation.

to maintain certain aspects of their non-agrarian culture (Bayly 1987, Satyanath 2001). Hence, what we identify as the cultural aspects of the agrarian system may often turn out to be the knowledge and skills of non-agrarian communities that have been integrated into the agrarian communities. By implication, it has become customary to treat the entire traditional knowledge system, be it agrarian, pastoralist, hunting or of other nomadic communities, as belonging to an agrarian knowledge system. It is this aspect of domination and appropriation of the knowledge systems of other communities by the agrarian system that also needs to be scrutinized and problematized in order to have a clear understanding of the knowledge systems of agrarian and non-agrarian communities.

A brief history of the changes that swept over south India is relevant here for the purpose of understanding the historical background of non-agrarian communities like the Kinnari Jogis. The beginning of the 11th century CE [Common Era] witnessed a significant structural change within the south Indian social and political systems. This has been pointed out as a vertical split between the 'right-hand' castes (principally agrarian) and the 'left-hand' castes (artisan and servicing castes) along with an increasing vertical mobility of the left-hand castes (Stein 1980). The impact of such change could be noticed in other spheres of cultural representations also. For example, the textures of Bhakti underwent radical changes that reflect such a shift. Whereas the Nayanars, the Shaivite saints belonging to 7th–10th centuries CE in Tamil Nadu, were conspicuously agrarians (right-hand castes), the Virashaiva saints in Karnataka during the post-10th century CE period constituted mostly artisan and servicing communities (left-hand castes). In addition, during the post-13th century CE period, the disintegration of powerful kingdoms in south India brought in an increasing inflow of pastoralists, nomads and hunters into the agrarian system. Accordingly, the post-13th century period witnessed a shift of power into the hands of feudal war-lords, often designated as Paleyakaras and Nayakas. This brought in significant changes within the newly developing composite agrarian system which is characterized by a tank-based irrigation system as against the earlier river-valley based agrarian system. It also introduced new knowledge and several skills of non-agrarian communities into the agrarian system. Hence post-13th century south India needs to be understood rather as a composite system with a blending of agrarian and non-agrarian knowledge systems.

The discussion so far suggests that the ecological changes that have been brought out by the river-valley based agrarian system, through a transformation of non-agrarian interface zones into agrarian ones, had far reaching consequences for the agrarian system itself. It brought forward structural, political, social, religious and representational changes within the tank-based irrigation system, which was jointly engineered by the erstwhile agrarian and the newly joined non-agrarian communities. Thus, the period of post-10th century south India witnessed changes in all walks of life, prompted initially by a conspicuous dominance and upward mobility of artisan and servicing castes on the one hand and a subsequent influx of non-agrarian communities such as the pastoralists, nomads and the hunters from the non-agrarian interface zones on the other. In particular, the changes and transformations that south India underwent during the post-13th century period has to be viewed and understood as a period in which the non-agrarian communities, their ideology and cultural aspects played a significant role in formulating the political, religious and cultural developments of the region. The need, and also, the pressure to accommodate, assimilate and rework the economic, religious and cultural aspects of this newly formulated ecosystem led to several changes. Such changes could also be seen in the representations of Bhaktas from the interface zone being incorporated into the agrarian system of Bhakti, and the changes in hagiography, *sthalapuranas* and other representation systems. It is with such an understanding of the post-13th century of south India that we need to understand an itinerant community such as that of the Kinnari Jogis. The theoretical background outlined above is essential for the study of Kinnari Jogis, as they not only constitute a religious community of an itinerant nature, but also, were an integral part of an eco-cultural system that was jointly developed and maintained by non-agrarian communities playing a significant role in it.

The Kinnari Jogis

Introduction

Kinnari Jogis, a term usually used to refer to a specific group of itinerant singers in Karnataka, are one among several types of Jogis who have been identified as belonging to a scheduled tribe. Among these groups, it is the Kinnari Jogis,[1] who as nomadic singers sing and enact the episodes from

---

[1] The word 'Jogi' also refers to the sectarian mendicants belonging to certain Tantric groups. Jogi–Jogini/Jogan also appears frequently in their sectarian literature as well as in the Sufi hagiographies.

the *Mahabharata* and other stories to the accompaniment of the *kinnari*, a string instrument.[2] There are usually five members in a troop (*mela*) in which there is a lead singer and the rest of them act as chorus. They may also interchange the role of the lead singer depending upon their expertise in the episode that they are singing. Sometimes, they may also dance while singing. Plate 8.1 shows a Kinnari Jogi from the Karnataka–Andhra Pradesh border.

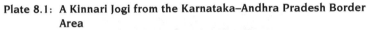

Plate 8.1: A Kinnari Jogi from the Karnataka–Andhra Pradesh Border Area

Source: Image courtesy of Dr S. M. Krishnaiah.

Cultural and Linguistic Aspects

An attempt has been made here to explore the nature of the relationship between the Kinnari Jogis, their performance and the construction of their texts. Unlike several Bhakti sects, the *natha* and *siddha* traditions

---

[2] In addition to stories from the *Mahabharata*, Kinnari Jogis also sing secular stories such as *rajahamsa-paramahamsa, shivashankina kumara, ashavati, shamasena, citrashekhara-somashekhara, basavakumara-lohitakumara, sati shilavati, virasena-kokile, gopammana kathe,* etc. (cf. Boralingayya 1997; Paramashivayya 1980).

have not left behind much information, thereby, making the reconstruction of their history a difficult task. It is exclusively through the material that is still available in the synchronic aspect of such performing traditions, that we need to understand such body-based mediaeval cults and reconstruct their history and cultural details. The detail outlined here is based on a performance of the Kinnari Jogis and an interview carried out in 1996.[3]

Kinnari is a string instrument and consists of three goads, two small ones and a bigger one. The bigger one is fixed in the centre and the smaller ones at the two ends of a bamboo staff, which is about four feet long. It contains 10 steps called *sare* (steps) that are controlled by putting the fingers on the strings. These steps are made from the quills of the porcupine and are glued to the bamboo staff. The strings are tied to the two ends of the bamboo staff with knobs to facilitate the tuning of the strings. In addition to *kinnari*, other instruments are also used: *dambarige* (a type of drum), flute, *gaggara* (a type of foot-bell) and *gejje* (foot-bells).

In order to understand the significance of a tradition, which eulogizes the exploits of a Jogi, we need to locate it within its context. Historically speaking, Karnataka and the Deccan have been regions in which the Kalamukha sect enjoyed extended political patronage from the rulers of different dynasties. The Kalamukha *mathas* (monasteries), located within the sectarian temple premises, remained as prominent centres of learning during this period (Chidanandamurthy 1968; Lorenzen 1969). Though their importance decreased after the 14th century CE, eventually resulting in their total disappearance from the region itself, their long presence in the region had far reaching consequences for the religious life of Karnataka. Tracing the influences of the Kalamukhas in the emergence of popular *yakshi* cults of Karnataka Jainism, Robert Zydenbos (1994) argues that it is the continuation of elements of worshiping woman as a source of spiritual power prevalent among the Kalamukhas that was responsible for the emergence of independent, popular and folk *yakshi* cults found today in the Jaina centres like Shravanabelugola, Humaca and

---

[3] I was able to watch this performance in 1996 while I was in Hampi as a visiting professor at Kannada University, Hampi, during 1995–97. The performers belong to Kurugodu village in the Raichur district, Karnataka. The troop is led by Manja, who originally hailed from Monakalmuru in the Chitradurga district. I sincerely acknowledge the performers and my colleagues at Kannada University, Hampi for making this performance and interview possible.

Karkala (ibid.). In addition, a look at the list of place names containing references to Jogi (cf. Jogimatha) and Siddha (cf. Siddhara-betta)
are densely scattered over the Kannada-speaking region.

The narratives of the Kinnari Jogis consider Shiva or Arjuna as their
primordial hero. Some versions say that it is Shiva who gave the initiation to Arjuna as the first Jogi. Accordingly, the Kinnari Jogis not only
consider Arjuna as their primordial Jogi but also believe that they get
their *kinnari* and initiation (*diksha*) from him. The exile of the Pandavas
(*vanavasa*) has remained as one of the most popular episodes for literary
and performing traditions of the Karnataka region including the Kinnari
Jogis. Furthermore, it has been pointed out that a special interest has
been shown by the poets of the Karnataka region towards the theme
of Kirata Shiva and ascetic Arjuna, in which they become engaged in a
fight in order to establish the right over a killed wild boar (Smith 1996).
Apart from the fact that Bharavi's *Kiratajuniya* was written in the court of
the Western Ganga King (Petterson 1991), Jaina (c.f. Pampa's *Vikramarjuna
Vijayam*; 932 CE), Brahminical (cf. Kumaravyasa's *Karnata Bharata
Kathamanjari*; c. 1450 CE) and Virashaiva (cf. *Shabarashankara Vilasa*;
c. 1670 CE) poets have repeatedly worked on this theme in Kannada. It
has also been pointed out that a majority of sculptural representations
and the Jaina textual tradition in Kannada appear to follow neither the
Sanskrit *Mahabharata* nor Bharavi's *Kiratajuniya* versions, but rather a
local (folk) tradition (Rao 1979).[4]

The versions of the Kinnari Jogi tradition also narrate Arjuna as a Jogi
going to Malayala (Kerala) on a pilgrimage and marrying the princesses
from the region, Citrangada and Ulupi. Similarly, Arjuna's disguise as
a mendicant (*yati*) and Subhadra's elopement with him has become a
very popular episode in the *yakshagana* plays, the traditional folk theatre of coastal Karnataka and has remained as a popular play during the
heyday of modern professional theatre. Furthermore, *sangita saubhdra*,
written by Anna Saheb Kirloskar in 1882, which became a highly popular
Marathi musical play performed by the Kirloskar Company during the
early part of the 20th century, was also one of the most popular plays in
the Kannada–Marathi bilingual areas of the north Karnataka region.

---

[4] For a detailed discussion see Satyanath (2009). In addition, Rao (1979)
has pointed out that local legends referred to hillocks near Kopalla and
Shankaraghatta (Shimogga district) as the Indrakila of *Mahabharata*, where
Arjuna performed his penance and fought with Shiva.

The Song of Arjuna Jogi

The Kinnari Jogis call their version of the *Mahabharata* as *Arjuna jogi kathe/hadu* (The story/song of Arjuna Jogi), which though it narrates the story of the Pandavas in general, gives a special treatment to the part of the story in which Arjuna wanders as a Jogi. It is the acts of Arjuna as an ascetic that becomes the celebrating element of the Arjuna Jogi performing tradition. It is against this background that we need to understand the performing tradition of the Kinnari Jogis. One of the episodes narrates the sectarian myth that the *kinnari* was made from the body parts of a demoness, thereby suggesting the tradition as a body-based knowledge system. In this sense, Kinnari Jogi tradition is a non-scripto-centric but performing tradition that makes use of the body homology at several levels. The details of the episode substantiate this point. According to the tradition, Arjuna killed Hiranya Rakasi and made a *kinnari* from her body parts: saffron colour for the cloth from her blood; thread from her hairs; *kamakshi* (the ear rings) from two of her hairs; the reed from her thigh bone; the two goads from her breasts; the bridge from her nose; the 16 steps of the instrument from her 16 teeth; the knobs from her fingers; and the strings from the nerves of her back (vertebral column).

Thus, the *kinnari*, narrative and Jogi become an integral part of the tradition. It is suggested that being body-based knowledge systems, such systems tend to use the homology of the body for their knowledge storage and retrieval, thereby structuring their tradition within an anthropomorphic format.

Performance: Details

The performance of the Kinnari Jogis typically starts with the playing of the *kinnari* first, followed by the *stuti*, which is an invocation mentioning the names of their favourite deities. Subsequently, the episode that has been requested for performance by the patron(s) is narrated and ends with the *stuti* that was performed at the beginning of the performance. The performance ends with the blowing of a *singinada*, an instrument made out of deer's horn, which generates a sound similar to that of a conch shell. Except for the episodes that they sing orally, additional information about the tradition does not come forward easily from the Kinnari Jogis. It appears that the tradition being a body-based knowledge system rather than a scripto-centric one and that the story belongs to a Tantric sect might be the reasons behind this.

Structural Aspects Of Epic Narrative

The Nature of Sectarian Knowledge

One of the characteristic features of body-based knowledge systems is that their sectarian details are codified in a body-based format and are not easily accessible to an introspection model of collecting information. After the performance was over, an inquiry was made by a participant-observer regarding the details of initiation (*diksha*) and the making of the sectarian instrument, the *kinnari*. Initially there was no reply and a long silence prevailed. The participant observer thought that the performers might not have understood his accent, which was different from that of the performers. Hence, he attempted to make his point clear by explaining it to them. The performers then told the observer that they were actually going to sing an episode to answer his query. It appears that the entire knowledge base of the Kinnari Jogis is a performance-based one and is codified in a body-centric format that is different from the dialogic textual mode of the scripto-centric format with which the observer was familiar. What followed as answer was the singing of the episode in which Arjuna kills a demoness and makes a *kinnari* from her body parts. The Kinnari Jogi version of this episode is as follows:

> Arjuna married Ulupi, Citrangada and Subhadra while he was wandering (*deshantara*) and visiting places of pilgrimage. When Draupati came to know about it she was upset and had a quarrel with him about it. Arjuna, being humiliated decided to bring the three newly wed wives to the palace where Draupati was living. This outraged her further. Draupati invited Arjuna to play the game of dice and it was agreed upon that whoever loses the game has to become a Jogi and go for a pilgrimage. Draupati prayed to Krishna for help and won the game.[5] Accordingly, Arjuna became a Jogi and assumed his wanderings. He arrived at the Indrakila Mountain, performed penance for Shiva and got valuable missiles from him. Arjuna also killed the demoness Hiranya Rakasi and made his Kinnari from her body parts.[6]

---

[5] In the version of the story that considers Shiva as the primordial Jogi, it is Parvati, his consort, who plays a similar role in making Shiva become a Jogi and go wandering.

[6] From a performance (1996) by a troop belonging to Kurugodu village in Raichur district, Karnataka. It was led by Manja, who originally hailed from Monakalmuru in the Chitradurga district.

Three important aspects need to be noticed here, which can provide clues to establish links between the Kinnari Jogi tradition and Tantric traditions on the one hand and to consider them as body-based systems on the other. Firstly, the aspect of providing a divine origin for the Kinnari Jogi tradition, whether the primordial Jogi is Shiva himself or Arjuna, a great devotee of Shiva. In either case, it is interesting to note that it is their female counterparts who are instrumental in their husband's transformation into the state of Jogi. Secondly, the genesis of *kinnari*, the sectarian instrument of the performing tradition is highly significant. It is made of highly polluting and sacrilegious materials. Not only are the goads used in making the *kinnari* conventionally used to store locally brewed liquor, which is also used in Tantric rituals, various parts of the *kinnari* are also made from the body parts of a slain demoness. Notice that the body of the demoness itself is transformed into the sectarian instrument. Furthermore, another version of the Kinnari Jogi narrative says that the first Jogi was made from the scuff of the body's dirt (sweat) of Shiva. The supremacy and extensive use of polluting agents, such as liquor storing goads, body dirt, blood, etc. on the one hand, and on the other, the body parts of a woman's body constituting different parts of *kinnari* are highly suggestive of Tantric links and create an inverse world order (*pratiloma*). Lastly, the tradition's manifestation that is based on a body-based knowledge system rather than a text-based scripto-centric one further substantiates this point.

Itinerary and Invocation

The Kinnari Jogis start their performance with an invocation (*stuti*) which mentions the names of the deities with their place names. On a closer look, the place names correspond to the annual migratory route of the Kinnari Jogis. Thus the itinerary and the invocation are actually one and the same and make the two a composite system. The itinerary of the Kinnari Jogis, which also covers the locations of the deities associated with the sect and the distribution of the clientele of the Kinnari Jogi tradition, comprises parts of Andhra Pradesh and Karnataka. Whereas the language of the home domain of the Kinnari Jogis is Marathi, suggesting the possibility of their visit to Marathi-speaking areas in Maharashtra, their itinerary involved Marathi, Kannada and Telugu-speaking areas. The Kinnari Jogis say that their ancestors used to visit the Marathi-speaking areas in Maharashtra, which has now been discontinued for the last two generations. Thus, Nasik in Maharashtra, Adavani in Andhra Pradesh, Molakalmuru in central Karnataka, Adichunchanagiri in southern Karnataka and Kadri near Mangalore in coastal Karnataka constituted important sectarian pilgrimages for the Kinnari Jogis and constituted their itinerary. The annual migratory route of the Kinnari Jogis as reflected in their invocation extends to parts of Maharashtra, Andhra Pradesh and Karnataka. The languages spoken in the region of their itinerary includes Marathi, Telugu and Kannada respectively. Similar to the overlapping of invocation and itinerary, the multilingual clientele of the Kinnari Jogis has brought in a multilingual repertoire and an oral translation strategy into their tradition.

Multilingual Repertoire and Translation

Considering the multilingual clientele mentioned previously, the most intriguing question that we need to answer is that with wandering in such a vast geographical area as a part of their itinerary, how is that the Kinnari Jogis who, it has otherwise been claimed, sing only in Kannada, were able to cater to the needs of different linguistic communities? On further inquiry, it was revealed that the Kinnari Jogis sing the same epic — an epic that extends for several hours — in Telugu during their itinerary in the Telugu-speaking regions. Their mother tongue being Marathi and Nasik being one of the important pilgrimage centres for the Kinnari Jogis implies that they also used to travel to Marathi-speaking regions and would sing the epic in Marathi. This multilingual repertoire of the Kannari Jogi narrative tradition provides us with a case of a multilingual oral translation tradition. The translation strategies that they adopt for the multilingual oral translation of the epic narrative are yet to be explored. However, it is important to realize that it is the itinerary through different linguistic regions and the languages of the clientele that has prompted such a bewildering multilingual and translation strategy of the Kinnari Jogi tradition.

Hybrid Nature of the Text

The multiple communities, to which the Kinnari Jogis cater, in fact, have been responsible for the emergence of a hybrid text. Although the entire oral text of the tradition is yet to be collected, a written text does demonstrate such hybrid characteristics. A cheap book version of the Arjuna-jogi episode is available under the title *Giliya-hadu mattu arjunana jogi-hadu* ('The song of the parrot and Arjuna Jogi'). The date of publication of the text is not available. Two reprints, published in 1992 and 1996 respectively, have been reported in the bibliographies. However, the original publishers of the text has been mentioned as the Vanivilasa Book Depot, Mysore, suggesting that the first edition may well go back to the later part of the 19th century. As a popular version, what makes the text interesting for our purposes is that Arjuna, in the guise of a Kinnari Jogi, visits a Muslim neighbourhood during his wanderings. This happens towards the end of the third chapter and all of a sudden, the language of the narrative suddenly shifts to Dakhani, a southern variety of Hindi. In fact, the text clearly mentions that 'Jogideva entered the street of the Musalmans speaking the language of their region (desha-bhashe, Dakhini)' (Nanjundapandita 1992: 72).

The narration continues to state that the maid servants (bandis) from the palace informed the wives (bubis) in the zenana about the arrival of Jogi. The women folk clad in ghosha stood behind the door and watched Jogi's dance with awe and wonder. The following verses in Dakhini clearly provide the nature of the language and the context of such a hybrid text:

> sultan bi jaldi ako jogi-ke haiso tamashe dekho
> jogi moti ka har galle-pe dalhe kar jokte nacteso deko (3.225).

Oh, Sultan's wife, come quickly and watch the tamasha (fun, play) of Jogi; watch him dancing with a necklace of pearls around his neck.

> hat me kinnari bajhate jogi-ke pavu-me gungar pukarte
> bat karte-kartese atke haste tarkhatatte tamasha dekho (3.226).

A kinnari being played in his hand and the foot-bells in his feet are inviting us; look at the magic of his hand-gestures while he sings.

> asman-me haiso chodko cand be dusre-duniya-ke ako
> asalke joti hakvem-haiso dekhyato hindu-musalman-me-naiso (3.227).

As if the moon in the sky has left his world and has come down to the earthly world; both the Hindus and Muslims watched Jogi dancing as if the original light itself has arrived on the earth (ibid.).

Summing Up

The nature of the itinerary and clientele on the one hand and the multilingual repertoire of the Kinnari Jogi tradition on the other, actually structures the construction of their epic narrative in terms of sacred geography, the multilingual translation and the hybridity of the narrative. It appears that peripatetic communities tend to structure and image their sectarian representations to cater to the demands of production and consumption of the sectarian community on the one hand and to the sectarian ideology on the other. All these suggest that we need to take a holistic approach and construct models from within the traditions for an appropriate understanding of such communities.

References

Bayly, Susan. 1987. *Saints, Goddesses and Kings: Muslims and Christians in South Indian Society, 1700–1900.* Cambridge: Cambridge University Press.

Boralingayya, Hi Chi. 1997. *The Story of Manteswamy.* Hampi: Kannada University.

Chidanandamurthy, M. C. 1968. *Kannaḍa Śāsanagaḷa Sāmskṛtika Adhyayana.* Mysore: Mysore University Press.

Lorenzen, David N. 1969. *The Kāpālikas and Kālāmukhas: Two Lost Śaivite Sects.* Berkeley: University of California Press.

Nanjundapandita. 1992 (n.d.). *Giṭiya-Hāḍu Mattu Arjunajogi-Hāḍu.* Mysore: Vanivilasa Book Depot.

Paramashivayya, G. S. 1980. *Kinnari Jogigalu.* Mysore: IBH Prakashana.

Patterson, Indira V. 1991. 'Arjuna's Combat with the Kirāta: Rasa and Bhakti in Bhāravi's Kirātārjunīya', in Arvind Sharma (ed.), *Essays on the Mahābhārata Vol. 1*, pp. 212–50. Leiden: E. J. Brill.

Rao, M. S. Nagaraja. 1979. *Kirātārjunīyam in Indian Art: With Special Reference to Karnataka.* New Delhi: Agam Kala Publications.

Satyanath, T. S. 2001. 'Problematizing Folk Popular Traditions: The Pastoralist Traditions of Mailara/Mallayya/Khandoba', in B. Ramakrishna Reddy (ed.), *Dravidian Folk and Tribal Lore*, pp. 236–58. Kuppam: Dravidian University.

———. 2009. 'Tellings and Renderings in Mediaeval Karnataka: The Episode of Kirāta Śiva and Arjuna', in Judy Wakabayashi and Rita Kothari (eds), *Decentralizing Translation Studies: India and Beyond*, pp. 149–70. Philadelphia: John Benjamins.

Smith, David. 1996. *The Dance of Śiva: Religion, Art and Poetry in South India.* Cambridge: Cambridge University Press.

Stein, Burton. 1980. *Peasant Society in South India.* Oxford: Oxford University Press.

Zydenbos, Robert J. 1994. 'Jaina Goddesses in Kannada Literature', in A. W. Entwistle and Françoise Mallison (eds), *Studies in South Asian Devotional Literature: Research Papers 1988–1991*, pp. 135–45. New Delhi: Manohar.

9

The Gullah of South Carolina and Georgia
Retention of Cultural Expression

Joseph McLaren

♋

The Gullah of the Sea Islands of South Carolina and the Georgia coast were the product of forced migration during the Atlantic Slave Trade. Despite the involuntary circumstances of their migration, they have maintained a distinct cultural heritage that reflects not only their particular African ethnic origins, but their cultural adaptations to New World communities, especially through language, folklore, and crafts. Known for rice cultivation, the Gullah were influential in transforming the agricultural viability of the area during the days of slavery and contributed immeasurably to the economy of the British colonies in North America. Gullah linguistic traditions are infused with African expressions, evidence of an Africanized English, which has been linked to Sierra Leonean creole and various African languages.

Gullah language, culture, and folkways can be found in a variety of sources, including oral tales, literary works, and films. Gullah experience has been the inspiration for a range of creative artists from Gullah story-teller Carolyn 'Jabulile' White to novelist Paule Marshall, to filmmaker Julie Dash. Furthermore, Gullah stories found in collected works of the 19th and early 20th century show how Africanized English has been used to promote 'American' folklore but not necessarily to validate Gullah retentions.

Gullah oral traditions can be paralleled to other oral heritages such as those found in India, where there is also an interest in preservation and valorization.

Oral traditions of folk literature, continuing vibrantly into present times, need to be accorded their due value by bringing them out of the shadow of the hegemonic 'written' literature. A suitable understanding of this phenomenon is needed by bringing it closer to scholarly attention, not as a separate area of study but alongside the tradition of 'written' literature (Kumar et al. 2005: 2–3).

In many respects, Gullah linguistic expression has remained within the 'shadow' because it has been viewed by some as a quaint folk expression of the plantation era, perhaps static and lacking Standard English qualities. Gullah has retained many of its tonal, linguistic, and lexical elements dating back to its origins; therefore, in a broader society that privileges progress and mobility, it might be seen as anachronistic. However, its resistance to assimilatory tendencies is the foundation of its cultural dynamics and its ability to retain African elements.

The African retentions of the Gullah can be found in an overview of the formation of their society. They are descendants of West Africans from various locations including the Senegambia region, the 'Gold Coast', and the Angola area of past times. The South Carolina planters were known to have preferred Africans from certain areas especially the Gold Coast and Gambia. A hierarchy of preferences was discernible, with the Ibo as the least preferred. Such preferences can be traced to skill in rice production. The establishment of Charleston, known as Charles Town in the early 18th century, is inextricably connected to the importation of Africans, who would eventually comprise the Gullah people (Pollitzer 1999: 41). The name Gullah may have been derived from Angola or an area between Sierra Leone and Liberia where the Gola resided. Another of the connections between the Gullah and Sierra Leone is Bunce Island, where Gullah representatives journeyed to its 18th-century slave castle. Three 'celebrated "homecomings"' were made by African Americans from the Sea islands in 1989, 1997 and 2005 to a site of British slave trading (Bunce Island Project n.d.).

Furthermore, the Gullah also had connections to the Caribbean as a result of the Middle Passage. Locations such as Jamaica and Barbados were places where Africans were 'seasoned', brought into the harsh realities of trans-Atlantic slavery. Many of those who are identified as Gullah may have first been arrivals in the Caribbean. 'There can be no question that there was a South Carolina–Caribbean connection', and this can be assumed from the similarity in, for example, Jamaican creole, 'similarities too numerous to be purely accidental' (Cassidy 1994: 16). The story of the Gullah is intertwined with that of the Atlantic Slave Trade as are the histories of other Africans brought into the Western hemisphere. How in particular have the Gullah retained their communities over time since cultural retention in diasporas is not unique to the Gullah? For example, older cultural traditions can also be found among South Asian or Indian descendants in locations such as Trinidad and Guyana on the South American coast, where Indian indentured labourers were brought during the 19th century. Evidence of their cultural traditions can be found in food, clothing, family organization, and language.

The region along the coast of South Carolina represented by the city of Charleston was the most prominent location for the disembarkation of Africans during the 18th century. The Gullah area can be defined as 'a coastal strip 250 miles long and 40 miles wide where low, flat islands, separated from the mainland by salt-water rivulets, feel the tides twice each day' (Pollitzer 1999: 4). Sullivan's Island, one of the many Sea Islands, was the African American Ellis Island. (Ellis Island refers to that small island in New York harbour where primarily Europeans entered the US (United States) during the late 19th and early 20th century. However, Ellis Island was also the port of arrival for numerous Caribbean migrants from Jamaica, for instance.) During colonial times, South Carolina was the wealthiest planter class location because certain planters had exploited the expertise of Africans skilled cultivating rice. 'The agricultural technology of rice production, especially in the early decades of settlement, was distinctly African' (Rosengarten 1994: 146). Clearly, the importance of the Gullah to the foundations of colonial moneyed interests is immeasurable because South Carolina became the leading exporter of rice. Because the Gullah resided in the numerous islands of the Low Country, they were able to maintain cultural traditions that might have been diffused had they resided primarily on the mainland. In short, the islands were conducive to rice production and became 'containers' for the retention of cultural traditions. The mainland, exemplified in films such as Julie Dash's *Daughters of the Dust* (1991), was the location where one could potentially lose one's cultural traits. Speaking Gullah rather than Standard English was comparable to speaking an African language and was a signifier of anti-assimilation.

The Gullah were specialized agriculturists, but as enslaved people they were viewed primarily in economic terms and not as cultural conduits of certain West African linguistic and craft traditions. African expressions in Gullah have been researched by linguists, especially Lorenzo Turner, whose *Africanism in the Gullah Dialect* (2002) is a classic text in which

Gullah names are shown to have West African origins: 'Even though my Gullah informants do not remember the meanings of these unmarked personal names . . . they continue to use them in naming their children because their older relatives and friends used them' (ibid.: 41). Turner cites the name 'aba', a 'name given to a girl born on Thursday' (ibid.: 43), and connects this name to Fante and Twi, languages of present-day Ghana. Other West African ethnicities such as Vai, Mende, Gola, located in the area of Sierra Leone and Liberia, were sources of Gullah language.

Although Turner recognized the linguistic linkages, non-Gullah speakers who first heard the Gullah language had certain negative perceptions, some thinking 'that the Gullah dialect was a simplified, corrupt English incorrectly acquired by ignorant blacks from British yeomen' (Pollitzer 1999: 8). Other characterizations of Gullah storytelling contained veiled complimentary remarks but with overtones of paternalism as in the descriptions by Ambrose Gonzales, who collected a number of stories in the 1920s. Gonzales considered Gullah language, which he called 'dialect', to be 'interesting, not merely for its richness, which falls upon the ear as opulently as the Irish brogue, but also for the quaint and homely similes in which it abounds' (Gonzales 1998a: 11). However, the linguistic investigations of the 1930s by people such as Turner showed 'a wealth of African words, numerals, grammar, and whole stories' (Pollitzer 1999: 8). Among the African words were '*cooter, goober, yam,* and *gumbo*', which have become part of 'American' English (ibid.).

Gullah Storytelling

Evidence of the retention of Africanisms by the Gullah can best be seen through historical and present-day manifestations of Gullah stories and folktales that have been passed down from the earlier generations. In the last decades of the 19th century in the US, the interest in collecting folklore led to the collection of Gullah tales such as those compiled by a mayor of Charleston, South Carolina — Charles Colcock Jones. (Jones was similar in interest to Joel Chandler Harris of Georgia, who was known for his collecting of Br'er [Brother] Rabbit tales and the Uncle Remus stories.) However, Jones's collections were not intended to valorize the Gullah but merely to show that 'America' could contribute to a growing interest in Europe and the US in folk peoples: 'Experts agreed that "the folk" could be characterized as "backward peoples", members of isolated illiterate societies with strong oral traditions' (Williams 2000: xx).

However, the 'Gullah' storyteller should be seen as a repository of wit and linguistic creativity, traits recognized by early collectors like Gonzales who also pointed out the 'philosophy of its users' (Gonzales 1998a: 11). Admittedly, the task of reading Gullah stories collected in the 19th century can be daunting because of the alterations in Standard English resulting in certain spellings intended to reproduce the original sounds and sometimes called 'dialect'. These Gullah linguistic sounds are certainly evidence of cultural retention.

In a story such as 'A Gullah's Tale of Woe' (Gonzales 1998b), one finds the folklorist-collector as the narrative voice in the opening, but soon this voice gives way to the story being told in the supposedly authentic voice of a Gullah speaker. Despite the ironies and complications resulting from the translation of Gullah speech by a non-Gullah collector, the theme of this story and others is discernible and relates to one of the characteristics of Gullah tales, to demonstrate trickster ingenuity and underlying intelligence. In 'A Gullah's Tale of Woe', Scipio Wineglass, a Gullah farmer, is depicted in his environment, where his 'few acres of land' and his humble dwelling are the 'net earnings of twenty-seven years of toil "sence freedom fus' come een"', referring to the years following the end of the Civil War and slavery (ibid.: 238). Scipio questions a white visitor passing by about whether a solicitor — a lawyer, whom he calls the 'puhlicituh' — can read. In the conversation, Scipio retells his experience with a case brought before a court and involving a hog stolen from him. In court, the confusion of his name with that of the person he has accused almost results in Scipio being convicted of stealing his own hog. The tale concludes with Scipio's remark, 'I did t'ink dat Mistuh Muffey, de puhlicituh, could'uh read' (ibid.: 241). The emphasis on literacy is of particular importance since those of African descent in the South were denied access to education, and even after the Civil War, opportunities were limited. Scipio inverts the power relations of literate versus illiterate and is able to claim knowledge of a judicial process gone awry.

The trickster motif is more apparent in another collected Gullah tale, which shows the retention of African linkages to the animal world. In 'How Come Buh Alligatur Nebber Sleep Fur From De Ribber Bank', the use of the alligator as one of the animal figures calls to mind a general familiarity by certain Africans with the crocodile, a 'relative' of the alligator. This connection is implied in the essay by Charles Colcock Jones, who remarks in 'The Negro and the Alligator', that to 'newly landed' Europeans the 'alligator was indeed a novelty' but that 'His [the African's] ancestors were well acquainted with the African crocodile' (Jones 2000: 161–62). Despite the generalization, Jones's observation shows why certain animal characters were adaptable to Gullah tales and were used to retain memories of their homeland. In the 'Buh Alligatur' folktale, Buh Rabbit, the well-known trickster figure, demonstrates to the alligator what 'trouble' means. Buh Rabbit wants to know, 'Enty you come pon trouble some time?' (ibid.: 1). When the alligator answers no, the trickster demonstrates trouble by setting a fire around the alligator while he is on the shore. Ultimately the tale has a hidden moral as well as a humorous reason as to why alligators are so alert and run into the water when hearing any sound. Within the context of ex-slave relations with white Southerners, the implications are numerous since Buh Rabbit is a representation of cunning and the ability to outwit the 'old master'.

With the contemporary interest in tourism in South Carolina, Gullah storytelling has become an important part of demonstrating cultural heritage. Local storytellers are hired to recite tales for gatherings of tourists. One of the popular Gullah story-tellers performing in Charleston is Carolyn 'Jabulile' White whose *Gullah Storyteller* (n.d.) contains numerous renditions including stories such as 'Old Black Man Goes to Charleston' and 'Wilhelmina and the Telyphone'. As in the collected stories from the late 19th and early 20th century, Jabulile's stories contain similar witty, ironic humour presenting a Gullah speaker in opposition to a white Standard English speaker, who assumes a certain degree of class superiority. The stories often show the cleverness of the Gullah character in not only understanding modern dilemmas relating to technology, for example, but in showing himself or herself as triumphant over attempts to belittle or minimize folk comprehension.

Most important, Jabulile poses in her introduction to the *Gullah Storyteller* the process of Gullah retentions. She learned Gullah stories as a child raised on what was a plantation. She attributes the source of 'these good old gullah tales' to her 'ancestors' and their acquisition or adaptation of language when

> Massa dem done take away all them drum, you know . . . couldn't make no signal with them drum no mo'. So they had to figure a way to talk to one another. They heard buckra talk a little bit of dat English and they mix em in too . . . When they went out in the field they got together . . . and Massa couldn't understand a thing they was talkin' 'bout . . . and would gather to tell the tales of what would happen (ibid.).

The storytelling also went on at night in the cabins, and the act of telling became a way that they 'made it through' the hardships of enslavement.

When Jabulile opens her storytelling session, she says, 'Lemme tell unuh somethin'. Buckra [the white man] like for here dem stories and when I done talkin', buckra got my check' (White n.d.). For the contemporary teller of Gullah stories, the commercial aspect is also relevant. Jabulile's stories told to tourists may seem like commodities, but in a sense, they serve a similar purpose as when they were told in the cabins during slavery days. Storytelling is a way to make it through the challenges of modern-day survival in South Carolina. However, the Gullah tales told for compensation have not lost their lessons of morality or their philosophical outlook concerning race relations then and now. Although some stories seem to be throwbacks to slavery and post-slavery plantation existence, they strike a chord among modern listeners. When she tells of the arrogant white Southerner who comes to town from James Island and asks directions of a Gullah speaker, the ultimate message of the tale is about respect, manners, and authority. She reminds listeners that manners even under conditions of deprivation were learned on the farm, thus raising questions about who actually is the 'civilized' individual. The use of humour is primary in Gullah tales, for it is a way of elevating one's station through mockery of assumed white privilege and power. When the black worker is asked several times for directions, his answers seem to suggest his misunderstanding of the terms. When asked, 'Where's the battery, referring to the military site in Charleston', he responds with a comment about a car battery. Similarly, when asked about the location of the jail house, he responds, 'Never been there, I ain't try fuh go there'. The jailhouse location has far reaching implications and unstated assumptions about the status of the black male in Charleston. Finally, when the black Gullah worker is told that he doesn't know anything about the town, he responds with authority, 'I know one thing. I ain't lost' (ibid.). Here the function of such tales is apparent; it elevates the Gullah farmer above white authority by showing his local knowledge. The story also suggests the civility of the Gullah man in relation to the arrogance and snobbery of the questioner.

In the tale 'Wilhelmina and the Telyphone', the context involves a white well-to-do woman who hires Wilhelmina as a servant to replace an earlier worker. When the white 'madam' goes out to play bridge, she instructs Wilhelmina on the use of the telephone, and Wilhelmina, being of rural folk stock, has little knowledge of its use. When Wilhelmina receives a call on the phone, we are simply told by the storyteller that Wilhelmina says 'Sho' is' (Sure is) and hangs the phone up. This seems odd and is repeated by the storyteller a few times to emphasize the mystery of Wilhelmina's response. The key to the story is that what has been said by the caller is not revealed. The 'punch line' occurs when the owner of the house returns and asks Wilhelmina if she had received any calls and messages. Wilhemina answers that the person on the other end simply kept saying, 'Long distance from Washington to Charleston'. So here her answer, 'Sho' is', is simply an affirmation of the fact. On the one hand, the story might show Wilhelmina's lack of knowledge of modernity, but on the other hand, it shows an assured authority on her part, the affirmation of her own knowledge of the world.

Gullah Traditions in Literature, Film, and Material Culture

Gullah sources have also been explored by writers and filmmakers. Portions of Paule Marshall's novel *Praisesong for the Widow* (1984) are set in South Carolina. The main character's later experiences on the island of Carriacou near Grenada are linked to a revival of the Gullah cultural elements. Avey Johnson had spent parts of her summers as a child with her great-aunt Cuney in South Carolina. Aspects of Gullah culture, such as the Ring Shout dance, are represented: 'Through the open door the handful of elderly men and women still left, and who still held to the old ways, could be seen slowly circling the room in a loose ring' (ibid.: 34). The novel can be seen as a 'Gullah initiation journey' (McNeil 2009: 186).

Later in the novel, there is a reference to various African ethnicities also in relation to a circle dance, a reminder of the formation of the Gullah from certain West African groups. Such ethnicities as Temne, Banda, Cromanti, Chamba, Moko, Arada are recalled (Marshall 1984: 237–39). Avey realizes the importance of 'a host of subliminal memories that over the years had proven more durable and trustworthy than the history with its trauma and pain out of which they had come' (ibid.: 244–45).

The use of Gullah heritage can also be found in documentary films such as *Family Across the Sea* (1991), where family lineage is traced through a return visit of a group of South Carolinians to Sierra Leone, and *The Language You Cry In* (1998), in which a song fragment becomes a link between Gullah and Sierra Leonean families. In the independent feature film *Daughters of the Dust* (1991), written and directed by Julie Dash, there is further usage of the Gullah culture and the location of Ibo Landing. The grandmother figure, Nana Peazant, and her granddaughters are the focus of the film. Nana, like Avey's great-aunt in *Praisesong for the Widow* (Marshall 1984), is the elder who strives to maintain and pass on Gullah traditions. The film's central dilemma — the return to the mainland of members of the younger generation who are out of touch with Gullah traditions — is developed through magic realism film techniques.

Of the many ways in which Gullah traditions have been retained, the craft of weaving is one that draws together symbolically the strands of history and culture. The West African skill of basket weaving was both functional and artistic, and like the Gullah tales, it was handed down from generation to generation. Craft markets in present-day Charleston exhibit the wares of these artisans, who weave while at the same time marketing themselves and their baskets. In various sizes and designs, their 'Sweetgrass baskets' are known widely as an authentic example of cultural production. Weaving for the Gullah had been a functional craft especially in the days of slavery where the fanner, a flat woven device, was used to separate the rice grain and the chaff. 'Low country fanners were used to process the first crops of rice raised in the New World' (Rosengarten 1994: 148).

The centre of Sweetgrass basket weaving enterprises is Mount Pleasant, South Carolina.

The coiled Sweetgrass basket is a historically significant example of African cultural heritage that was transported across the Atlantic by enslaved African people. Africans from the Windward or Rice Coast of West Africa had knowledge and experience with rice cultivation and were, thus, particularly sought after in the Atlantic Slave Trade to the Low country. Fearing that they might never return to their homeland, these enslaved people brought their culture with them in their minds and spirits and in treasured objects hidden away on their bodies (Mount Pleasant/Isle of Palms Visitor Center n.d.).

One practising weaver, William Rouse, who sells his crafts outside one of the entrances to the main market in Charleston, explained as he wove effortlessly, the origins of the craft from 'West Africa during the 1700s'.[1] He is the fifth generation of weavers in his family. Another weaver, Laura Mack, identified one of her stitch patterns as she also wove while sitting alongside her numerous items (Plate 9.1).[2]

---

[1] Interview with William Rouse, Charleston, South Carolina, 24 July 2008.

[2] Interview with Laura Mack, Charleston, South Carolina, 24 July 2008.

Plate 9.1: Laura Mack, Gullah Sweetgrass Basket Weaver, Charleston, South Carolina, July 2008.

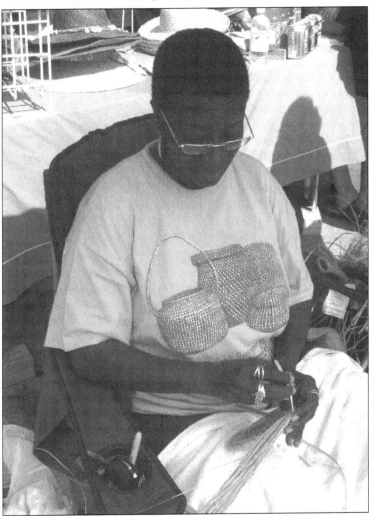

Source: Photographed by the author.

In addition to Sweetgrass baskets in the market, one can find in Charleston art galleries, paintings of Gullah culture and life. One of the internationally known artists, Jonathan Green, is recognized for his unique style. Scores of his paintings are available as prints ranging in size and price. Green has brought great recognition to Sea Island fine arts; he goes beyond such labels as folk art.

Gullah culture has been retained through oral, written, visual, and material cultural productions. The relationship between the oral tradition and the literate one was demonstrated in July 2008 at the Toni Morrison Society Conference in Charleston — 'Toni Morrison and Modernism' — dedicated to the work of Nobel Laureate Morrison. Perhaps the most distinguished African-American writer of our time, Morrison was honoured in conjunction with a special Maafa Ceremony on Sullivan's Island, where a bench was placed to honour ancestors and a wreath was released into the water. Morrison's 'Bench by the Road' project is another way of connecting the wider interest in African-American history with a material artefact that can stand as a symbolic marker.

The 'Bench by the Road' on Sullivan's Island denotes a point of arrival of countless Africans. It is also a reminder of the ongoing existence of the Gullah, whose language, stories, and arts will continue to motivate writers, filmmakers, and artists. With a firm knowledge of their roots in West Africa, the Gullah have resisted cultural homogenization, and like their Sweetgrass baskets, they too are a complex interwoven pattern. They realize the necessities of modern existence but are unwilling to relinquish their historical connections across the Atlantic.

References

Bunce Island Project n.d. 'Friends of Sierra Leone'. Harrisonburg, VA.

Cassidy, Frederic G. 1994. 'Gullah and the Caribbean Connection', in Michael Montgomery (ed.), The Crucible of Carolina: Essays in the Development of Gullah Language and Culture, pp. 16–22. Athens: University of Georgia Press.

Gonzales, Ambrose E. 1998a. The Black Border: Gullah Stories of the Carolina Coast. Gretna, LA: Firebird Press/Pelican Publishing.

———. 1998b. 'A Gullah's Tale of Woe', in The Black Border: Gullah Stories of the Carolina Coast, pp. 238–41. Gretna, LA: Pelican Publishing.

Jones, Charles Colcock. 2000. Gullah Folktales from the Georgia Coast. Athens: University of Georgia Press.

Kumar, Sukrita Paul, Vibha S. Chauhan and Bodh Prakash (eds). 2005. Cultural Diversity, Linguistic Plurality, and Literary Traditions in India. New Delhi: Macmillan.

McNeil, Elizabeth. 2009. 'The Gullah-Seeker's Journey in Paule Marshall's Praisesong for the Widow', Melus, 34(1): 185–209.

Marshall, Paule. 1984. Praisesong for the Widow. New York: Dutton.

Mount Pleasant/Isle of Palms Visitor Center. n.d. 'Sweetgrass Baskets of Mount Pleasant, South Carolina'. Mount Pleasant, South Carolina.

Pollitzer, William S. 1999. *The Gullah People and Their African Heritage*. Athens: University of Georgia Press.

Rosengarten, Dale. 1994. 'Spirits of Our Ancestors: Basket Traditions in the Carolinas', in Michael Montgomery (ed.), *The Crucible of Carolina: Essays in the Development of Gullah Language and Culture*, pp. 133–57. Athens: University of Georgia Press.

Turner, Lorenzo Dow. 2002. *Africanisms in the Gullah Dialect*. Columbia, SC: University of South Carolina Press.

White, Carolyn 'Jabulile'. n.d. *Gullah Storyteller*. CD.

Williams, Susan Millar. 2000. 'Foreword', in Charles Colcock Jones, *Gullah Folktales from the Georgia Coast*, pp. xi–xxxv. Athens: University of Georgia Press.

Films:

Daughters of the Dust, 1991, dir. Julie Dash, Kino International.

Family Across the Sea, 1991, dir. Tim Carrier, California Newsreel.

The Language You Cry In, 1998, dir. Alvaro Toepke and Angel Serrano, California Newsreel.

10

Nomadic Writing
The 'Blind Spot' of Caribbean Fiction
Judith Misrahi-Barak

The unfortunate thing . . . is that it's up to the different ethnic groups to write their own history and culture. To me, that's outrageous, because that reveals a kind of a self-apartheid. . . . I speak objectively in view of the massive ignorance that we entertain about our Amerindian, and our Indian, and our Chinese and Portuguese heritages. Obviously, we have to correct that, otherwise how can we boast about being a tapestry of peoples and cultures? That can just be rhetoric, and basically, what it would mean is that we are still offspring of Britain. We don't talk about Indianness or Amerindianness because we don't make the effort to understand those languages and concepts.

(Kwame Dawes 2001: 199–200)

The Caribbean is most often associated with the Middle Passage and slavery. As a result, it has also been associated for a long time with alienation and the loss of memory, with deracination and the memory of loss. This aspect of Caribbean history has been so pregnant that it has tended to occult the indigenous people who had originally conquered

---

* Parts of this chapter have been used in a longer version, written with a different focus and published online as 'Amerindian *ante*-Coloniality in Contemporary Caribbean Writing: Crossing Borders in the Caribbean with Jan Carew, Cyril Dabydeen and Pauline Melville', *The Journal of Postcolonial Writing*, 47(3): 309–19.

the Caribbean, having come from South America in the first place, nearly 6,000 years ago. In many ways, the Amerindian is the blind spot of Caribbean literature, but one that may yield a few surprises.

The destruction of those indigenous societies in the Caribbean certainly was a rapid process once the Europeans had arrived in 1492. Most of the indigenous peoples did not survive the period of conquest, at least in the Greater Antilles. So much so that the idea according to which the indigenous peoples had completely been erased has been held a well-known truth for centuries. That period of erasure is well documented, but it is only fairly recently, a couple of decades ago, that *survival* was deemed as interesting as *erasure* and the emphasis was gradually put on survival more than on erasure, thanks to historians and anthropologists like Peter Hulme (1986, 2000), Samuel Wilson (1997) or Maximilian C. Forte (2006). When post-colonial literatures began to emerge in the 1950s, in the Caribbean as elsewhere, all the focus was on socio-political and sociological issues, on the development of the young nations, on the relationships with the Mother Country, on post-coloniality, etc. It soon became clear that the interest for the African part of Caribbean history, for the Middle Passage and the Plantation period, was going to take up all the space, not leaving any room for the few descendants of indigenous people who had indeed survived, against all odds. In many ways, it is as if the indigenous peoples were killed off a second time since for a long period only marginal breathing space was granted them in the historians' studies. The Caribbean is made up of all the migrations, major and minor ones, of people who went to the Caribbean, from the first colonization almost 6,000 years ago to that undertaken by Europeans 500 years ago and which led to the forced migration of Africans to the world of the Plantation — a 'tapestry of people' as Kwame Dawes has suggested (ibid.). The original migration of Amerindians coming to the Caribbean from the South American mainland did not lead to permanent settlement right away. As Samuel Wilson suggests, 'through the centuries, there was probably a good deal of coming and going, with new migrations and continuing interaction with mainland people even after European contacts' (Wilson 1997: 2). This original nomadic component of the Amerindian culture in the Caribbean has not been focused on as it should have been.

Considering that Dominica has an Amerindian population of about 4,000, all residents of the 3,700 acre Carib Territory set aside for them in 1903 in the north-eastern corner of the island, and that St Vincent has an Amerindian population of about 1,500, the numbers are inconsequential and the physical presence is scant. Nowadays even in Guyana, which is one of the few countries on the mainland that have not experienced a complete wiping out of the Amerindian population, the Amerindians comprise a little under 7 per cent of a population of about 718,000 (Guyana News and Informations 1996), i.e., about 49,000 people. Although the numbers are very small, I would like to read the Amerindian history in the Caribbean as one of survival, not one of extinction. I will go along with Wilson when he states:

> ... [D]espite the ravages of five centuries of European conquest, the indigenous people of the Caribbean have survived. The role they have played in the formation of the Caribbean culture is immense, and the voice of their descendents is growing ever stronger in the modern Caribbean (Wilson 1997: 8).

And also: 'Had the archipelago been uninhabited in 1492, the modern Caribbean would be radically different in language, economy, political organization and social consciousness' (ibid.: 206–7).

Because I am not a historian, nor an anthropologist or an archaeologist, I am not going to try and show how the Tainos and the Kalinagos living in the Caribbean between 1000 and 1492 CE are the descendants of the Saladoid people who had come to the Caribbean from the South American mainland in waves of migration between 500 and 250 BCE, and how they have overlapped one with the other. Rather, I am interested in the ways the writers of the contemporary Caribbean have explored the Amerindian presence, thus reinforcing that very presence and foregrounding it in our contemporary consciousness. This will hopefully highlight the reasons why it is of vital importance to foreground the Amerindian presence in the Caribbean today.

Indeed, just as was the case in the 1950s and 1960s at the time of the independence period, it is again through and thanks to literature that a new focus is being gained, and a new vision is arising. Over the past few decades, several Caribbean writers have started to go back to Amerindian history, underscoring the most forgotten aspect of the forgotten. Why have those writers recently extracted those themes, stories and characters from the abyss of memory? Is it only for the sake of the past? How is it that it has been gaining ground? It is not only because some of those elements belong to those authors' family biography — could they be telling us something about the Caribbean itself, that very Caribbean where the presence of the Amerindians has been said to have been erased, but in fact has not been? What is the form used by those writers in order to speak about the original migrations, before the one that was such a deep and everlasting trauma? The Middle Passage post-traumatic period has, understandably, gathered a lot of attention, but what about the original trauma linked to the first European migration and settlement? Where has the nomadic presence of the Caribbean gone and is it of any interest for the Caribbean today? The nomadic presence that existed in the Caribbean several thousand years ago was almost totally annihilated by the European settlers and indeed, the world of the Plantation is the absolute contrary of any form of nomadism. I am going to suggest that contemporary Caribbean literature is one of the few sites where, through the blind spot of Amerindian presence-absence, the nomadic element in the Caribbean has been granted a renewed quality and ethos. In order to reclaim that ground, however, contemporary Caribbean writers have displaced the nomadic — it does not only pertain to space anymore. It has become attached to the mind- and timescape, imagination and writing, and to a general slippage of boundaries. We will have to wonder what exactly this slippage means for the Caribbean at large, and how it participates in the Caribbean struggle against dispossession and disinheritance.

Wilson Harris, of course, was a pioneer in bringing to the foreground the Amerindian history and stories, the surviving Amerindian presence, but he did not have many disciples or readers at first and his readership has been quite restricted because he is often considered a difficult author.[1] If Wilson Harris can be said to be the Caribbean writer in whose writing the Amerindian element is the most vibrant and dominant, writers like Pauline Melville, Cyril Dabydeen, Marie-Elena John or Kevin Baldeosingh also integrate the Amerindian element in their writing. I would like to bring them together here, in spite of the fact that they all have very mixed backgrounds, and do not necessarily have Amerindian ancestors. This may be precisely one aspect of the point I want to make: fusing the Amerindian into the Caribbean may allow the ethnic and historical boundaries to become blurred into the background instead of being constantly projected to the foreground.

---

[1] Hena Maes-Jelinek was one of the critics who endeavoured to make Wilson Harris's writing accessible to a larger reading public. One can refer to her many books and articles.

Kevin Baldeosingh's novel *The Ten Incarnations of Adam Avatar* (2005) chooses to include the Amerindian element among others in order to try and paint a saga of Caribbeanness: Adam Avatar, living in the contemporary Caribbean we know today, takes the advice of a shrink to decide whether he needs psychiatric help. He complains he has been suffering from delusions that lure him into believing he has been leading several lives, always dying at 50, each time being reincarnated as a different human being, living in different periods. His 10 lives cover more or less exactly the span of Caribbean migrations and waves of conquest. He is in turn Taino, Conquistador, African slave, planter, indentured labourer, stick fighter, etc. The final chapter is entitled 'Human', making the message quite clear. If a little too obvious at times, the novel's structure has the advantage of starting with the Taino, juggling with the notion of identity as origin and root. The juxtaposition of all those first-person narratives offers a multiplicity of perspectives on and from the Caribbean, those perspectives that have been aggregating to compose the archipelago's unicity.

Marie-Elena John also plays on the Amerindian element in her fiction, which mostly has to do with the descendants of Maroon slaves in Dominica, their relationship with the few Amerindian survivors, and more generally, the settling of one's past. Just like *The Ten Incarnations of Adam Avatar*, but in a more sustained and adventurous way, *Unburnable* (2006) also weaves a web of links between past and present, moving forward and backward from one chapter to the next. John brings together the West African and the Amerindian origins of the Caribbean. Lillian, a young Caribbean woman who was sent to the US when she was 14 so as to shield her from her past and the scandals that affected her family, goes back to Dominica some 20 years later so as to settle her debts and make her peace with the ghosts that keep haunting her. Lillian is the daughter of Iris, half-African and half-Carib, born to the West African Matilda and the Carib Simon:

> Iris died in 1971 in a Roseau jail, where she was being kept overnight for the crimes of disorderly conduct and disturbing the peace . . . The isolated place where Iris's navel was buried didn't appear on a map until 1950, after it had already ceased to exist, when it was recorded as « Noah ». Before that, it was known only as « Up There » — with the rest of the phrase, « where Matilda lives, » left unspoken, understood.
> "Up There" was where she was born to Matilda and Simon the Carib . . . the people who lived Up There, every last one of them of unadulterated African descent, knew that not even sixteen forested and

mountainous miles opposite their enclave, over on the Atlantic side of the island, lived a small group of people left over from the time before the white people and before the black people. But while most Dominicans were accustomed to seeing the red people with the dead-straight hair, few of those who lived Up There had ever set eyes on a Carib until the middle of the 1920s, when one appeared in the person of Simon (John 2006: 2–3).

Through the character of Simon, John tries to grasp something of the ancient Amerindian nomadic migrations around the islands, so completely antithetic to the Reserve that was set up for the 400 Amerindian people left in 1903:

> [Simon] recalled that the entire Atlantic Ocean had been his ancestors' property, and the two percent of Dominica where he lived was not enough for him to call his own. His people had moved in their numbers from Island to Island in long canoes, all the way from Trinidad in the south up to Puerto Rico, Jamaica, and beyond in the north (ibid.: 21).

Lilian has resolved to investigate the reasons why Matilda was accused of murder, why she was hanged for a murder Lillian believes her innocent of. Several layers of history are gradually unearthed, the official and the unofficial. Instead of simply being the story of how her grandmother was hanged for killing the white man who had jilted her daughter Iris (Lillian's mother), the story that emerges is that of the descendants of the Maroon slaves of Dominica coming into contact with the last few remaining Kalinagos. Matilda was not guilty of the death of the people whose skeletons were found at the top of the mountain, Up There. The revelation will come at the very end of the book.

Generally speaking and when it is focused on in fiction, the Amerindian presence is made palpable through the deep and intricate association between diegesis, human character, natural landscape and myth, almost in such a way that they merge and fuse into one element. Wilson Harris was the first writer who in the 1950s grounded his fiction writing in the Guyanese earth and water specificities, history and myth being indissociably wed to geography. Cyril Dabydeen is also associated with this attraction for the *hinterland*, so different from the ethos of the islands, character being shaped by landscape, diegesis by landscape, landscape and myth fusing into one, foregrounding the fact that the Amerindian myths still work their magic on us and have a meaning for us. His novel *Dark Swirl* (1989) focuses on the character of Josh, a young boy who is unavoidably attracted to the fantasies he is extracting and creating from the creek. The multi-hued serpent, the *massacouraman* of the Amerindian myths, is haunting him, pulling him down into the creek of his dreams and nightmares:

> Josh turned and twisted, frantically kicking out and twisting his hands in a vain swimming motion as he felt something pulling him down to the bottom of the creek. Vast ripples surged its length. A mighty board-stiff tail swayed, creating waves that reached the houses nearest the banks, rocking them as in an earthquake. Large emerald eyes belched fire as a head surfaced. Then it plunged to the bottom before quickly tearing up through the mud and decaying vegetation. Water splashed high in the air. A gurgling sound that never seemed to end roared in his ears (Dabydeen 1989: 19–20).

Things are made more complex when a European zoologist settles in that part of the Guyanese forest and starts looking for specimens, not making it possible anymore for the people of the village to tell Josh off because he's imagining things — the ambiguity is there to stay:

> It was something they had always feared in a dim, unspecific way, yet now that they thought the stranger was looking for it, they were sure that it couldn't really exist, that it was just a local legend. And then, without knowing why, they simultaneously wanted it to be real, and not to be there, afraid that it might end up in one of the stranger's crates (Dabydeen 1989: 35).

In Pauline Melville's novel *The Ventriloquist's Tale* (1997), it is also Amerindian myth that gives its backbone to the story, again interrogating the present via the past. The novel, just like John's *Unburnable*, spans three generations, starting with Chofy McKinnon of the third generation of a Wapisiana Amerindian family of Guyana. Chofy, on one of his trips to Georgetown, meets Rosa Mendelson, a British academic researching Evelyn Waugh's stay in the Rupununi in the 1930s. Thinking they can extract information from Chofy's aunt, Wifreda, Rosa and Chofy talk her into delving into the past. As her memory turns to the past again and unlocks it gradually, the prophecy spoken by Beatrice, Wifreda's sister, comes true and Wifreda is struck by a severe bout of blindness. This blindness allows the tale of the past to be told and the secret of the Wapisiana family gradually becomes unearthed, the repressed memories of the older generation coming out into the open, again just as in *Unburnable*. Travelling through myth along generations brings the reader to the story of Danny and Beatrice in the 1920s. They are the children of the Scotsman Alexander McKinnon and of Maba of the Wapisiana tribe in the south savannahs of the Rupununi. Their settlement is at Waronawa near the Kanaku mountains, but the novel is traversed by the nomadic journeying of the different Amerindian tribes who live in Guyana — the Macusi of the north savannahs, the Wai Wai of the forests in the south.

In the chapter entitled 'The Master of Fish', it is made clear how the Amerindians' everyday life is ruled by the constellations and the myths attached to them:

> During the month of May, the slow dive of a certain constellation takes place in the night sky, headfirst and arching steadily backwards over the western horizon. It signals the advent of the rains and in the Rupununi district of the Guianas, in the red, parched savannahs, the fish-runs begin.
>
> The constellation is called Tamukang, the Master of Fish, because he orchestrates the silver battalions that come leaping along the rivers at this time. To Europeans, that same configuration of stars is known as the Pleiades, the Hyades and part of Orion. But the constellation of Tamukang does, indeed, look like the skeleton of a fish, head and backbone rolling through the singing blackness in a descent towards oblivion. The moaning winds, they say, are Tamukang blowing his flute. He remains out of sight until his resurrection over the eastern horizon in the months of August and September.
>
> It was one particular cluster of stars in the constellation, the one that the Europeans called the Hyades that was thought to control the tapirs which were so plentiful during the rainy season.
>
> . . . What made [Maba] uneasy was that the patch of tapir stars seemed to be getting brighter as she watched. Everybody knew that the snifflysnouted, short-sighted, night-trotting tapir was too lazy to mate outside its own family. The stars seemed to be confirming what she suspected (Melville 1997: 175–76).

The Wapisiana believe that man and nature were one, until an eclipse separated them:

> They believed that a brother came secretly to his sister at nights. She enjoyed this but not knowing who he was, blackened his face with the magical genipap to identify him. In his shame he rose to the sky and became the moon. That is why the moon has dark patches on its face (ibid.: 82).

The Taruma version has it that the brother started to chase his sister and she transformed into the moon and he into the sun:

Whenever he catches her and makes love to her there is an eclipse. Demons come from the forest and rivers to attack people. Those massive camoodies in the rivers raise their heads from the water to see why the sky has gone dark (Melville 1997: 194).

Even an anthropologist's version is ironically worked into the story — one Michael Wormoal from the University of Berne whose research field is Amerindian mythology and whose presence in the novel, coming into contact with Rosa in the first part of the book, offers an ironical comment on anthropology and structuralist ethnology. It is one of the many modulations that the myth is shown as going through.

The whole novel is kept abuzz with all kinds of Amerindian myths concerning the creation of the world, Wapisiana, Taruma, Wai Wai and Macusi myths of how the constellations used to be beings who lived on earth and went up to the sky to avoid persecution. It is also the value of myth to circulate from tribe to tribe and from generation to generation; like the ventriloquists of the novel's title: 'they can make their voice sound as if it's coming from somewhere else' (ibid.: 200). The myths also circulate from the Amerindians to Western readers who are made particularly aware that the unravelling of the family secret of incest echoes what is happening to the younger generation in Georgetown, struggling against a background of eco-imperialism, with mining and logging multinationals wrecking the environment. The story of the older generation trying to work against fate is, it seems, only a metaphor for the present-day situation. As Jan Shinebourne remarks in an article about Melville's novel:

> In the novel, incest is a metaphor for a multitude of phenomena including myth, science, magic, fate, destiny, desire and love — in short, existence and humanity's struggle for knowledge and survival in the race to stave off catastrophe. Danny and Beatrice's incestuous relationship is foretold oracle-fashion by the circulating myth (from the Bering Straits to Guyana's Rupununi and Brazil) that links the phenomena of eclipse and incest, both of which have the power to disturb the balance of nature and society and to defy the desire of science and religion to order and control existence (Shinebourne 1999: 183).

The material of both writers, Melville and Dabydeen — and one could, of course, include Wilson Harris first and foremost — is myth and imagination and how we come into the possession of ourselves through a circuitous journeying into the archives of the past and imagination. This is the kind of nomadism of the mind and sensitivity that the Amerindian presence in Caribbean literature has provided for us, Western readers. E. K. Brathwaite formulated this in a particularly pertinent way:

> In the Caribbean, whether it be African or Amerindian, the recognition of an ancestral relationship with the folk or aboriginal culture involves the artist and participant in a journey into the past and hinterland which is at the same time a movement of possession into the present and future. Through this movement of possession we become ourselves, truly our own creators, discovering word for object, image for the Word (Brathwaite 1970: 44, quoted in Welsh 1999: 164).

In the novels mentioned previously, the Amerindian element is structural in the diegesis and the organization of plot, as all the narratives move freely between past and present, between the different zones of the past and of consciousness, thus composing a sort of nomadic way of inhabiting both time and consciousness, our pasts and our presents, all our *hinterlands*. All the novels also oscillate in-between genres, the historical novel, the confessional novel, the murder story, the detective novel, real page-turners in John's and Melville's cases. This nomadism of the mind, of imagination and writing — and this is what I have been meaning to get to — has taken over the nomadism in space that disappeared so long ago. It is expressed, organized and foregrounded in the Caribbean through the Amerindian element in a way that is both specific and general and whose impact has to be understood for the whole Caribbean today. The narrative visions of Baldeosingh, John, Dabydeen and Melville are made of all the permutations of the stories, of all the cross-cultural explorations, the multiple meanderings of imagination, the modulations of dream and myth woven into the web of the diegesis. The result provides the sense that the self is fluid but has to take into itself the trace of its previous belongings in order to be whole. Melville's fiction resembles this sense of self in that it is similarly 'syncretic, multiple, overlapping, constantly contesting categories or oppositions such as time and space, life and death, the natural and the supernatural' (ibid.: 148).

The Tainos and Kalinagos may well be the *Other* of the Caribbean, but an *Other* that may paradoxically bring the Caribbean closer to itself. Trying to gain access back to the Amerindians also sends a vibrant message across the whole of the Caribbean. As Maximilian C. Forte (2006) suggests, the relationship of the Amerindians to nature may well contribute to a stronger bond between the land and the people in the Caribbean at large. As is suggested by Dabydeen and Melville, ecoimperialism is definitely one of the main challenges that have to be faced today in the Caribbean. The relationship to one's history is also part of what the Caribbean may learn from the Amerindian survivors: would forgetting about the Amerindian past and present not be the equivalent to what happened to the African past that was denied and despised for so long? And finally, the Amerindian culture could be a renewed symbol of a shared identity, and not one based on discrimination and hatred. So there is a lesson to be learned in all three aspects (environment, history, culture). The last element would certainly be, more generally speaking, a symbol of resistance to any form of external domination, and we all know that domination and colonization are not over in the Caribbean. This strategy of the nomadic detour, foregrounding the Amerindian culture and history in order to speak of the Caribbean as a whole, is certainly one of the most pregnant aspects of Amerindian-Caribbean literature. One hopes that, through such a cross-cultural nomadism of the mind, the national cohesion will be strengthened as well as the awareness of the Caribbean's multiple legacies.

References

Baldeosingh, Kevin. 2005. *The Ten Incarnations of Adam Avatar*. Leeds: Peepal Tree Press.

Brathwaite, Edward. 1970. 'Timehri', *Savacou*, 2: 44.

Dabydeen, Cyril. 1989. *Dark Swirl*. Leeds: Peepal Tree Press.

Dawes, Kwame (ed.). 2001. *Talk Yuh Talk: Interviews with Anglophone Caribbean Poets*. Charlottesville: University of Virginia Press.

Forte, Maximilian C. 2006. *Indigenous Resurgence in the Contemporary Caribbean*. New York: Peter Lang.

Guyana News and Informations. 1996. 'Amerindian Policies', National Development Strategy (NDS), http://www.guyana.org/NDS/chap22.htm (accessed 7 December 2009).

Hulme, Peter. 1986. *Colonial Encounters: Europe and the Native Caribbean — 1492–1797*. New York: Methuen.

———. 2000. *Remnants of Conquest: the Island Caribs and their Visitors 1877–1998*. Oxford: Oxford University Press.

John, Marie-Elena. 2006. *Unburnable*. New York: HarperCollins.

Melville, Pauline. 1997. *The Ventriloquist's Tale*. New York and London: Bloomsbury.

Shinebourne, Jan. 1999. 'The Ventriloquist's Tale', *Ma Comère*, 2: 182–86.

Welsh, Sarah Lawson. 1999. 'Pauline Melville's Shape-Shifting Fictions', in Mary Condé and Thorunn Lonsdale (eds), *Caribbean Women Writers*, pp. 144–71. New York: St Martin's Press.

Wilson, Samuel M. 1997. *The Indigenous People of the Caribbean*. Gainesville: University Press of Florida.

11

From Migrancy to Malignancy

What Ails the Yaaku?

Mumia Geoffrey Osaaji

♋

I begin with a question asked by Lee Cronk in his book *From Mukogodo to Maasai: Ethnicity and Cultural Change in Kenya* (based on an anthropological study he conducted among the Yaaku over two decades in the 1980s and 1990s): 'Can one change one's ethnicity? Can an entire ethnic group change its ethnicity?' (2004: xi).

In this chapter, I focus on the strategic manipulation of ethnic identity by the Yaaku (*Mukogodo Maasai*) of Kenya. It is notable that changes brought on by the British colonial government led the Yaaku away from their traditional life as independent hunters and gatherers into the orbit of the 'high status' Maasai, whom they began to emulate. Today, the Yaaku form the bottom rung of a regional socio-economic ladder of Maa-speaking pastoralists. An interesting by-product of this sudden ethnic change has been to give the Yaaku women, who tend to marry

---

*In this chapter, I am tracing the root of this 'malignancy' and explaining it within the post-colonial perspective. I explore the land alienation and ethnic segregation policies of the British colonial government as well as the education practices of successive post-independence regimes — and how they affected the Yaaku. I also examine how negative ethnic attitudes and socio-economic influences of the more populous Maasai contribute towards the endangerment of the Yaaku language, culture and identity. Finally, I outline the efforts being undertaken by the UNESCO, the government of Kenya, the Yaaku themselves and other actors, to restore the Yaaku identity.

'up the ladder', better marital and reproductive prospects than Yaaku men. Yaaku parents have responded with an unusual pattern of favouring daughters over sons, though they emulate the Maasai by verbally expressing a preference for sons.

Cronk (2004) notes that, before the 1920s, the Yaaku were hunters and gatherers. They spoke the Yaaku language and lived a semi-nomadic existence, making their homes in caves and under rock shelters. For subsistence, the Yaaku gathered wild foods, hunted wild game, and kept bees. They described their diet as one of 'honey and meat', and they lived a materially adequate if not abundant existence.

Under British colonial rule, the Yaaku found themselves increasingly in close contact with the Maasai. The Yaaku were, however, looked down upon by the pastoralist Maasai neighbours, who saw them as dirty, poor and uncultured. This marginalization forced the Yaaku to make a remarkably swift transition in virtually all aspects of their lives and cultural patterns. Over the course of a decade (mid-1920s to mid-1930s), they switched from hunting and gathering to herding cattle; they settled in Maasai style huts and villages; they even dropped their native Yaaku language to become Maa-speaking. In effect, they became Maasai. Yet the Maasai do not accept them as Maasai. To them, the Yaaku are still *il-torobo*, a pejorative term with connotations of poverty, pollution, and powerlessness.

In 1969, only 28 per cent of the Yaaku had some rudimentary knowledge of their old language. The shift in language was precipitated by the fact that the Yaaku were so few, necessitating that everyone at least becomes bilingual. The Maa spoken by the descendants of the Yaaku does retain bits and pieces of the old language. According to recent research by UNESCO and the Kenya Network for Research on Indigenous Knowledge (KENRIK), what remains of the Yaaku is a small population of just three fluent speakers down from 250 in 1983. These are two women called Roteti and Yapanoi NeSakaya and an old man called Lengunai. This is a sad picture of a language, a culture and a heritage that is close to extinction (UNESCO and KENRIK 2006: 12).

How the Yaaku View Themselves

The Yaaku reject the *il-torobo* tag, a derogatory label used by the Maasai and Samburu to describe them. They see themselves as the centre of their own universe, a world in which they were the first inhabitants, a world in which the Maasai are just the latest in a long series of groups to pass through their territory. They view hunting and gathering as a complete way of life that predates the arrival of the pastoralists in East Africa (Cronk 2004: 52).

Perhaps a good way to express the Yaaku hidden transcript is the story recorded from the Yaaku by Cronk about two Maasai warriors and a single Yaaku. The Yaaku man was returning from a honey-gathering trip when two Maasai confronted him with an intent to kill him. The Yaaku asked to be allowed to eat his honey so that he could die satisfied. As he ate, he asked his captors whether they too ate honey. They did and while their hands were covered with the sweet liquid, the Yaaku quickly washed his hands with dirt, grabbed one of the Maasai swords and stabbed one of his captors. The other Maasai, unaware of the Yaaku trick of washing the slippery honey with dirt, tried to grab his spear but could not firmly hold it. The Yaaku stabbed him, picked his honey and left. Thus, a Yaaku with his honey can easily outwit two menacing Maasai warriors (ibid.: 55)!

As Cronk notes, the traditional Yaaku language and culture are very rich. Making a living in the forest involved an elaborate and complex body of knowledge and the language with which to express it that had taken centuries to develop. The Yaaku had knowledge and skills necessary to maintain themselves, their culture and their language for many centuries. If we realize that the Yaaku were a long-lasting, well-adapted group, with its own language, culture, social organization, and subsistence patterns, all of which had served them well over the centuries, then the transition to Mukogodo Maasai is a puzzle. After all, other hunters and gatherers such as the Hadza of Tanzania and the Okiek of Kenya have not entirely abandoned their traditional hunting and gathering, language, ethnic identity and cultures (ibid.: 60).

British Policies

In the 1920s, the British created a *Dorobo* (derived from *il-torobo*) reserve in Mukogodo division of Laikipia district as a safe haven for the Yaaku. While justifying this decision, a colonial administrator, D. G. Worthy, wrote that '*Wandorobo* (Yaaku) were, and presumably still are, the victims and prey of more powerful groups. We sought to give them a chance to retain their very unusual identity as people who predated the later immigrants' (ibid.: 68).

The British colonial policy in Kenya involved identifying a limited number of ethnic units, associating certain parcels of land with those ethnic units, and ensuring that people live in areas where they share cultural affinities. This resulted in the creation of cultural native reserves. People who did not fit the cultural profile of a certain region were forced to move to that which the administrators deemed more appropriate.

The most important goal of creating native reserves was to limit the amount of land available to ethnic groups while at the same time, creating more space for European settlers and infrastructure projects such as railways and roads. The first British–Maasai treaty of 1904 bifurcated the expansive belt occupied by the Maa-speaking groups into the northern and southern reserves. The subsequent British–Maasai treaty of 1911 obliterated the northern reserve and obligated the Maasai to move to the southern reserve around Kajiado and Narok.

This policy created some difficulties with some of the Maa speakers refusing to shift to the southern reserve and choosing instead to move into the Yaaku reserve in Mukogodo. According to Cronk, the British were forced to effect up to 21 deportations of non-Yaaku ethnic groups from Mukogodo area between 1912 and 1959 (2004: 69).

If the goal of the British policy was to protect the Yaaku against contact with other communities, it proved an utter failure! The alienation of land for settlers had forced the displaced communities into Mukogodo, where they intermarried, and had a profound impact on the Yaaku. As a result of the initial intermarriages, the British deportations of non-Yaaku groups proved futile, since they could easily return and be hidden by their newly found in-laws.

Non-Yaaku in-laws offered livestock for bride wealth while the Yaaku men could only manage a beehive. With time, livestock became more attractive than beehives and Yaaku families were soon finding it more attractive to marry their daughters to the non-Yaaku in exchange for livestock. Sooner, Yaaku men who failed to become pastoralist found it difficult to marry, and because of their patrilineal system of descent and inheritance, failed to produce legitimate heirs. For instance, Cronk found out that all men in the Yaaku lineages of Suaanga and Biyoti failed to make the transition to pastoralism and these lineages no longer exist (ibid.: 72).

Endangered Language

There is widespread fear that the Yaaku language is currently endangered. An endangered language, according to the UNESCO, is a language headed for extinction. A language is in danger when its speakers cease to use it; when its speakers use it only in an increasingly reduced number of communicative domains; and when the speakers cease to pass it on from one generation to the next. In other words, there are no new speakers, either adults or children (UNESCO and KENRIK 2006: 2).

An endangered language is, therefore, a language without monolingual speakers, people who speak only that language. It is a language spoken by a minority of people in the nation and for that reason, it is held in low esteem, causing its speakers to avoid using it or passing it on to their children. Many endangered languages today have only a few remaining speakers, usually elderly, who will take that language with them to the grave (ibid.: 3).

The following factors are used to gauge whether or not a language is endangered. These include the absence or presence of intergenerational transmission, the number of absolute speakers, the proportion of absolute speakers within the total population, shifts in domains of language use, response to new domains and media, presence or absence of materials for language education and literacy, government policies and attitudes, the speech community's attitude towards their own language, and the type and quality of documentation (ibid.: 10). These foregoing parameters fit the current state of the Yaaku language.

When the Yaaku became aware of the advantages of the cattle economy, they promptly started ranking languages according to a prestige scale, with the Maasai language of the wealthy cattle keepers on top and Yaaku (largely associated with hunters and gatherers) at the bottom. This language shift was considered necessary in order to adopt their life to a new value system (Heine 1977: 90). To borrow Ngũgĩ wa Thiong'o's words,

> [l]anguage is power. Language has power to upset, to uproot, and to shackle . . . If you name the world, you own it. If you are dominated, you see the world through the eyes of the conqueror, effectively burying your memory under the conqueror's memory (2005: 41).

We may also perceive the Yaaku as a dismembered language. While explaining language dismemberment, Ngũgĩ observes that:

> the domination of a people's language by another leads to the separation or severance of the community's soul from body. This dismemberment takes a speech community further and further away from itself to other selves, from their world to other worlds, which can lead to spiritual subjugation. In other words, the dominant linguistic group has planted its memory on

top of another memory, their linguistic layer on top of a smaller layer. To address this situation, Ngũgĩ calls for 're-membering' these broken and scattered parts (Thiong'o 1986: 19, 2005: 37).

The loss of the Yaaku language is worrisome because language embodies a people's culture while serving as the vehicle for its transmission. Therefore, 'a community may easily lose its sense of identity when its language gets lost because such identity is closely associated with language' (Osaaji 2006: 2). If you lose your language, you have lost your world view. The history tied up in a language will go unrecorded; the poetry and rhythm of a singular tongue will be silenced forever. Loss of a language is, therefore, a loss of the original ethnic and cultural identity. Similarly, people from other cultures are also impoverished when any language dies anywhere in the world (Töpfer 1999: xi). This brings us to Joast Smiers's view that language contributes towards the development of a people's cultural identity while demarcating their difference from others.

It is instructive to note that the successive post-colonial governments of Kenya, through the Ministry of Education, have not succeeded in empowering indigenous languages. For example, vernacular is taught only in primary schools, and just up to the third year of basic education. Beyond this level, the education system encourages only English and Kiswahili. English is the language of instruction throughout the learning process, while also retaining the status of the co-official language of government business alongside Kiswahili. Kiswahili is also the national language, but is not widely used as the language of instruction in the education system, in which it is only taught as one of the disciplines up to secondary level. Beyond this point, it becomes an optional course.

This lopsided arrangement has hit minority languages even harder: the small population of native speakers has not motivated the government to publish basic education materials in these minor languages. Hence, children from minority linguistic communities such as the Yaaku are compelled to learn the languages of dominant communities during the first three years of basic education. This policy has aggravated the endangerment of languages such as Yaaku.

Language is not the only precious asset the Yaaku lost after contact with the Maasai. The pastoralist lifestyle of the Maasai quickly replaced the traditional Yaaku hunting and gathering. According to Cronk, 'the importance of honey to the Yaaku is reflected in the seriousness with which they treated honey theft' (2004: 37). To illustrate, Cronk shares a cautionary tale that was narrated to him by several informants. The story is that long time ago, a boy from one lineage was found stealing honey from another lineage's hive. Violence ensued and in the confusion, an arrow put out the eye of the honey thief's mother. Notwithstanding its gender insensitivity, the moral of the story is to remind future generations of the seriousness of honey theft (ibid.: 37).

The Yaaku are classified by anthropologists as 'delayed-return hunters and gatherers', a term which describes a group that invests a great deal in tools and equipment such as traps and beehives. They defend their territories and store their excess food: all these are examples of 'delayed-returns', that is, investments of time, materials and energy that will not pay off immediately until sometime in future. On the other hand, 'immediate-return hunters and gatherers' do not invest time and energy in large elaborate structures or tools; they do not store food; they consume what they hunt and gather rather immediately. An example of this type is the Hadza of Tanzania (ibid.: 50). However, the contact with Maasai has forced the Yaaku to adopt pastoralism and its dietary lifestyle. For instance, in the pre-transition period, the Yaaku concept of food, *daa* consisted of honey: today, *daa* is defined not as honey, but as milk (ibid.: 51).

Another noticeable cultural change attributed to the Maasai–Yaaku contact, is the adoption of the rigid age set system associated with the Maasai. The key event in this system is circumcision, which begins the transition of a boy from childhood to a *murrani*. Later, *a murrani* will become an elder. When the Yaaku adopted the Maasai age sets, they initially followed the names given by the Maasai before switching to those of their northern neighbours, the Samburu.

Traditionally, the Yaaku referred to their god as *Yecheri*, who was believed to reside on top of Mt Kenya. The holiest place among the Yaaku is the hill, Ol Doinyo Lossos. During worship, the leader of a family would climb to the top of Ol Doinyo Lossos, and make offerings of honey, blood, milk and fat to *Yecheri*. Other Yaaku holy places include a small hill in Siekuu valley, and a particular tree in Mukogodo forest known as Hindadai (ibid.: 50). The current Yaaku noun for god is *enkai*, which is borrowed from the Maasai. And due to pastoralism, the older Yaaku worry that their ancestors will not recognize their worship and sacrifices offered away from their known traditional shrines. In the absence of a written tradition, their archives and libraries are sacred valleys, hills, mountains, caves, rivers, groves, gigantic trees, forests, giant stones, and burial sites (UNESCO and KENRIK 2006: 11).

Ethnic Switching for Survival

Why did the Yaaku change their way of subsistence, their language, their religion, and their customs? There are no new answers, since much has already been provided in the foregoing discussion. However, there is need to emphasize the main key points. The decision to switch from hunting and gathering to pastoralism, and from Yaaku to Maasai, was driven by necessity. This switching was part of the practical things that had to be done if one wanted to make a living, marry, and talk to new neighbours. These were also the ways of shedding the *il-torobo* stigma. As the rates of intermarriage increased, people realized that they could no longer count on the Yaaku language to communicate with their neighbours or even their own grandchildren. They may have also found Maa language more developed to handle the new lifestyle of pastoralism than Yaaku whose vocabulary was limited to hunting and gathering. The transition was rapid, taking just a decade from start to finish. It was also thorough, sweeping aside not only the old subsistence pattern but also the Yaaku language and many other aspects of Mukogodo culture (Cronk 2004: 82).

The elderly Yaaku who survived the transition are nostalgic of the days when they spoke pure Yaaku. To illustrate this point, Cronk brings out the findings of Matthias Brenzinger, a German linguist who has studied the Yaaku language, and who recalls a poignant and rather melancholic story during his interview with a Yaaku man. One day, Brenzinger played back a tape with some Yaaku phrases the same old man had spoken during an earlier interview. At first the old man was delighted to hear the old language; and not fully attuned to the principle of the tape recorder, tried to engage it in conversation. But soon, it became evident that the radio could not carry on conversation in Yaaku. The old man first became frustrated, then angry, and finally began to weep (ibid.: 83).

Since the transition, the Yaaku have behaved very much like the Maasai. Their clothing and jewellery are in the Maa style. They also speak a variety of the Maa language common among the southern Maasai. They follow the religion and customs of the Maasai. In 1971, the elite among the Yaaku petitioned the Government of Kenya to legalize their identity name as *Mukogodo Maasai*. By demanding to be called *Mukogodo Maasai*, the Yaaku elite were claiming to constitute a new Maasai section equivalent to the Kisongo or Purko Maasai of southern Kenya and northern Tanzania respectively (ibid.: 140).

Conclusion

Kenya is a signatory to the UNESCO convention and UNESCO's Universal Declaration on Cultural Diversity, both of which provide a framework for preserving and sustaining linguistic and cultural diversity, while binding state parties to do everything in their power to maintain and perpetuate language diversity as a basic principle for fostering peace and security, enhancing universal respect for justice and respect for human rights and fundamental freedoms for all the peoples of the world without distinction whatsoever. The UNESCO encourages the maintenance, development, revitalization, and perpetuation of endangered languages.[1] Therefore, Kenya has an obligation to invest more resources to preserve, restore and sustain the endangered languages and cultural heritage of communities such as the Yaaku.

While the Internet is increasingly becoming a useful and reliable tool for preserving endangered languages, it is interesting to note that the website of the Ministry of Culture and National Heritage has not been active for more than a year. This is a useful resource that could host the diverse materials on endangered minority languages and cultures in Kenya, hence, contributing towards their continuity.

In Kenya, there has been an explosion of FM radio stations broadcasting in vernacular or indigenous languages. These have followed the trend set by the state broadcaster, the Kenya Broadcasting Corporation (KBC), which started such programmes in ethnic regions in the 1960s. However, neither the private stations nor KBC broadcast in the smaller languages! While economic reasons and smaller audiences could explain this scenario, there is need to rethink such practices in order to accommodate the minorities.

Other innovative practices include deliberate effort on the part of the government to support language training in the endangered languages and by providing curriculum materials in the endangered languages. Such measures may contribute towards the revival of the Yaaku language, through its re-introduction, fortification, and maintenance.

Select References

Cronk, Lee. 2004. *From Mukogodo to Maasai: Ethnicity and Cultural Change in Kenya.* Boulder, CO: Westview.

---

[1] http://www.unesco.org (accessed 17 December 2007).

Ethnologue. n.d. 'Extinct and Endangered Languages', http://www.yourdictionary.com/elr/nextinct.html (accessed 5 December 2007).

Heine, Bernd. 1977. 'Linguistic Minorities and Language Shift in Kenya', in *MILA: Journal of the Institute of African Studies*, 77: 87–98.

Hotz, Lee Robert. 2000. 'Linguistic Potpourri: The Impassioned Fight to Save Dying Languages', http://www.yourdictionary.com/library/article004.html (accessed 6 December 2007).

Osaaji, Mumia. 2006. 'Performance and the Disappearing Present'. Paper presented at the UNESCO Regional Conference on Safeguarding Endangered Oral Traditions in East Africa, 3–4 October, Nairobi.

Parry, Benita. 1997. 'The Postcolonial: Conceptual Category or Chimera?', in Andrew Gurr, Philippa Hardman and Lionel Kelly (eds), *The Yearbook of English Studies: The Politics of Postcolonial Criticism*, pp. 3–21. Leeds: W. S. Maney and Son.

Posey, Darrell A. 1999. 'Culture and Nature: The Inextricable Link', in Darrell A. Posey (ed.), *Cultural and Spiritual Values of Biodiversity*, pp. 3–18. London: Intermediate Technology.

Smiers, Joast. 2003. *Arts Under Pressure: Promoting Cultural Diversity in the Age of Globalization*. London: Zed Books.

Thiong'o, Ngũgĩ wa. 1981. *Writers in Politics: Essays*. Nairobi: Heinemann.

———. 1986. *Decolonising the Mind: The Politics of Language in African Literature*. Nairobi: Heinemann.

———. 2005. 'Homecoming Address', in Henry Indangasi and Masumi Odari (eds), *The Nairobi Journal of Literature*, 3: 36–43.

Töpfer, Klaus. 1999. 'Foreword', in Darrel A. Posey (ed.), *Cultural and Spiritual Values of Biodiversity*, pp. xi–xii. London: Intermediate Technology.

United Nations Educational, Scientific and Cultural Organization (UNESCO). n.d. 'Oral Traditions and Expressions including Language as a Vehicle of the Intangible Cultural Heritage', http://www.unesco.org/culture/ich/index.php?lg=en&pg=00053 (accessed 4 April 2012).

———. n.d-a. 'Safeguarding Endangered Languages'. http://www.unesco.org/culture/ich/index.php?pg=00136 (accessed 15 December 2007).

United Nations Educational, Scientific and Cultural Organization (UNESCO) and Kenya Network for Research on Indigenous Knowledge (KENRIK). 2006. *Safeguarding Endangered Oral Traditions in East Africa*. Research Report, United Nations Educational, Scientific and Cultural Organization, Nairobi.

12

The Story of an African Enlightenment

A Cameroonian Myth of Separation and its Relevance for Human Autonomy

A. O. Balcomb

♋

In every myth of human origin there is an episode in which the deity departs and a gulf appears between creator and creation. This departure is premised on human beings performing some act of rebellion, disobedience, or stupidity. One of my favourites goes like this.

Once upon a time heaven was near earth and (the deity whose name was) Bumbulvun lived with men. Heaven was so near that men had to stoop to walk; yet they did not have to worry about what to eat, they only had to stretch out their hands and tear off pieces of heaven for food.

But one day, a young girl, a chief's daughter, who was a *mukuwan* (a naughty girl who did everything the wrong way and the opposite of what others did), instead of taking bits of the vault of heaven to feed on, started looking on the ground and choosing grains she found there. Then she made a mortar and pestle to grind the grains she chose. Each time she knelt down and raised her pestle, it would hit against heaven and also against God. Frustrated in her work, the young girl said to heaven, "God, won't you move just a bit?" Heaven moved a bit further, and the young girl was able to stand up. And she went on and ground her grain; she raised her pestle still higher. Soon she implored heaven for a second time; again heaven moved a bit further. Then she began to throw her pestle up in the air. When she asked for a third time, heaven became outraged and moved far away to its present location.

From that time on men have been able to stand up and walk. They no longer feed on pieces of heaven, but have become millet eaters. In addition, God does not appear as he used to, long ago, when every evening, he would come and act as their arbitrator. Now men are left alone to settle their problems; hence there is war (Mana 2002: 38).

Myths of creation explain why things are as they are. One of the things we need to know is why things are not all as they should be. Why there is pain, suffering, and evil, and, more prosaically, why there is work. The assumption is therefore made that once upon a time things were not as they are now. It cannot be that things were not always less than perfect. This would give some permanent ontological status to imperfection, evil, or what I would prefer simply to call not-all-rightness. This is impossible for the human mind to accept. The deity (for there must have been one to bring about things in the first place) must have originally made things better than they are now and must have had reason to depart because something had gone wrong. Someone must have been the cause of this. This could not have been God because God, by definition, is perfect. So the cause must have been on the human side. More often than not a woman is blamed. We are expected to believe that women are, after all, the cause of most problems in the world.

But there is always a double-edged meaning to separation myths. Not only do we need to know why things are not all right. We need to know that it is difficult to conceive of a situation that is better than the one that we have to live with. We need to know, in other words, that it is alright that everything is not all right and that the departure of the deity was a necessary one and that there is still a possibility of salvation in the situation that we find ourselves in. The myth, predictably, puts the blame on a young girl, which mitigates the seriousness of the original sin from the perspective of the rest of the human race, justifying the situation by reminding us that young girls are the silliest of creatures. But it also elicits a sense in which the present state of affairs was somewhat inevitable and therefore is one which the best must be made of. A closer reading might even suggest that there is reason to admire this young woman. But this would depend on whether we place any value on independence of thought and initiative, especially of young women. Since the myth itself is an explanation of how independence of thought came about in the first place it means that such independence existed when the myth was conceived so a certain level of recognition, if not admiration, is permissible. Further justification for the less than perfect situation could be conceived on the basis that we might not have learned certain things if the original state of unity with the deity continued to exist. We would not have learned, certainly, to invent the mortar and pestle and to pound grain. It is not so bad being a millet eater, though what we picked from the sky might have been better. There are worse things we could be eating. Moreover, it is not such a bad thing that we can now stand up, and not crawl around or walk in a cramped position. Is it not true that, when all things were considered, the deity was really taking up a little too much space anyway? We could even go so far as to say that this young woman taught us to take responsibility for our lives, to discover the meaning of human dignity and the dignity of work. In a word, she might have opened the door to freedom, with all the rights and responsibilities that this entails.

But recognition of all of these things would depend on a certain degree of enlightenment, an acceptance of the value, however limited, of individual autonomy.

Thus does this story essentialize some of the basic issues around the project of the autonomization of the individual. It graphically demonstrates that while unity with the divine is necessary for the origin of life, continuing such a unity might be detrimental to the integrity of the human being. A Freudian interpretation of the myth would be that while the unity of the foetus with its mother is necessary for its life the most fundamental of separations has to take place at birth with the cutting of the umbilical cord, from which time the development of the child's ego can take place.

What interests me more about this story, however, is the way in which it resonates with the story of the autonomization of the human being as it has been enacted in the history of Western civilization. I am talking here about the story of the European Enlightenment, that period of history starting in the early 17th century and reaching its climax later on in the following century in the French Revolution when Europe finally invited God to absent himself from the everyday affairs of human life — especially those to do with politics and work. The early rumblings against the authority of the Catholic church in the scientific discoveries of Copernicus and Galileo, leading to outright revolution against the church by the French *philosophes* and finally culminating in the blood bath of the French Revolution gave Europe democracy, the secular state, and the culture of the rights of the individual human being. This does not mean that God was completely banished. But it did mean he was kept at a distance, just as the African story suggests. The scientific discoveries of Newton, Boyle and Bacon and the philosophical musings of Descartes did not exclude God but they popularized a deist conception of God which meant that he was a far-off creator who began things and then absented himself, rather like the watchmaker who creates the watch, winds it up, and then leaves it to tick away by itself.

It was left to the atheist revolutionary Robespierre to institutionalize the political implications of deism through the cult of the Supreme Being. He did this because of the atavistic forces of revolution, released partially as a consequence of rejecting the authority of the aristocracy, the church, and God, and the invention of the notion of power to the people, from where we get our idea of democracy — literally a combination of the words *demos* (people) and *kratos* (power). What the revolutionaries did not bargain for, Robespierre included, was the destruction by the revolution of the very fabric of society itself. He calculated that power needed to transcend the Hobbesian Leviathan of the secular state and that the idea of a supreme being would do this, and, hopefully, this would bring some order and sanity to the bloodbath that had erupted. Unfortunately, this did not happen soon enough to prevent Robespierre himself from losing his head. Deism, however, has ever since then become the preferred theology of politicians who wish to have God close enough to call upon to give legitimacy to their political agendas and far enough not to interfere too much with these agendas.

Much of this resonates, quite startlingly in many ways, with the Cameroonian myth of separation. Here is a deity who simply has too much sway in the lives of human beings. The African version depicts this graphically in terms of the actual space taken up by God, leaving human beings to stoop or crawl. The European Enlightenment depicts it in terms of a recognition, first incipient but becoming increasingly emphatic, of the need to remove religious belief from the world of work and politics. But not completely. We still call upon bishops to throw holy water on building projects when they are finished, or give divine legitimacy to politicians and royalty by being resplendently present at inauguration ceremonies. They even make their appearance at those bastions of the enlightenment legacy — the western university.

But the essential message of the Cameroonian myth — the need for the deity to be removed so that the human being can be truly human — is precisely the message of the European Enlightenment. The fact that a young woman features in both — one in the form of that wielder of pestle into mortar and the other in the form of the symbolic young woman called liberty who leads the peasants of France to war against their oppressors — is also profoundly significant. Both stories choose a young woman as the archetypal symbol of liberation.

As prescient as this Cameroonian myth of separation is there is irony in the fact that it does not reflect the reality of the African situation with regards to secularism. Africa is known to be 'incurably' religious and continues to live in what Max Weber called an enchanted universe, as much as the European West is known to be post religious and lives in a disenchanted universe. Indeed the scientific project of the West was premised on the disenchantment of the universe which had to be rid of all agency or what Darwin called caprice, if nature was to give up its energies to control by technology. Africa is not known for its scientific achievements. But then Europe is not known for its spirituality. The postmodern project of the re-enchantment of the universe, which could be interpreted as indicative of disillusionment with the modern secular project and an emergence of an inchoate yearning for the lost state of unity with the divine, demonstrated in the current fascination in the West for things supernatural, spiritual and transcendent, and with its more serious western advocates in science, theology and philosophy, may do well to look to the east and to the south for some inspiration, but this is the subject of another paper.

Reference

Mana, Kä. 2002. *Christians and Churches of Africa Envisioning the Future*. Oxford: Regnum Africa.

13

The Dasse's Story and The Crow's Story

The Interdiscursivity of /Xam Bushman Literature

Michael Wessels

♋

/Xam was the language of a Bushman people who, in the opinion of 19th-century evolutionist thought, were doomed to vanish from the face of the earth. The /Xam people were a museum piece, a living fossil in the modern world and the study of their language, culture and mythology might even provide a link between the evolution of apes and humans (Bank 1999: 15, 2006: 40; Moran 2009: 67–78). Such ideas seem to have motivated, in part at any rate, philologist Wilhelm Bleek's successful request to governor Henry Barkly to have released into his custody for research purposes some of the /Xam convicts who were held in Cape Town's harsh Breakwater prison for offences such as stock theft, poaching and manslaughter — even the colonial magistrate recognized that Dia!Kwain and Kasin's killing of a white farmer was in self-defence (Bank 2006: 69–71). /A!kunta, the first of these prisoners, arrived in the Bleek household in 1870. For a decade Bleek and his collaborator, sister-in-law and successor (Bleek himself died mid-way through the /Xam project) recorded the /Xam language as well as a substantial body of its literature and other materials such as history and biography.

The /Xam language did indeed cease to be spoken. The /Xam themselves, though, and we might assume, something of their culture, became part of the Afrikaans-speaking rural proletariat of the Cape, indistinguishable to outsiders at any rate from the rest of the Cape Coloured population. They were not exterminated although many were murdered and the settler strategy of separating children from their parents was a brutal act of social destruction (Szalay 1995: 79). Even if Bleek had been able to recognize that tangible forces which might have been opposed were to blame for the 'disappearance' of the /Xam rather than the incontestable logic of evolution and, anachronistically, had become an activist in the /Xam cause, it is doubtful that the /Xam language would have remained a living language in the context of 19th-century frontier politics.[1]

It might well be asked how the /Xam themselves viewed these events and their changing circumstances. Did they see themselves as fated to perish? It is clear from an examination of the historical and biographical materials in the Bleek and Lloyd notebooks that all the /Xam informants had been drawn into the wider colonial economy in the years that preceded their incarceration in the Breakwater prison. One can detect in the accounts of conflict with Korana groups, for example, the impact of events further south as more and more groups migrated north out of the settler areas in an earlier period. Nowhere, though, do the notebooks offer a direct /Xam interpretation of late 19th-century historical events in the Northern Cape. This view has to be reconstructed. As Anne Solomon (2009) argues, reading the materials through the lens of a contemporary political outlook can be misleading. A post-colonial interest in detecting anti-colonial elements in the texts has led several commentators to interpret Dia!kwain's well-known extract about the broken string as a metaphor for land dispossession and subsequent cultural alienation. The evidence of the text itself, though, and its relationship to the /Xam cosmology and beliefs that can be discerned by the careful reader in the rest of the Bleek and Lloyd archive suggests that the broken string re-lates primarily to 'the severed connection between Dia!kwain's father and the *spirit*-rainmaker with whom he enjoyed a special relationship' (ibid.: 35–36). The difficulty in discovering a /Xam perspective is not a question of a paucity of sources — the Bleek and Lloyd collection[2] consists of close on 13,000 notebook pages that were recounted/dictated by /Xam individuals — but one of exegesis. The problem is not solely due to the

---

[1] Anthony Traill (1996) provides a thorough account of the reasons for the disappearance of the /Xam language.

[2] The archive of /Xam materials is 'still officially known as the Bleek collection' (Bank 2006: 400). It is generally, though, referred to as the Bleek and Lloyd collection or the Bleek–Lloyd collection, in order to acknowledge Lucy Lloyd's pivotal contribution. It is also sometimes referred to the /Xam archive or collection.

strangeness of the sources or their obscurity, in my view, but because of the inadequacy of existing modes of interpretation, the influence of contemporary intellectual preoccupations and certain misperceptions about the nature of the archive. We cannot assume, for example, that the Bleek and Lloyd materials present a consistent /Xam view of things. For a start, the informants did not experience or see the world in the same way.

If the historical and biographical materials in the archive are difficult to interpret, we might reasonably expect the narratives that comprise the bulk of the collection to present an even greater analytical problem. Stories, after all, fall within the category of what we generally call literature.[3] Literature invites interpretation but never offers unambiguous and univocal meaning. By its very nature it eludes the interpretation that it provokes. This brings me to the chief business of this chapter, a discussion of the interpretation of the /Xam narratives, texts that exhibit all the ambiguity and discursiveness of literature. This complexity is compounded by the fact that the /Xam narratives have their basis in traditions of oral performance but are only available to interpreters in a transcribed and translated form. The situation is not helped, of course, by the absence of living exponents of the /Xam literary tradition whom critics could consult.

Even before we examine the way the texts work and generate meaning, there is the question about their nature. The answer to this question greatly influences their interpretation. The narratives are usually placed in particular categories that have remained fairly constant over the years since Lucy Lloyd first used them in *Specimens of Bushman Folklore*, the selection of materials from the notebooks that was published in 1911. Although no-one has disputed that the /Xam narratives (as distinct from the /Xam materials which include personal history or cultural information, for example) are literature, they are always described as literature of a certain type: mythology, folklore, legend, fable or traditional oral literature. Once these categories have been established — and in the case of the /Xam archive this has been accomplished with little debate or contention, the interpretation of the texts becomes relatively uncomplicated in terms of the functionalist, comparatist or structuralist questions that have commonly been asked of them. The chief concern of

---

[3] Anne Solomon (2009) notes that there is a general tendency in the interpretation of the /Xam materials away 'from the attention to indigenous meaning that had reached some depth (notably in Hewitt's work) to understanding the /Xam testimonies as "some of the earliest accounts in southern Africa of colonization from the perspective of the colonized" (Brown 1998: 36)'.

a functionalist analysis is not so much what the stories mean or how they generate meaning but how they contribute to social cohesion. The answer generally is the same as that which would be offered for any body of traditional mythology. They serve to reinforce the social order by articulating certain values (often after showing the consequences of their infraction) and, in the form of charter myths, sanction the status quo by investing it with a sacred origin. In terms of comparatist methodology, the meanings of texts emerge once they are collated with others of the same type in the region and beyond. By the logic of this approach, these meanings reside in general, if partly concealed, patterns. A specific /Xam narrative becomes the local instance of a widespread story. Subterranean and broad meaning is also the province of the structuralist interpretations that have been applied to the /Xam narratives, although in this case these meanings are articulated with broader patterns and themes within /Xam culture itself, especially in the commentary of Roger Hewitt (1986). Some of the assumptions of these modes of interpretation were first questioned by Mathias Guenther (1999) who argues for the multivocality of the narratives and for their location within a foraging ideology that foregrounds ambiguity and flexibility. Crucially, in my opinion, Duncan Brown (1995) has reminded us that /Xam narrative is discourse; it belongs to a historically and culturally grounded set of discursive practices. In this chapter I should first like to reconsider the /Xam narratives' position as literature and then propose a way of approaching a single narrative by seeking to situate it within /Xam discourse.

Literature

In modern class society, the literary is separated from ordinary fiction by its quality and its relationship with an elite group of consumers. It exists by virtue of a value judgement that is sanctioned by university departments and book prizes. Above all, it is separated from mass or popular culture. The idea of high and low culture has in western culture (but not only in western culture) been a calibrating procedure which helps to legitimate and sanction the class structure. The sign of the popular serves to endow the literary or the artistic with value, rather like the way exclusive suburbs derive their value from the existence of other, less desirable, residential areas. The distinction between high and low culture is less secure, of course, in the postmodern era in which the borders between high and low culture and the commercial and non-commercial are frequently transgressed. Nevertheless, the division is still maintained, as bookshop shelves and university curricula attest.

Materials such as the /Xam narratives are not positioned as literature in opposition to the non-literary in this way. Oral narrative is always literature, but of a special type. This in itself is unremarkable. Literature is a broad umbrella term that only becomes more specific when it is qualified by period, language, genre or region. It is a universal. All peoples have it just as they have a social structure and religion. But traditional literature is not generally distinguished from other literature in the same way that say Elizabethan drama would be from the 19th-century German novel. It is generally characterized as folklore or mythology (separated in some schemes but interchangeable when it comes to Bushman literature). It tends to be positioned outside history and also, to a lesser extent, outside a geographical place that is historically delineated. The category of traditional literature is not defined in terms of an opposition to popular or commercial culture but to its difference from contemporary literature. It is assumed also that it is to some degree a collective product rather than the self-conscious creation of gifted individuals. One might note that modern literature has seldom elicited the sort of functionalist or comparatist treatment that is commonly applied to traditional literature. One could also note that in Isidore Okpewho's opinion the term 'traditional' has replaced the unfashionable and offensive term 'primitive' (Okpewho 1983: 225).

Many of the common assumptions about traditional literature such as the /Xam narratives do not hold when examined more closely, I would suggest. The /Xam stories are more historically situated than the term 'traditional' would allow, although they are clearly embedded in a /Xam discursive tradition. Contemporary events in the colony and in the household often prompted Bleek and Lloyd's narrators to recount a particular narrative or supply a specific piece of cultural information (Bank 2006: 258–69, 287). Individual narrators also possessed distinctive interests (Hewitt 1986: 235–47). It has even been suggested that some of the narratives can be read as allegories for interactions with outsiders (Brown 1998: 62; Hewitt 1986: 229). The mode of composition was not the verbatim repetition of set pieces handed down unchanged from age to age but more akin to jazz (see Hewitt 2007).[4]

---

[4] The /Xam themselves appear not to have attached much importance to the distinction between different types of discourse. They used the term *Kukummi* to refer to all kinds of speech: stories, conversation and news (Hewitt 1986: 47). Even the historical and biographical materials in the collection include elements of what has been termed legend, mythologized real events or historicized mythology.

While some of the notions that are generally entertained in relation to traditional oral literature and mythology should be treated with caution, in my view, it cannot be denied that /Xam literature was produced in a completely different social, economic and historical environment from that in which contemporary literature occurs. It seems reasonable to ask whether the products of such disparate cultural, economic and historical circumstances can usefully be placed together under the umbrella term 'literature'. Contemporary literature, as we have seen, is supposed to display certain complex aesthetic characteristics as opposed to the simple commercial imperatives of popular culture. Is it at all appropriate to seek to find these characteristics in traditional literature or does it owe its status as literature (even of a certain type) purely to its curiosity and historical value as traditional? In order to further explore these questions in relation to the /Xam narratives, I should like to briefly consider the place of some of these concepts in the literary criticism of Italo Calvino, a producer of literature that has a strong metafictional character, and an admirer of traditional literature.

The Unassailable Literariness Of /Kaggen

Italo Calvino's incomplete and posthumously published text, *Six Memos for the Next Millennium* (1996), concerns itself with the intrinsic value of literature, the value it contains within itself, independent of socio-historical contexts of cultural production and consumption. The test of the literary value of a work occurs in the unique laboratory of the artist-critic's aesthetic sensibility. Calvino identifies, in a range of texts, the particular literary qualities that he prizes above all others. His chosen texts are drawn, in the main, from the high European literary tradition but also, interestingly in the context of this chapter, from Europe's folk tradition, in the European context, a pre-industrial version of popular culture that was regarded with some disdain by the educated religious elite.

He begins by asserting the future of literature in terms of its capacity to offer unique gifts: 'My confidence in the future of literature consists in the knowledge that there are things that only literature can give us, by means specific to it' (ibid.: 1). An opposition is brought into play between literature and that which is not literature. The precise nature of literature's alter ego is not as stable and obvious in Calvino's work, though, as it might have been for T. S. Eliot (1951), say, or Matthew Arnold (1869). It is not necessarily mass or commercial culture. Elsewhere, Calvino (1993) celebrates the mythic force that popular Hollywood movies exerted on his adolescent imagination and discovers inspiration even in the Parisian system of refuse disposal. Nevertheless, his chief position is that literature can give us something nothing else can. And the gift it bestows is of superior value. Other kinds of textual production, and, by implication, other kinds of cultural experience, cannot offer satisfactions of a similar order.

Calvino elaborates on the literary qualities he treasures in detail, devoting separate chapters to each of them (he died before writing the last chapter). He loves, above all, a quality he calls 'lightness', 'the subtraction of weight' (1993: 3). In 40 years of writing fiction, he states, 'I have tried to remove weight, sometimes from people, sometimes from heavenly bodies, sometimes from cities; above all I have tried to remove weight from the structure of stories and from language' (ibid.). 'Lightness' isn't so much a question of levity or absence of artistic seriousness and depth as the enlistment of 'the liveliness and mobility of the intelligence' (ibid.: 7) in the escape from life's 'unbearable weight' (ibid.). This sort of deployment of the intellect enables a change of 'approach' (ibid.) and helps accomplish a seeing of 'the world from a different perspective, with a different logic and with fresh methods of cognition and verification' (ibid.).

There is a 'lightness' of frivolity and a 'lightness' of thoughtfulness, the latter figured for Calvino in Boccaccio's account of the poet Guido Cavalcanti whom he presents as 'an austere philosopher' (ibid.: 10). One day Cavalcanti is 'walking meditatively among marble tombs near a church' (ibid.) when he is challenged by a group of Florence's *jeunesse dorée*. They dislike him for his refusal to join their group and for his suspected impiety. When they question him aggressively,

> Guido, seeing himself surrounded by them, answered quickly: "Gentlemen, you may say anything you like to me in your own home". Then, resting his hand on one of the great tombs and being very nimble, he leaped over it and landing on the other side, made off and rid himself of them (ibid.: 12).

This is the very image of 'lightness': 'the sudden agile leap of the poet-philosopher who raises himself above the weight of the world' (ibid.).

In literature, Calvino maintains, 'lightness' is, above all, a question of language:

> [T]hroughout the centuries two opposite tendencies have competed in literature: one tries to make language into a weightless element that hovers above things like a cloud or better, perhaps, the finest dust or, better still, a field of magnetic impulses. The other tries to give language the weight, density, and concreteness of things, bodies, and sensations (ibid.: 15).

Calvino values both weight and lightness but prefers and aspires to 'lightness', in which 'meaning is conveyed by a verbal texture that seems weightless' (ibid.: 16).

Calvino then leafs 'through the books in (his) library, seeking examples of lightness' (ibid.: 18). He quickly finds Mercutio, Puck and Ariel. More surprisingly perhaps, Hamlet qualifies on account of the way he and other Shakespearean characters 'distance themselves from their own drama, thus dissolving it into melancholy and irony'. He discovers more examples of 'lightness' in the pages of Cyrano de Bergerac and Swift.

The /Xam character /Kaggen, the Mantis, cannot, of course, be found in the pages of the European classics or even in collections of European folklore.[5] He is, nevertheless, an extraordinary exemplar of 'lightness', as Calvino describes it. He is a master of leaping away from tight situations: 'And the Mantis sprang aside and ran away, because he felt he could not bear it any longer. Then he called to the quiver and his shoes, that his things should follow him home' (Bleek 1923: 13). This action occurs in an encounter with the Will ó Wisp, another exponent of 'lightness'.

> Then the Mantis jumped out of the bag and got feathers; he flew up into the sky. The Ichneumon threw him up into the sky and he went along calling to the Hartbeest-calfskin bag. He said, as he went up into the sky: 'O shoes, you must come! O Hartbeest's children (to the bag), you must come. O quiver, you must come. O kaross, you must come! The cap must come' (ibid.: 16–17)!

'The Mantis quickly got feathers, he flew away. He called to the Hartebeest-skin bag: "O Hartebeest's children, leave here, we must fly"' (ibid.: 19). There are numerous similar examples in the Mantis stories of the Bleek and Lloyd collection.

Lightness, for Calvino, is more a question of the mind than of the body. /Kaggen, too, is a practitioner of mental agility: 'His thinking strings quickly told him to take off his shoe and throw it up into the sky, for the shoe to light up the earth for him' (ibid.: 4). Mobility of intelligence, the seeing of things from fresh angles, is his forte. It leads him into

---

[5] This, according to Carlos Valiente-Noailles (1993: 188), was not the case with the Kua of the central Kalahari who learnt stories off by heart and repeated them as accurately as possible. If true, this illustrates once again how careful one should be to avoid the quite common habit of referring to the Khoisan cultures of the region as though they were a single culture with only insignificant variants.

many unpredictable situations. But he is always light and quick enough to extricate himself from them.

The language of the /Kaggen narratives, even in a sometimes laboured Victorian translation exemplifies the linguistic qualities Calvino identifies with 'lightness'. The characters are precise in their speech and actions. Their words have the immediacy and concreteness of actions. Then there is the lightness of the /Kaggen stories of the First Times themselves, which are often amusing and seldom threatening. There is no death, permanent injury or essential evil. Instead there are transformations, abrupt reversals and miraculous reconstitutions.

Each of the other literary qualities Calvino discusses in his book could as easily be applied to the Mantis stories. The many qualities Calvino imputes to 'quickness', for instance, are evident in even a cursory reading of a /Xam narrative. 'Quickness' in language results in logical leaps and in statements that defy explanation. It involves digression: 'a strategy for putting off the ending, a multiplying of time within the work' (Bleek 1923: 46). Digression is one of the /Xam narrative most recurrent and striking. Perhaps the most important feature of 'quickness', though, is speed of narrative time. Consider the following passage from the story entitled, *The Dasse's and the Crow's story* (ibid.: 47):

> Kwammang-a once went visiting. They were two, he and the Mantis, and they went to the Bee's house, when the Dasses lived with the Bees.
>
> Then a young Bee offered Kwammang-a his ostrich egg-shell, out of which Kwammang-a drank; while a young Dasse offered the Mantis his ostrich egg-shell, into which he had put dirty water. So the Mantis drank out of the Dasse's egg-shell. When he tasted the Dasse's dirty water, he cursed the young Dasse.
>
> Then the Mother Dasse, who was on the hunting-ground, sneezed, and drops of blood came from her nostrils. Therefore stones rolled. The stones said "V v v v v," because stones which had stood fast were falling.
>
> Then the young Bee spoke to his Grandfather Kwammang-a; he said: "You should go to this gambro (a sort of cucumber); mother has made a hole in it. You get into it, for the Mantis was really with you, that man who has been teasing. Therefore hard things are falling upon you; for the Mantis who was teasing was really with you."
>
> Then Kwammang-a arose, he went quietly along, and quietly reached the hole in the gambro; he went to sit in it, while the Mantis was outside, because he had come later. He was covered up fast; the stones fell covering him up fast, while Kwammang-a lay loose.
>
> The women (at home) said: "What can be the matter? You ought to send the ring-necked Crow, that it may go and see where the people are."

And the ring-necked Crow went; it had on its neck a little piece of fat which was very small. It went and ate up the fat half-way and it turned back (ibid.: 47).

The events in this extract move with extraordinary alacrity. There are at least four shifts of physical location. Characters move rapidly in and out of the action. The text abjures explanation and explication, any element that would detract from the speed of the action. Perhaps the most important aspect of quickness for Calvino in the folktale is 'economy of expression' (ibid.: 37). As the extract just cited demonstrates, one of the features of the Mantis stories is the paring down of the stories to bare essentials. This accounts not only for much of their vitality but also for their mystery. It is the source of many questions whose answers are not immediately apparent. In relation to the last paragraph of the extract just quoted one might ask, for example, why it is the ring-necked crow in particular that should be sent. One might also wonder why the crow has a piece of fat on its neck and why eating this fat causes it to turn back.

What is the value, if any, of reading a /Xam text with these sorts of considerations in mind? Such an exercise, in my opinion, is useful insofar as it transports certain kinds of cultural production from the historical and generic ghetto of traditional mythology to the sphere of contemporary literary and cultural concern. The usual hierarchy between dominant, mainstream cultural systems and marginalized ones is to some extent unravelled. The aesthetic technologies and artistic resources of /Xam literature begin to emerge more clearly when they are treated as literature rather than as a prehistoric oddity. This move also illustrates that the usual tools of folkloristic analysis are by no means the only ways of reading the sorts of texts that have been traditionally their preserve. All of these are salutary effects. The problem, though, is that the /Xam narratives are still approached in terms of a general category that is extrinsic to them. Literature has replaced mythology or folklore. This is an improvement, in my opinion, but there is still the disregard for the way that /Xam discourse generates meaning in terms peculiar to it and also a lack of attention to the way that it positions itself for exegesis. As Karin Barber notes, all literary texts, verbal and written 'are set up to be interpreted in particular ways; they engage the hearer in specific kinds of hermeneutic activity' (1999: 28). In the remainder of this chapter I shall explore some of the ways in which the /Xam extract that I have already quoted (ibid.: 47) can be positioned within an intertextual field of signification that is also a field of interpretative possibility.

The Interdiscursive Character of /Xam Narrative

What happens if we try to read the story in terms of /Xam discourse itself? The first point to note is that some of the literary effects noted above could disappear. Many of the gaps in such a text result from our unfamiliarity with the /Xam interdiscursive field. The audience for these stories in the centuries and decades that preceded their telling in Mowbray would have been what Mathias Guenther describes as a 'high context group' (1996: 81). The references to the crows would have triggered many interlocking significations for them that are unavailable to a contemporary person who is not steeped in /Xam discourse as a living medium and for whom a /Xam narrative is divorced from the context of a performance and from all the non-verbal signifiers that would have attended such a performance.

The extract from the story I cited is not taken directly from the notebooks but from Dorothea Bleek's *The Mantis and His Friends*, an edited selection that Wilhelm Bleek's daughter published in 1923. She has intervened in particular ways in the story. Her version contains more incidents than the notebook versions by /Han≠Kass'o but also contains less repetition: 'some I have shortened by leaving out wearisome repetition' (Bleek 1923: Introduction).[6] She considerably underplays the scale of her manipulation of the texts. She does not, as she rather disingenuously suggests, simply provide a selection from the materials in the notebooks with needless repetition removed. She rewrites the language, in many instances. In addition, and much more controversially, she actually combines different texts into new texts. In effect, she takes it on herself to

---

[6] /Kaggen, the Mantis, is a character who occurs in the /Xam stories of the early formative times. This period is usually referred to as the First Times or the First Order and its inhabitants as the people of the Early Race, the First People or the First Bushmen. /Kaggen lives with his family in a time when animals were still people. The Dassie is his devoted but critical wife. Their adopted daughter, Porcupine, her husband, Kwammang-a (associated with the rainbow, in which he can be seen) and their son, the Mantis's grandson, Ichneumon (a type of mongoose), feature prominently. The Ichneumon is fond of the Mantis but is also able to criticize him. Between the Ichneumon and /Kaggen, as between all children and their grandparents, there exists a joking relationship. The Ichneumon often voices his father's concerns. As /Kaggen's son-in-law, Kwammang-a has an avoidance relationship with him and may not address him directly.

improve the narratives as they were presented by the informants: to make them better written literature, texts for readers rather than listeners. Her failure to signal her own part in the rewriting of the /Xam texts in the Bleek and Lloyd collection (already themselves a writing and a rewriting — a transcription of a verbal account that has been translated) could be seen as self-effacing. Dorothea Bleek is simply the editor, according to the title page, of a selection of Bushman folklore collected by Wilhelm Bleek and Lucy Lloyd. Her 'editing' could also be considered in a harsher light, of course: it is an example, perhaps, of a hegemonic ethnographic power to present and represent subjugated people for external consumption, a milder version of the brutal appropriation of their land and bodies by colonial forces.

Dorothea Bleek's versions, one could say at the very least, should be treated with caution since they misrepresent the narratives in the notebooks to varying degrees. I should like here to offer a partial defence of them, however, not in order to defend Bleek's editorial procedure as such but to support the proposition that a /Xam narrative should not be read in isolation from other narratives and from /Xam discourse in general. In forming a story from different texts in the collection, Bleek is following, not necessarily deliberately, the /Xam practice in which narrators continually rearrange themes and plots into narratives that are both new and also recognizably reinterpretations of other stories. The two texts from which she chiefly draws are in any event contiguous in the notebooks and are clearly related. The first (L.VIII.2: 6146–64)[7] contains the section that occurs in Dorothea Bleek's text about the ring-necked crow going out to look for the men who have been covered over by stones.[8]

---

[7] I follow common practice when referencing the Bleek and Lloyd notebooks. The letter L or B indicates whether the notebook was compiled by Wilhelm Bleek or Lucy Lloyd. The Roman numeral refers to the informant. For example, //Kabbo is consistently accorded the numeral II, Dia!kwain is indicated by the numeral V, and /Han#kass'o by VIII. The number following the Roman numeral indicates the number of the notebook collected by Lloyd from a single informant.

[8] By removing the 'wearisome repetition' she also transposes the story even more firmly into writing. Repetition with its dramatic opportunities is a distinguishing feature of /Xam oral narrative. Bleek herself included excerpts from this narrative in one of her *Bantu Studies* articles in order to illustrate the /Xam use of particular types of speech for certain animals, a technique that would have been much enhanced by repetition and one which disappears in translation (Hollmann 2005: 349–55).

On the way it eats most of the sheep fat that was placed on its neck to replenish it on its journey. It fails to find the men as does a second ring-necked crow. As a consequence of this primal event the ring-necked crow has today only a thin band of white around its neck. A pied crow is then sent out. It finds Kwammang-a and the others covered by the pile of stones and leads the rescuers to them. It does not touch the fat around its neck. The result of this restraint is that the Pied Crow today has a large band of white around its neck and on its chest.

The second major source for Bleek's version of the narrative, also by /Han#Kass'o, recounts the incident, some of which I quoted earlier, in which /Kaggen, the Mantis and Kwammang-a visit the bees. Kwammang-a enjoys the sweet honeyed water that the young bee gives him but /Kaggen curses the young Dasse (generally spelt as dassie nowadays) for giving him dirty water to drink. The Dasse's mother who is out on the hunting ground responds to her child's being cursed by sneezing drops of blood. These turn to stones that roll on /Kaggen and Kwammang-a and cover them. This narrative excludes the section about the crows altogether. It proceeds instead to describe how Kauru, the Dassie and the Mantis's wife (not to be confused with the mother in the story, spelt Dasse by Bleek) and his adopted daughter, the Porcupine are accompanied by the Giraffe, Elephant and Rhinoceros to the hunting ground where they remove Kwammang-a and the Mantis from under the pile of stones. Importuned by the Porcupine the 'people' first remove Kwammang-a as gently as possible so as not to hurt him. They are tempted to leave /Kaggen under the stones since he caused the trouble in the first place. /Kaggen's wife begs them to rescue him: he is her husband, after all, and his childlike nature means that he is not really responsible for his actions. They do rescue him but pull him out roughly. They soften a bit on the way home and anoint his wounds so that they begin to heal. /Kaggen's sister, the Blue Crane, is especially distressed to see his wounds when he reaches home.

Finally, /Kaggen is subjected to a series of admonitory lectures. His grandson, the Ichneumon, scolds him on behalf of Kwammang-a who, as /Kaggen's son-in-law may not address him directly. /Kaggen had especially violated the rules of visiting and interacting with strangers by complaining about the water he was given to drink. In so doing he put not only his own safety in danger but also that of Kwammang-a. /Kaggen had been warned about this sort of infraction countless times before but had failed to listen.

/Han#Kass'o's discourse about the crows from which Bleek draws for her composite narrative is a hybrid text that moves between fiction and non-fiction, the First Times and the present, aetiology and cultural information; it straddles narrative and the presentation of knowledge. It begins by supplying information about the naming of birds. The crow story follows on directly from a piece about why the secretary bird is called 'carry-feathers'. Much of the information about crows is located in the First Times since it deals with the origin of the appearance of the different crow species and also mentions the discovery by the pied crow of Kwammang-a under the stones, an event that occurs in the same First Time story of the Mantis, /Kwammang-a, the Dassie and the Bees that forms the backbone of Bleek's integrated version (she thus can be seen to be following /Han#Kass'o in integrating the two narratives since he links them in his first piece even though it is only in passing and he omits the crow incident in the second). But /Han#Kass'o's discourse about the crows also goes on to relate crows to springbok hunting as part of present hunting experience and practice.

This generic hybridity is common in the /Xam materials and presents particular difficulties for those would like to place the /Xam materials into categories — mythology, narrative, cultural information. It is no doubt partly attributable to the /Xam informants' not drawing the same rigid distinctions between fact and fiction, past and present and the real and the imaginary as their commentators do but also, and crucially for interpretation, to the fact that they were relating their narratives to an audience who were not steeped in /Xam culture and interdiscursivity and who consequently required a great deal of background explanation. In effect, the /Xam informants delivered a commentary on the narratives they recounted. Thus, the reference to the crow's finding Kwammang-a and /Kaggen that Bleek includes as a central incident in her version of the story (even using it in the title) is accompanied by a long discourse on the role of crows as messengers and intermediaries in /Xam hunting practice. We can ourselves augment this direct explanatory material by exploring the other references to crows in the collection. In this way, a sense of the intertextuality that a /Xam auditor experienced can to some extent be obtained.

There are two extended disquisitions on the role of the pied crow as instrumental in the finding of missing men in the /Xam archive; both display the same sort of mixing of genres and of 'fiction' and 'non-fiction' that characterizes /Han#kass'o's piece about the crows. !Kweit ta //ken's relates directly to husbands who have gone missing while hunting and like /Han#kass'o's goes on to give intricate detail about children, crows and springbok hunting. Her discourse also contains a reference to stones falling on men and to fluids connected with bees and dassies, in this case their urine. Dia!kwain's piece (BXXVI.2473–86) brings many of the same elements together with a piece of near contemporary history. Once again two different kinds of crow are sent out to look for husbands who have not returned from the hunting grounds. The women put sheep fat around a /xuru (ring-necked) crow's neck. When it returns without finding the men, they transfer the meat to a /kagen (pied) crow's neck. It finds vultures devouring the corpses of the men. They had been murdered by Boers (Dutch-speaking farmers).

These texts are directly and obviously linked to the events in the narratives. There are also other references to crows in the materials, though, that could be investigated, especially relating to the more sinister and ambiguous figure of the black crow, often accused of spying for lions (Hollmann 2005: 41–44) but also sometimes providing a warning of their presence, a role that can in some ways be contrasted with the ring-necked crow's neutral stance towards humans and the pied crow's benign one.

So what do we make of the signifier 'crow' in this story? In the very limited space of this chapter, I can only give some indications. Perhaps to a comparitist the first and most obvious point to note would be the correspondence between the roles of crows in the story and the role of crows in other literature. The story of the crow as messenger in the biblical story of Noah's Ark comes to mind, for a start. It is one with which, incidentally, the /Xam narrators might well have been familiar. It is not surprising that widespread and general patterns of meaning that relate to crows exist if we take into account their wide distribution and certain obvious characteristics about them: their cawing, their predilection for coming close to men, the divide they span as carrion eaters between the living and the dead. The position of the crow in the regional literature is another stratum of investigation that would provide further indications as to the way that the sign crow might be signifying in the story. Most important, though, in my opinion is a detailed investigation of the signifier in the /Xam interdiscursive field itself. We are not only dealing with the universal sign 'crow', after all, but with particular species of crows in a specific environment. In the same way, we need to investigate how the signifier 'crow' (and there are at least three terms in the materials for three different species) generates meaning in /Xam discourse itself.

This picture becomes especially complex when we consider the field of signifiers that are interconnected with these signs and the intertextual links that they in turn provoke. In this story we have links with fat, missing husbands and submersion by stones. When we consider the piece by !Kweit ta //ken, we have in addition, a recurrent association with dassies and bees which corroborates Dorothea Bleek's bringing of her two texts together. The web of connotations that link fat, bees and honey in the archive is enormous. For a start each of these signifiers is heavily linked to relations between the sexes and to female sexuality. Although the signifier 'springbok' does not appear in Bleek's text it occurs in both /Han#kass'o's and !Kweit ta //ken's discourse about the crows. Even if not directly present in a particular narrative it would have still continued to signify through its association with crows. It is a potent multivocal sign.[9]

As I have mentioned several times, the role of the crows in finding the men is not referred to at all in the main text from which Bleek constructs the story. Had she omitted the crow materials, as she might easily have done without any damage to the story, then the detailed investigation of the crow signifier would not, it might be assumed, have been necessary. The information gap about the crow that I referred to earlier in the context of Calvino's comments about literature would not have arisen in the first place. It is quite likely, though, that the sign 'crow' would still have emerged as one to be considered in the course of the examination of some the other signifiers in the story just as the signifier 'springbok', as I remarked previously, soon emerges when the intertextual field is explored.[10] A search connected to submersion by stones, for example, would immediately lead to the linking of crows with the events in the story. 'Crow' as an absent signifier would, in all likelihood, have been present for a /Xam auditor through a familiar web of interdiscursivity. Bleek, it could be argued, makes explicit for non-/Xam readers what was implicit for /Xam auditors.

A consideration of this wider discursive field also points to its consistency across the categories into which commentators have placed the /Xam materials. The piece with the crows used by Bleek, as I have already

---

[9] A considerable amount of work has been conducted on the resemblances between narratives in the southern African region, especially between those that belong to the different Khoisan traditions (see, for example, Barnard 1992; Guenther 1989; Schmidt 1989, 1996). This has been attributed to borrowing, a pan-Khoisan worldview and even to common shamanistic experience.

[10] For an extended discussion on the sign 'springbok' in /Xam discourse, see Wessels (2007).

mentioned, moves from 'mythological' time, the submersion of the First Time character Kwammang-a with stones to springbok hunting in the 'present', the everyday world of the /Xam before the arrival of the settlers into their territory in the mid-19th century. !Kweit ta //ken's piece also refers to the mythological Dasse and Bee characters in the same discourse as looking for lost husbands and springbok hunting. We cannot, in any event, easily separate the cultural information from the obviously literary materials. Did /Xam women really capture crows, tie sheep fat around their necks and send them out to find lost husbands, a motif that recurs in Dia!kwain's account of a Boer massacre? Surely this invites a literary interpretation as much as do the events in the First Time narrative in which 'Kwammang-a is Found by Crows'?

An investigation of the whole Bleek and Lloyd corpus provides, then, a wider context for the reference in the story to the crows. It is this wider context that in my view provides the best resource for interpreters who wish to investigate the /Xam texts more closely. The Bleek and Lloyd archive provides a huge reservoir of cross references.[11] In addition, the narratives and other pieces in the collection are often accompanied by explanations or elaborations by the informants, usually in the form of notes recorded on the reverse sides of the pages of the notebooks. In this way we do have access to some degree an indigenous exegesis. Although we can never know what sort of questions a /Xam listener might have asked of a performance or how he/she might have interpreted these answers we can to some degree surmise what answers a /Xam informant might have given to our questions.

I have only discussed a small part of the story in the limited confines of this chapter. To do justice to this text, it would require a much broader investigation of its signifiers. The characters that appear in it, such as Kwammang-a, /Kaggen, the Porcupine and the Blue Crane, feature in many narratives. Their roles in this narrative have to be related to this wider context. But the most detailed work concerns the investigation of the signifiers in the story. The list is very long. It includes fat, honey, blood, sneezing, stones, the elephant and the giraffe. The works of

---

[11] Cross-referencing is a procedure that has become a lot easier now that the archive is available online, thanks largely to the efforts of Pippa Skotnes and her team (http://www.lloydbleekcollection.uct.ac.za/ [accessed 9 April 2012]). The digitalized collection is also available on a DVD that accompanies Skotnes (2007).

Roger Hewitt (1986), David Lewis-Williams (1996, 1998, 2000), John Parkington (2002), Jeremy Hollmann (2005) and Alan James (2001), among others, provides very useful leads about how some of these signs signify in /Xam discourse, although the main resource remains, in the absence of living /Xam informants, the notebooks themselves.

While I argue for the location of signs like 'crow', 'sneezing' and 'fat' in the web of /Xam signification, I do not mean that the /Xam stories occur within a hermetically-sealed system. The stories do have relationships with other literatures and can be compared with them, as my earlier discussion of them in terms of Calvino's categories illustrates. It is this relationship that allows them to be read or heard with enjoyment by readers or auditors who have little acquaintance with their discursive context. The stories undoubtedly exhibit literary qualities that need to be described and celebrated. I would argue, though, that these aesthetic properties are in fact often a consequence of their interdiscursivity. Storytellers can take shortcuts, omit explanation and use allusions because of the location of their auditors within a wider discursive field. The multivocality of the materials, and thus their literariness, exists by virtue of their location within a wider /Xam intertextual field. Calvino concludes his book by celebrating the literary quality of multiplicity. He relates this property especially to the encyclopaedic character of some contemporary novels which work 'above all as a network of connections between the events, the people, and the things of the world' (Calvino 1996: 105). My argument in this chapter is that /Xam discourse itself displays the property of multiplicity. It comprises a network of connections that span individual stories and which are endlessly capable of new formations. A consideration of this network provides new insight into the way that narratives generate meaning. But the fact that the signs exist not as themselves but as part of a shifting network of signifiers also makes the meanings we do uncover difficult to hold as they rapidly multiply, change and disappear before our eyes.

References

Arnold, Matthew. 1869. *Culture and Anarchy: An Essay in Political and Social Criticism*. London: John Murray.

Bank, Andrew. 1999. 'Anthropology, Race and Evolution: Rethinking the Legacy of Wilhelm Bleek'. Paper presented at Seminar, 14 April, University of the Western Cape, http://scnc.ukzn.ac.za/doc/SOC-cult/Race-Racism/Bank-A_Anthropology_race_evolution_Wilhelm_Bleek.pdf (accessed 4 April 2012).

Bank, Andrew. 2006. *Bushmen in a Victorian World: The Remarkable Story of the Bleek-Lloyd Collection of Bushman Folklore*. Cape Town: Double Storey.

Barber, Karin. 1999. 'Poetry, Obscurity and Exegesis in African Oral Praise Poetry', in Duncan Brown (ed.), *Oral Literature and Performance in Southern Africa*, pp. 27–49. Oxford: James Currey.

Barnard, Alan. 1992. *Hunters and Herders: A Comparative Ethnology of the Khoisan Peoples*. Cambridge: Cambridge University Press.

Bleek, Dorothea. 1923. *The Mantis and his Friends: Bushman Folklore from Material Collected by the Late Dr. W. H. I. Bleek and the Late Dr. Lucy C. Lloyd*. Cape Town: Maskew Miller.

Bleek, Wilhelm and Lucy Lloyd. 1911. *Specimens of Bushman Folklore*. London: George Allen.

Brown, Duncan. 1995. 'The Society of the Text: the Oral Literature of the /Xam Bushmen', *Critical Arts*, 9(2): 76–108.

———. 1998. *Voicing the Text: South African Oral Poetry and Performance*. Cape Town: Oxford University Press.

Calvino, Italo. 1993. *The Road to San Giovanni*. New York: Pantheon.

———. 1996. *Six Memos for the Next Millennium*. London: Vintage.

Eliot, T. S. 1951. *Selected Essays*. London: Faber & Faber.

Guenther, Mathias. 1989. *Bushman Folktales: Oral Traditions of the Nharo of Botswana and the /Xam of the Cape*. Wiesbaden: Franz Steiner Verlag.

———. 1996. 'Attempting to Contextualise /Xam Oral Tradition', in Janette Deacon and Thomas Dowson (eds), *Voices from the Past: /Xam Bushmen and the Bleek and Lloyd Collection*, pp. 77–99. Johannesburg: Witwatersrand University Press.

———. 1999. *Tricksters and Trancers: Bushman Religion and Society*. Bloomington: Indiana University Press.

Hewitt, Roger. 1986. *Structure, Meaning and Ritual in the Narratives of the Southern San*. Hamburg: Helmut Buske Verlag.

———. 2007. 'Reflections on Narrative', in Pippa Skotnes (ed.), *Claim to the Country: The Archive of Wilhelm Bleek and Lucy Lloyd*, pp. 161–67. Johannesburg: Jacana.

Hollmann Jeremy (ed.). 2005. *Customs and Beliefs of the /Xam Bushmen*. Johannesburg: Witwatersrand University Press.

James, Alan. 2001. *The First Bushman's Path: Stories, Songs and Testimonies of the /Xam of the Northern Cape*. Pietermaritzburg: University of Natal Press.

Lewis-Williams, David. 1996. '"A Visit to the Lion's House": The Structures, Metaphors and Sociopolitical Significance of a Nineteenth-Century Bushman Myth', in Janette Deacon and Thomas Dowson (eds), *Voices from the Past: /Xam Bushmen and the Bleek and Lloyd Collection*, pp. 122–41. Johannesburg: Witwatersrand University Press.

———. 1998. 'The Mantis, the Eland and the Meerkats : Conflict and Mediation in a Nineteenth-Century San Myth', *African Studies*, 56(2): 195–216.

———. (ed.). 2000. *Stories that Float from Afar: Ancestral Folklore of the San of Southern Africa*. Cape Town: David Philip.

Moran, Shane. 2001. 'Specimens of 'Bushman' Studies', *Wasafiri*, 34: 46–51.

———. 2009. *Representing Bushmen: South Africa and the Origin of Language*. Rochester, NY: University of Rochester Press.

Okpewho, Isidore. 1983. *Myth in Africa*. Cambridge: Cambridge University Press.

Parkington, John. 2002. *The Mantis, the Eland and the Hunter*. Cape Town: Krakadouw Trust.

Schmidt, Sigrid. 1989. *Catalogue of the Khoisan Folktales of Southern Africa*. Hamburg: Helmut Buske Verlag.

———. 1996. 'The Relevance of the Bleek/Lloyd Folktales to the General Khoisan Traditions', in Janette Deacon and Thomas Dowson (eds), *Voices from the Past: /Xam Bushmen and the Bleek and Lloyd Collection*, pp. 100–21. Johannesburg: Witwatersrand University Press.

Skotnes, Pippa. 2007. *Claim to the Country: The Archive of Wilhelm Bleek and Lucy Lloyd*. Johannesburg: Jacana.

Solomon, Anne. 2009. 'Broken Strings: Interdisciplinarity and /Xam Oral Literature', *Critical Arts*, 23(1): 26–41.

Szalay, M. 1995. *The San and the Colonization of the Cape 1770–1879 Conflict, Incorporation, Acculturation*. Cologne: Rüdiger Köppe Verlag.

Traill, Anthony. 1996. '!Khwa-Ka Hhouiten Hhouiten, "The Rush of the Storm": The Linguistic Death of the /Xam', in Pippa Skotnes (ed.), *Miscast: Negotiating the Presence of the Bushmen*, pp. 161–83. Cape Town: University of Cape Town Press.

Valiente-Noailles, Carlos. 1993. *The Kua: Life and Soul of the Central Kalahari Bushmen*. Rotterdam: Balkema.

Wessels, Michael. 2007. 'The Discursive Character of the /Xam Texts: a Consideration of the /Xam "Story of the Girl of the Early Race Who Made Stars"', *Folklore*, 119(1): 307–24.

14

The Adverse Effect of Migrant Fishing on Students' Competence in English in the Niger Delta of Nigeria

Macaulay Mowarin

♋

The Niger Delta region of Nigeria is associated mainly with the exploitation of crude oil which accounts for most of the nation's revenue. This chapter discusses the state of education in Nigeria with a focus on migrant farmers in the Niger Delta region. It discusses the adverse effect of migrant fishing on the education of the children of migrant fishermen who relocate to Kpakiama and Torugbene in the Burutu Local Government Area of Delta State during the fishing seasons. These fishermen go to the two communities to fish with their children who are either primary or secondary school pupils. They therefore miss the first and third terms which span September to December and April to July respectively. When these children return to school, they find it difficult to cope academically. The chapter observes that migrant fishing is the main cause of the high failure and drop-out rate of students living in the creeks in the region. It proffers solutions to this problem by advocating the establishment of mobile schools in these communities during the fishing seasons.

The Faulty Education System in Nigeria

Another factor that acted as a barrier to the flourishing of creative minds in Nigeria is the lack of innovation in our system of education. Over a hundred years after education was introduced into Nigeria by the missionaries, the nation's educational system from primary to tertiary levels still focuses on producing administrative staff for government ministries, parastatal organizations and the private sector just as it produced catechists and interpreters for missionaries, and clerks and administrative officers for colonial administrators about a century ago. The nation's system of education can, therefore, be aptly described as *certificated education* since it focuses on rote learning where students cram and struggle to pass. The bottom line of this system of education is the acquisition of a certificate and not the acquisition of knowledge. This is the main reason for the spate of examination malpractice and certificate racketeering. This system of education encourages the production of arts and social sciences graduates at the expense of science education. Obsolete science equipment in the nation's educational institutions does not expose the few science students to the modern scientific gadgets of a technologically-driven economy. This obsolete, uncreative and non-innovative educational system has increased graduate unemployment, since most Nigerian graduates have been shut out of the globalized labour market. Until the nation's educational system conforms to the 1990 world declaration on education which outlined the salient qualities of good, innovative and creative education, Nigeria will remain shut off from modern knowledge.

Language Deficiency in English

Language deficiency in English can be attributed to the dominance of the policy of 'English mainly' as the language of education and the lack of qualified English teachers in most of the nation's primary and secondary schools. In addition, the lack of good instructional materials like teaching aids and textbooks also engenders language deficit in English. 'English mainly' as the language of education in Nigeria introduces pupils — from Pre-Primary to Primary 1 — to English as the language of instruction despite the fact that some of these pupils are being introduced to the English language for the first time. The national policy on education (Federal Republic of Nigeria 1971), revised in 1981 (Federal Republic of Nigeria 1981), states that pupils should be taught in their mother tongue from Primary 1 to Primary 3. However, introducing English as the language of instruction from primary 1 has increased semi-literacy and the illiteracy rate in Nigeria. The concomitant of the language deficiency for most children from rural areas and urban slums manifests itself in truancy, poor performance in examinations, examination malpractices and a high drop-out rate among the two classes of children identified above. The few children exempted from the problem of language deficiency in English are those of the élite. These children are exposed to English in their homes before they enrol in primary schools. They constitute a minority among Nigerian children.

Francis Egbokhare (2004: 10) grimly observes the adverse effect of 'English mainly' as the language of instruction on the nation's educational system thus:

> An English only or even an English mainly policy necessarily condemns most people and thus the country as a whole to a permanent state of mediocrity, since people are unable to be spontaneous, creative and self-confident if they cannot use their first language (ibid.).

Incompetence by most Nigerian children in the language of instruction serves as a barrier to the acquisition of creativity and innovation skills because it adversely affects cognitive processes like positive operative thought, formal languages and elaborated codes. Competence in English is imperative for Nigerian children since it is the nation's official language and the default language of science and technology. If properly introduced to primary school pupils as a second language, English would serve as a catalyst for the churning out of young creative and innovative Nigerians, thereby launching the nation into the knowledge era.

Education in Southern and Northern Nigeria

The level of education in southern Nigeria is believed to be higher than that in northern Nigeria. Some reasons given for the gulf between the two regions are discussed in this section.

First, southern Nigeria was introduced to western education by the missionaries in the 19th century and the first primary and secondary schools in Nigeria were established in Lagos, Abeokuta and Calabar in southern Nigeria. Second, the introduction of free education by the premier of Western Region, the late chief Obafemi Awolowo, in 1958 also furthered the rise of western education in southern Nigeria. Third, Christianity was introduced mainly to southern Nigeria and this religion is regarded as a forerunner of western education. In fact, the earliest schools established in southern Nigeria were set up by Catholic, Anglican, Methodist and Baptist missionaries and by philanthropists.

In northern Nigeria, on the other hand, the main religion was Islam, since the region was first conquered by Othman Dan Fodio. So, Islamic education took precedence over western education. Western education is therefore a recent development in northern Nigeria. The fact cannot be gainsaid however, that there are Christians in parts of northern Nigeria. These Christians are found mainly in the middle belt region which is closer to southern Nigeria. However, they constitute a minority when compared with the Moslems in northern Nigeria.

The fact that southern Nigeria imbibed western education earlier than northern Nigeria is also buttressed by the establishment of four of the first five universities in Nigeria. While the University of Ibadan, the University of Lagos, the University of Nigeria, Nsukka, and the University of Ife (now Obafemi Awolowo University, Ile-Ife) are in southern Nigeria, Ahmadu Bello University, Zaria, was the only university in northern Nigeria before 1976.

Education in the Niger Delta Region

However, there is also a disparity in the level of educational attainment in the three geo-political zones in southern Nigeria. While the level of education is highest in the south-west zone, it is lowest in the south-south zone or the Niger Delta. The spread and quality of education is not evenly distributed and the terrain of the region can be used as the parameter for assessing the disparity between the levels of education in the region. The quality of education as well as the number of schools in the dry land in the Niger Delta region is higher than in the riverine area of the region. The main reason why the quality of education is very low in the riverine area of the Niger Delta is the inhospitable nature of the terrain. There is a lack of water, electricity and affordable means of transportation. Due to the above-mentioned deficiencies, many teachers refuse postings to these inhospitable terrains. In addition, almost all the tertiary institutions in the region are found in the dry lands of the region. A minute number of the higher institutions in the region are found in the creeks. Using Delta state as an example, three universities, are owned by the federal government, one is owned by the state government and one is privately owned. The state government also established three Colleges of Education and three Polytechnics. Incredibly enough, none of these institutions was established in the riverine area of the state, which comprises six out of the 18 local government areas.

Ironically, most of the gas and crude oil found in the Niger Delta is located in the creeks. The deprivation of the indigenes of the creeks of basic social and educational amenities is the main cause of the militancy in the region; most if not all, of the militants fighting for the emancipation of the Niger Delta are from the creeks.

Oil exploitation has brought about a dramatic change to the erstwhile environmental-friendly Niger Delta region. With oil exploitation, the numerous rivers and creeks became polluted; fish and other aquatic creatures met their untimely death. Loss of aquatic life also connotes the displacement of people from their natural habitats once their rivers are polluted. Since they can neither fish, bathe, cook nor wash in the polluted water, their logical option is to relocate from their natural habitat to a new and strange one. Many activists from the region who opposed the poverty and environmental degradation were either jailed or executed. A patent case is the trial of the Ogoni Nine and their eventual execution on 9 November 1995. This date is now tagged *Black Friday*. For daring to draw world attention to the devastating effects of environmental pollution in the Niger Delta, Ken Saro-Wiwa and other eight prominent Ogoni activists paid the supreme price with their lives. This execution was the precursor to the military regime in the region.

The lack of basic social amenities like cheap means of transportation, electricity, and pipe-borne water coupled with the environmental degradation of the region caused by unbridled exploitation of crude oil and gas has resulted in the lack of cottage industries in these parts of the Niger Delta region. While the intractable terrain and the environmental degradation of the creeks is one of the main reasons why education is at a low ebb in the creeks of the Niger Delta region, migratory or itinerant fishing is another important factor.

Fulani Cattle Herdsmen from the North and Migrant Fishermen in the Niger Delta

Two groups of people whose means of livelihood involve itinerancy are the Fulani herdsmen from the north and migrant fishermen from the Niger Delta region. The Fulani are cattle rearers who lack a permanent abode. Their place of abode is premised on the availability of grass pasture to feed their cattle. During the dry season, they migrate, with their cattle from the north to the southern part of the country. Those who remain in the north migrate to river banks since there is lush vegetation around the banks for the cattle to feed on. Even within the southern part of Nigeria, the Fulani cattle men do not become permanent residents but camp in a particular area for about two to four weeks and then relocate to another area.

The nomadic livelihood of these herdsmen has adversely affected their children educationally. Rather than change school on a monthly basis, these children are not encouraged to attend school at all; the boys learn the art of cattle rearing from their father while the girls learn the art of preserving and selling milk from the cattle known as *fura do nunu* from their mothers. The illiteracy rate among these people is astonishingly high.

However, the federal government has come to the aid of the children educationally by establishing the Board of Nomadic Education. The schools are mobile and the teachers follow the herdsmen from one camp to another to teach their children. Due to the establishment of Nomadic education, the level of education of the children is increasing rapidly. However, the level of education of these children is quite below that of children of non-itinerant parents.

Migrant Fishing in Burutu and Bomadi Local Government Areas of Delta State

As stated earlier, numerous oil spillages have decimated aquatic life in the rivers and creeks of the Niger Delta region. Yet fishing still remains the main occupation of most indigenes who live in the riverine areas. Like subsistence farming, fishing is also a seasonal occupation in the region. The two fishing seasons are May to July (first season) and October to early December (second season). These two periods are at the onset of the rainy season and the beginning of the dry season respectively. It is believed that before the pollution of the region's rivers and creeks, fish were found in the region. Due to environmental degradation, fish are now found in large quantities in a few designated areas.

It is to these areas that fishermen migrate during the fishing season. In Bayelsa State, the designated fishing settlements are Bennet Island and Bass, and in Delta State the two designated fishing camps are Torugbene and Kpaiama, both in Burutu Local Government Area. During the fishing season, families migrate to these two fishing settlements to fish. Those that fish are mainly adult males and females and most of them are husbands and wives. However, children of school age between the ages of six and 18 also accompany their parents to these fishing settlements.

Unfortunately, there are no schools in these settlements since they are occupied for four months in a year at most.

These four months are, however, crucial to the nation's academic calendar. While the first season is part of the nation's third term which ends with promotion examinations, the second season is part of the first term in the three-term academic calendar. As stated earlier, educational institutions in the riverine areas are poorly staffed and infrastructure like classrooms and learning materials are in a state of disrepair and short supply respectively.

Even students who attend school regularly throughout the academic year have rather poor results compared to those of other students in other parts of the state. The fact cannot be gainsaid that the results of these students will be worse than that of their counterparts in dry land. The poor performance of the students, who either follow their parents or go to the settlements on their own to raise money for their upkeep or their education, can be attributed to the following reasons.

For students that have just gained admission into Primary 1, they spend only about a month at school and then follow their parents to the settlement. Basic knowledge in English language and other subjects that they would have acquired during the first term is lost. They come back to school in January, which is the beginning of the second term, and having lost the basic knowledge they were supposed to have acquired during the first term, they find it difficult to cope. At the beginning of the third term, they go back to the fishing settlements with their parents. In three years at school, they lose interest and end up as drop-outs.

The fate that befalls these Primary 1 pupils also befalls those who have just gained admission to Junior Secondary Schools (JSS) because they will also find it difficult to cope. While the girls end up going into marriage as minors the boys become miscreants.

The adverse effect of migrant fishing is quite obvious in the case of students who continue their education until they write their external examinations. These include primary school pupils in Primary Six who are reading to write their Primary Six leaving certificate examination, those in JSS III who are ready to write their JSS III examination and the final year senior secondary students preparing for their senior secondary school (SSS) certificate examination.

The results of these students are always woeful when compared to those of their counterparts in other parts of the state or in the country in general. The intermittent periods when the students leave school to fish adversely affects them academically because they miss part of the curriculum every session. So, when they sit for external examinations their performances are always woeful. Many of these students do not continue their education after they see their poor results. This is why these riverine areas have very few graduates from tertiary institutions.

Revitalizing the Education of Children of Migrant Fishermen

The problem of the poor performance of the children of migrant fishermen can be solved if the following measures are taken. First, a new town can be built around the fishing settlement to make the fishermen permanent residents of this town. This new community would definitely have standard and well-equipped primary and secondary schools for the children of these fishermen and women. However, the problem that might emanate from this solution is the fact that the fishermen and women might not want to stay after the fishing season since they engage in other occupations like trading and farming when the fishing season is over.

Secondly, a commission could be established for migrant fishermen in the same way as it was established for Nomadic Education. The commission should be known as 'The National Commission for Migrant Fishing Education'. The purpose of this commission would be to set up mobile schools which would be in session during the fishing seasons. Students would be taught from Primary 1 to SSS III. With the establishment of this commission, the drop-out rate would reduce drastically and their performance in external examinations would improve dramatically since they would not lose any weeks in school because they migrated to the fishing settlement. For this commission to be successful, teachers that will be employed by the commission should be given incentives to encourage them to do their work effectively. If this commission is not set up, the people in the riverine area will remain backward educationally in a globalized world which is now a global village.

Conclusion

The close connection between literacy and development, on the one hand, and illiteracy and underdevelopment, on the other hand, has been a recurring theme. This chapter has discussed the high illiteracy rate among children of migrant fishermen in the Niger Delta region. It took an overview of the faculty education system which has stalled the nation's socio-economic and technological development. It undertook a comparative analysis of education in southern and northern Nigeria and gave reasons why the level of education in southern Nigeria is higher than that in the northern part of the country. The chapter analyzed the adverse effects of nomadic and migrant fishing on education and, finally, it proffered solutions to the problem.

References

Egbokhare, Francis. 2004. 'Breaking Barriers: ICT Language Policy and Development. Interdisciplinary Discourse of the Postgraduate School'. University of Ibadan.

Federal Republic of Nigeria. 1971. *National Policy on Education*. Lagos: NERC/Federal Government Press.

———. 1981. *National Policy on Education*. Lagos: NERC/Federal Government Press.

———. 2004. *National Policy on Education*. Lagos: NERC/Federal Government Press.

15

Gender Relations in Marginalized Communities

A Case Study of Women in Maasai Oral Literature

Helen Oronga A. Mwanzi

♋

According to Ole Ntimama, a prominent Maasai leader who is also a senior politician:

> The Maasai lost their lands to the colonizers. They were banished from their ancestral lands of the Rift Valley and driven to the malaria and tsetse fly infested southern reserves like the Red Indians of North America. There were no schools, no primary health care services and no infrastructure at all. It was human suffering for over one hundred years. For all the suffering, for all the marginalization, for all the dispossession, for all the degradation of our culture and our environment . . . it is the woman and the child who became the main sufferers, and it is the indigenous woman who was perpetually glued to poverty, hunger and diseases (Mwanzi 2006: 3).

This speech leads me to the point of my argument: the Maasai are marginalized and the marginalized position of the tribe is doubled in the case of the women of that tribe. I state this in the light of Ole Ntimama's assertion — 'it is the women and the children who became the main sufferers' (ibid.: 2). Being 'perpetually glued to poverty, hunger and disease' is the worst form of marginalization. It is tantamount to being denied the right to life itself. That Ole Ntimama recognizes this in his anthropological writing about his people is in itself an admission on the part of the dominant male that things have not been right for the womenfolk;

yet as the analysis of the community's oral literature will reveal, these marginalized folk are the bedrock of the life of the community as one of human beings endowed with sense, sensibility and soul and mind as well as flesh and blood.

The Maasai are nomadic pastoralists whose present day abode is the Great Rift Valley of Kenya. The term 'marginalization' is almost synonymous with the life of certain pastoral tribes, the Maasai being the largest such group. This chapter is guided by the assumption that the marginalization of a community spells double marginalization for that community's womenfolk. Further to this is the view that the oral literature of a people does hold a mirror to the gender relations within that community. I, therefore, intend to analyze three narratives with a view to documenting the way women among the Maasai, a marginalized community, are regarded and regard themselves. The chapter also intends to discuss what I view as the portrayal of the Maasai woman in these selected stories.

First of all, we recognize the fact that among the Maasai, women are viewed with respect, as three of the four narratives cited in this chapter will demonstrate. They are portrayed as human beings who are capable of making decisions that should be respected. This image is, however, blurred in one narrative: the fourth story in which the woman is presented as a muffled voice; otherwise the dominant image of the women is positive.

One such narrative has it that the first Maasai ailed and died; he was buried, but he did not rest in his grave. Instead of resting and protecting the clan, he kept sending his apparition in the form of a snake to the clan. Everyone who saw this apparition screamed and ran off for dear life. However, one day a woman saw it and instead of screaming and running for dear life, she took courage and gave the snake a second look. She noticed that it was hungry, so she gave it some of the milk she had with her. The snake accepted; then she recognized something special about it though she could not tell exactly what it was. She shared this information with fellow women; and from that day, women have been recognized to be the feeders of the spirits of departed elders and medicine men — the only two categories of people who traditionally were accorded burial as the rest of the Maasai were left unburied for carrion animals and birds to eat.

I find this image of women to be an emboldening one. Listening to this oral narrative, young women are bound to see something special about their role. The courage with which this primeval woman of the narrative faced the snake, approached and even fed it is memorable; it draws a mental image of courage and valour, kindness and self sacrifice. That it is a woman to whom this enviable image is assigned is indicative of the esteem with which women are held in the Maasai community. Further to this is the extension of the narrative to include the clause, 'and from that day women have been recognized to be the feeders of the spirits of departed elders and medicine men' (Hollis 1905: 172). This voice of the narrator suggests the awe in which women among the Maasai are held. It suggests that the world of women among the Maasai is one clouded with mystery and wonder: a world where men dare not tread carelessly. This regard seems to highlight gender roles in such a way that one is likely to see women as the spiritual half of the community while the men are the physical half, engaged in providing physical security, including livelihood. In this highlight one can read a respect for the symbiotic relationship between the two sexes: an informed recognition of the important role each sex plays in the life of the community in the harsh environment they live in.

A closer examination of the image of the woman and the snake communicating in a social context in which the narrative has stated that everyone ran away for dear life reminds one of Eve's encounter with the serpent in the Garden of Eden. Adam had certainly seen this creature several times; he had even named it 'snake/serpent', but he had not noticed its interest in communicating with human beings. However, when Eve came across it, she held a conversation with it; special communication took place between human and reptile. The curiosity of the Maasai woman in the story and that of Eve in the Garden resemble one another. The difference lies in the actions of the two: in one it is the Serpent which offers the woman delicious food (a rare fruit that must not be eaten), and in the other it is the woman who offers the snake delicious food (milk).

Stretched further, this story yields interesting symbolic information about the woman's psyche. In this case, one is thinking of the shape of the snake, the gender of the snake and the fascination for the same animal in both stories. The oblong shape that resembles that of the male sexual organ is of as much significance as is the male gender of the snake in both stories. In the primitive mind of young girls, the male sexual organ is likened to all sorts of ordinary thick and long/oblong objects such as cassava (a Luhya riddle: 'The cassava in your father's garden' — 'A penis'). Thus, the Maasai woman's response to the snake and Eve's response that both resemble the Luhya woman's response tell the audience about the freedom of thought that these women exercise when faced with the wonders of their world *vis-à-vis* that of the men.

In addition, it is noteworthy that in both the Maasai and the Hebrew narratives the two snakes and the two women are associated with the first human beings and the first reptiles on the earth. This narrative, therefore, presents the audience with a woman as being the first to appreciate the difference in the two sexes of the human species and to take interest in that difference. Viewed from this angle, this old narrative has liberating force in it even as it suggests voluntary decision to serve the male with delicacies — milk. It is a rich narrative.

The second narrative that I would like to connect to the portrayal of women in Maasai oral literature, is the myth about the voices and sounds of lowing cattle around Dony Erok or the mountain of smoke (Hollis 1905: 189). Here it was believed that voices of people and lowing of cattle could be heard, and women took there gourds of milk and left them there for these beings to drink. I find this myth portraying women as peculiarly religious and, in a community that is remarkably religious (ibid.: 10), this fact says something positive about how the women regard themselves *vis-à-vis* the mysterious, the divine or the invisible. In this myth they go out to meet the invisible and to give the invisible their best and most valued possession: milk, their lifeline. That the myth shows them as the sole decision makers in this matter underscores their independence of mind; hence their character and status: they are courageous, and they are adventurous besides being generous and religious.

A critical evaluation of this act of bringing milk to invisible people who are presumably herders of cattle highlights the way Maasai women regard themselves in the harsh environment they inhabit. Milk is a delicacy among the Maasai. That they should take it to people invisible to them is intriguing; yet it is remarkable when we consider similar acts of devotion in other cultures. Christians, for instance, bring various foods from their harvest to the altar and leave them there; church offerings are left at the altar and the givers do not look behind to find out who has used these things. Many communities have the tradition that involved men in offering food to invisible ancestors; women did not participate in this in practice. Thus, the myth that depicts the women of the Maasai community as the ones going out of their way to be close to the voices of the invisible beings and to offer them their 'harvest' — milk — reinforces the important role the women play in the religious life of the community. They, it can be safely argued, commune with the spirits; they are sensitive to the voice of the invisible. In other words women are depicted as being the clairvoyants of the community, the interpreters of voices.

One is further reminded of the practice involving the Maasai traveller and his spear. A Maasai seeking a house to rest in after a long journey is welcome to eat and sleep in the home of any of his numerous age-set members (*rika*) so long as he leaves his spear prominently stuck upright in front of the house in which he is resting or sleeping. The entertainment is not restricted to feeding and providing accommodation. However, in the event that pregnancy occurs, the traveller is fined a bull if a son is born; there is no fine for the birth of a girl, for the family into which she is born is the family that stands to benefit when she eventually marries and dowry is given for her.

In addition to the myths above, we shall refer to the story entitled 'The Warrior and his Sister' or 'Why Free Love Is Permitted among the Maasai' (ibid.: 120–22). In this myth, a warrior decides to take his father's cattle to the salt-lick against all odds; his elder sister accom-panies him while his younger sister remains at home. He asks her to watch out for smoke issuing forth from the salt, for this will be sign that he and his sister are safe; absence of smoke should be taken to mean death of the warrior. The two leave for the salt-lick. While there, the warrior leaves his sister behind to look after the kraal as he takes the cattle out to graze. This she does, but one day warriors from the enemy tribe come to the kraal, and they make love to the girl and walk away. On his return, the brother notices the footprints of the warriors and he decides to eavesdrop in order to know what exactly they are up to. He overhears his sister plot to betray him. She tells the strangers that she will sing as her brother milks the big cow; they should take her away and the cows too at that moment. He prepares for the enemy's act, and when they launch it in the evening, he attacks first and kills six of them; the rest flee without either the girl or the cattle. He burns the bodies. The girl's treachery is reported to her father, and he seeks out a man to marry her.

We note that once again, the story is underscoring the woman's inde-pendence of thought. The absence of the idea of coercion is significant: the warriors did not apply any pressure. She is an active participant in matters that concern her private life, and she makes the choice to love and be loved. Her brother discovers, to his horror and dismay, that his sister is a traitor; she is heard plotting against her own brother and family property. Her preference for the strangers who have made love to her is uniquely individualizing; it distinguishes her as a character capable of making decisions that define her as a person with personal needs and interests that override mass/family loyalties.

The young woman's father seems to appreciate her action as one that is making a statement that is stronger and clearer than any rush judgement can make sense of. He allows her to have her way: to get attached to a man to continue having access to what she has already acquired for herself, without seeking either parental or brotherly permission — intimate relationship. Thus, the story presents to the audience a society that views their women as persons with a right to make choices affecting their lives. At the same time, both the father's and the brother's responses indicate willingness to live with women as equals in decision-making in issues that are pertinently female. This presentation contrasts with Ciarunji Chesaina's submission that 'The position of women as voiceless subordinates begins from childhood' (1994: 87) for in it we have a voiced young woman who not only decides to follow her brother to the hostile salt-lick but also discusses with the enemy the strategy of taking off with her and the wealth — her father's cattle. This is daring.

In addition to the young woman displaying independence of mind, she comes through as a symbol of courage and valour. It is important to note that this is the only family that has their animals going out to the salt-lick, as every other family is afraid of being attacked and killed by warriors of the neighbouring tribe with whom they were at war (Hollis 1905: 120). The boy's decision exemplifies great courage as he makes up his mind 'to take them to the salt-lick, and die with them if necessary' (ibid.: 121). The girl's decision to accompany her brother to the salt-lick also exemplifies great courage. Besides, the esteem in which the society holds both its boys and girls is highlighted. The story immortalizes the people's value for courage and sacrifice.

Besides displaying courage through her decision to follow her brother to the wild, the girl shows an independence of mind that sharply contrasts popular hearsay that is common about the Maasai: women have no say in anything. Here, without consulting her brother, she entertains a stranger and eventually goes with him as his wife. In other words, she makes the statement that she is the only one who knows when she is ready to get into a relationship and get married.

Another story that I shall analyze is the one entitled 'The Demon and the Child'. In this story a Demon kills all people and their animals, but one woman manages to hide herself and her son successfully. The Demon retires after he convinces himself that there are no people to kill and swallow. The woman hides her child until maturity; then one day the woman tells his son the story of the way the Demon had destroyed their village that had been so crowded with people before the murderous act. The young man decides to go out and hunt for the Demon; he feels strongly obliged to take his revenge. His mother discourages him, but he is adamant. Finally, his mother joins him. Together, they climb a tree and light a fire. This fire attracts the Demon who in turn smells smoke and realizes that there must be a human being around. He decides to go straight for the human being, but smoke deters him. The boy embarks on shooting arrows at his face. This act of shooting at him takes a long time, but eventually the Demon surrenders. He tells the boy that he is going to die, and after he dies the boy should cut open the tip of his index figure; he should also cut the forehead of the Demon. He dies and the boy proceeds to open the finger and the forehead. As soon as he cuts the finger, the whole village of people and domestic animals comes out of the opening in the finger; the cut on the forehead allows the chief to come out. Finally, the village is restored and the people choose their rescuer to be the chief.

It is clear that it is the mother's intelligence, courage and the exercise of the freedom to express her thoughts that save the village and its property as well as propelling her son to the highest position in the restored village: that of chief. The rescued chief is told to respect the people's saviour and accept to be led. This decision is a vindication of the woman's role in the plot and action of killing the Demon and rescuing the people.

In this story about the disappearance and restoration of the village, the audience has several aspects of the image of the woman highlighted. The first one is that of the woman as the enduring force of life: the mother is the think-tank of the plot to subdue the terrible adversary and save her son and herself. She eludes the Demon's destructive hand by hiding herself and her son. The Maasai tell the story for the purpose of conveying to the audience the central role women play in the survival of the community as nomads. As a people exposed to elements of nature during their movement from one district to another in search for pasture, the Maasai are often at risk; and as people who take pride in going on cattle raids, they have composed narratives that depict the bedrock of their survival: actively thinking women of great intuition, invention and tact.

While the four narratives analyzed in the chapter succeed in affirming that the image of women in Maasai oral literature is that of thinking and expressive beings, one narrative provides a different image altogether. It is the story about the entitled 'Father of Marogo' (Hollis 1905: 170–71). Because of its uniqueness, I shall use this narrative to say something about the portrayal of men and the male child in the community, however briefly.

In this narrative, Marogo was an only child of her parents for a long time. Being a greedy man, the father of Marogo resented her presence for he 'provided food for her' (Hollis 1905: 170). Fortunately for him, one day, a suitor gave him dowry and married her. The two lived happily as her husband had a large kraal. Meanwhile Marogo's mother conceived and gave birth to a baby boy. Then one day Marogo's husband sent word that he was going to slaughter a bullock and would like his parents-in-law to be present to enjoy the meat with his family. This news was received with a great deal of excitement and expectation from the father of Marogo. On the way to their daughter's kraal, the father let go of the child, and the boy was carried downstream, never to be seen again. Meanwhile his pot, in which he expected to carry left-over meat was supposed to be carefully held across the river. When the wife wept for her child, the husband told her to keep quiet as the child would be picked 'lower down' the stream and be given to her. He tricked her into believing that there were people downstream whom he was requesting to pick the baby for him. When the wife finally discovered that he had been lying to her about the safety of the baby, she cried bitterly, but he rebuked her, thus: 'You women are such fools! Even if this child is lost, won't you bear another one?' (ibid.). As they approached the homestead, he hit her with his club while excitedly making gestures about the slaughtering of the bullock; blood gushed out, but he plastered the wound with earth (ibid.: 171). He apologized and told her not to tell anyone that he had hit her. Furthermore, he told her, 'Now that you have no child, you can take home whatever you don't eat' (ibid.). He also tells her, 'if [sic] you are offered plenty of meat, don't refuse. Put it aside on one side, and give it to me afterwards, for I shall not get enough' (ibid.). At the end of the feast, the woman 'took away some of the meat that was left over for the husband to eat at home' (ibid.).

In the course of listening to this story, one is persuaded to see the relationship between the man, his children and his wife. The gender relations here are clearly portrayed, and the man is shown as one who regards himself as the unquestionable leader of the trio. He views his wife as a being who has no opinion, and should she have it, she should be controlled so that she does not air that opinion. This attitude of the man comes through in the three crucial episodes in the narrative: when he lets the baby drown so as to allow him to have more meat than he would have had had the baby been allowed to live and be present at the feast; when he hits his wife until blood gushes out; and when he shamelessly tells his wife to carry the meat which the baby would have eaten home for him to use it later. Except for the crying that is promptly suppressed, we do not get any protest against these repeated atrocities. What the audience is treated to is a coerced conspiracy of silence, a voiceless woman whose existence seems to be justified by her ardent support and protection of her husband. He views her as voiceless, and she accepts this view of his. This view is of concern, for it contrasts with views of the men characters of the other narratives that are analyzed in this chapter.

An examination of this story infers something about men in the Maasai community. The greed that the story assigns to the father of Marogo is inexorable. It reminds one of the ogre and hyena stories, where the characters' appetites are difficult to satisfy. In the father of Marogo, the audience is confronted with an anti-life force; the audience comes face to face with a human character whose greed surpasses even that of ogres and hyenas. Initially he hates his daughter because she eats of the food he provides. Thus, it is a relationship that is puzzling given that a father always stands to benefit from the presence of a daughter in the family since he is the one who receives the bride wealth/dowry upon her marriage. If we take the father of Marogo to be representative of men in Maasai oral literature, then we are moved to conclude that the narrative gives a grim image of men whose selfishness is a threat to the survival of the community.

The negative image of the father is later accentuated by his treatment of the baby; he lets the baby slip off his arms and fall into the fast flowing river. The reason for this strange act is that he longs to eat the meat which the baby would have been served when they arrive at Marogo's home and start feasting. The mother's concern is met with derision and then a strong rebuke. Here, then, he is being portrayed as being an enemy of the family as well as posterity. This contrasts sharply with the hyena in a Luhya narrative which expresses horror on learning that she has been tricked into boiling her own cubs ('The Hyena and the Goat', Nandwa and Bukenya 1986: 89). In this Maasai narrative, the father of Marogo comes across as a human being who is worse than a hyena; it is the image of a base being that we have at the end of the journey to his son-in-law's home.

Before getting in the homestead for the feast, the anxiety which drives him to utter such words as, 'Now that you have no child, you can take home whatever you don't eat' (ibid.: 171) is shocking. The portrayal of the man here is demeaning. It is an image of a being that is so base that he has no thought for any other person apart from himself; a being that is so base that he is able to see the death of his son as an opportunity to have more meat for his stomach. This portrayal of the man as all stomach and no brain or sense has not been examined before, though it is a significant angle to the study of gender relations in Maasai oral narratives.

The baby boy in this story is easily disposed of. This in my view says something about the community and the boy children. It is universally accepted among them that boys are the backbone of the community's security; in other words, they are communally owned; they are communal property. Compared with the girls who bring wealth directly to the family into which she is born, the boy's value is shared by all. It is for this reason that the father of Marogo tolerates his daughter's eating the food he provides until she grows up, matures and gets out of his way and into her own home. He receives dowry, and he gets invited to bullock parties by her husband; hence, she is of immediate material value. The baby boy is portrayed as an endangered species even as we admit that this story has certain uniqueness in the way it presents women.

Finally, it is important to focus on the way the father of Marogo relates with his wife. She is the mother of Marogo, 'the goose that lays the golden egg', so to speak. From the story we can tell that she has nurtured this girl through difficulties placed in her way by her greedy husband who sees the presence of this girl as a symbol of loss, the dowry that he finally receives at her marriage notwithstanding. The utter misery of the life of the mother of Marogo, which is caused by her relationship to her husband, is exemplified in the episode where the greedy man drowns their only son and then rebukes her for mourning the death of her son. Here, the audience is treated to an image of an insensitive imbecile who does not seem to understand the process of conception, birth and child care. The statement, 'Even if this child is lost, won't you bear another one?' (Nandwa and Bukenya 1986: 170) portrays him as inhuman. One would expect a sympathetic statement even if it is not coming from the bottom of his heart.

Hence, the study of this narrative leads me to compare the portrayal of the man as a husband with that of the Luhya, which is expressed in songs that refer to men as ogres:

Solo: The cow, is taking me
        The cow is taking me to the land of ogres
        The cow is taking me
        Eh! The cow is taking me to the land of ogres.[1]

The Chorus repeats the stanza. This song is sung over and over again with the final words posing the rhetorical question, 'Where will you

---

[1] Narrated by Khahechia Muhando, May 2003.

sleep? Where will you sleep today?'. I feel that the story about the father of Marogo sounds like a narrative version of this Luhya wedding song. The portrayal of a man as an ogre who causes danger to the life of the woman is similar though in this story the callousness of the man has gone a notch higher: he not only kills the child the woman has borne into the family, but he also derides and insults the woman for mourning the death of her son, the only child the couple has in the home after the marriage of Marogo.

In the marriage of Marogo I find subtle rebuke for the greedy man's behaviour. There is an ironic twist where the very man who hated the growing child, Marogo, for the mere fact that she was eating the food which he brought home, is eager to go to the same child's (Marogo's) home to eat and feast on a whole bull. The narrow-mindedness of the father of Marogo is highlighted. Juxtaposed with his wife about whom there is expressed love for her children in spite of the odds in her way of displaying total protection, the man turns out to be typical of his class: the class of the greedy and selfish whose vision of the future is blurred by what they perceive to be the immediate gains or losses. Thus, examined from this angle, this narrative has a serious moral lesson for the men of the community: children must not be denied their right to eat and grow since they too are destined to be provident when their time comes.

The analysis of the gender relations done, this chapter will now focus on the portrayal of women in this story. To start with, this narrative reveals several attributes of women seen through the mother of Marogo. First of all, she is portrayed as strangely naïve. The first example of her strange behaviour is noted when the death of her son is greeted with grief that is quickly checked successfully by the killer. The story is silent on any efforts to rebuke the man for being careless in the way he handles the child while crossing the river, for being greedy and for being sly. This naiveté portrays her as one socialized to ask her husband no questions even when what he is doing is bizarre.

Later in the story, she is easily persuaded to save her husband's repu-tation by remaining silent about hurting her through greedy expectations translated into wild gestures with his baton. This silent suffering portrays her as a pitiable person who has long effaced herself for the sake of pro-tecting her husband's strange character. This quiet suffering, whose sole end is to give a semblance of a harmonious family, is seen in her presence at the feast. In other words, the story gives the audience a character that has nothing to speak of, a character who has sacrificed all at the altar of her husband's reputation, at the altar of appearance, the reality of their life being too painful and ugly to expose to the world.

Flatness of character is belaboured further during the feast. It is intriguing that the mother of Marogo agrees to the arrangement to keep the meat which the dead son would have eaten for the father to eat later on when the couple arrives back home. Under normal circumstances, this arrangement would be seen as oppressive, but the mother of Marogo is presented as one who is neither ready to oppose it nor to seem uncomfortable with it. It is a negative portrayal of women, holding a mirror to the worst lot of the sex.

This portrayal is subtly condemned by the events of the narrative. The death of her son is a condemnation of her flatness of character. Symbolically the narrative is conveying the warning that such a character is not fit to be a mother; that in the harsh environment of their lives Maasai women must be ready to defend their own brood like the mother of the boy in the story about the resurrection of the village.

Thus, the mother of Marogo's naïveté and flatness of character seem to be as unique as they are strange, for several myths that have been collected among the Maasai present the audience with women of character as well as women who are endowed with the ability to make decisions about their life, their future.

Finally, one is obliged to comment on Marogo. Though the title bears her name, the audience does not hear her say anything throughout the whole narrative, neither is she depicted as doing anything to anyone or even to herself. The minute she survives her father's tyranny, which she says nothing about, she is killed by the composition. It is her husband who invites her parents to her home to eat the bullock. In this way, she fits the stereotypical image of a quiet traditional woman who must be seen and not heard. It is an image of a woman, like that of her mother's, who cannot support life in the harsh environment in which the Maasai live and have lived for centuries.

This chapter is led to conclude that four out of the five narratives referred to have shown that though marginalized communities are conventionally expected to subject their women to greater marginalization, the Maasai community seems to have risen above this stereotype, giving the women the voice to express their innermost desires and act on them. In this conclusion, I would state that the story of the father of Marogo is unique in its portrayal of the woman, and this goes to show great variety that is to be expected in a community that sprawls the length and breadth of the Great Rift Valley, covering both Kenya and Tanzania.

References

Chesaina, Ciarunji. 1994. 'Images of Women in African Oral Literature: A Case Study of Kalenjin and Maasai Oral Narratives', in Austin Bukenya, Wanjiku Mukabi Kabira and Duncan Okoth-Okombo (eds), *Understanding Oral Literature*. pp. 85–91. Nairobi: Nairobi University Press.

Hollis, Alfred Claud. 1905. *The Maasai, their Language and Folklore*. London and Oxford: Clarendon Press.

Mwanzi, Henry. 2006. 'William ole Ntimama and the Politics of the Maasai'. Paper presented at an international conference on 'The Native and the Indigenous', March, Sweden.

Nandwa, Jane A. and Austin Bukenya. 1986. *African Oral Literature for Schools*. Nairobi: Kenya Literature Bureau.

16

Experiential History *vs* Objective History

A Literary Study of Lambada Aphorisms

Mohan Dharavath

♋

Folklore is a fossil which refuses to die.

(Anonymous)

The research work I am currently involved in gives a clear picture of the Lambani community (the names 'Lambada', 'Lambani' and 'Banjara' could be used interchangeably to refer to the same community). The research started on the basis of my course work, which provided an absorbing account of their culture and tradition. The first day of my field work started in Apparajupally, Govindapuram of Warangal District in the month of March 2009. I gathered materials from Thanda Nayakas (sometimes referred to as the storyteller and alternatively as the village head) and many other people from the villages of Joshithanda, Dubbathanda, Janguthanda, Amanagal, and Samyathanda, which are in and around Apparajupally and Govindapurum. It is known that the Lambani community has had a culture of aphorisms since the ancient period. I spent some time with this community and discussed their aphorisms with them.

Lambada tribes in India have a rich tradition of oral literature, which includes folksongs, tales, riddles, myths, aphorisms, and legends which have been told and preserved in their community from past generations. The oral tradition illustrates their culture and life-style. The word 'oral' signifies 'orally transmitted' and is opposed to that which is written; it also contrasts with what is not verbal. The word 'tradition' refers to the way of doing things and the process of handing down practices, insights, ideas and values, which belong to the whole community.

The Lambanis have been living in India like this for many years. Earlier Lambanis lived in the northern states of India, but at present they can be found anywhere in India. In olden days, the economic condition of Banjaras was very good. Since they migrated to the southern states, they have been treated as tribes and dalits. Until three or four decades ago, Banjaras were not given any opportunity to take part in development but were the victims of circumstances.

The oral tradition of the Lambadas is still authentic in their context, though personal variations occur during its rendition. I want to posit that most anthropologists who 'study' Lambada culture eschew Lambada history. Their aim in many cases is for personal purposes — publishing an article, a book or obtaining a PhD. It is time for the history of the Lambadas to be written and translated. Do anthropologists take notice of this aspect? Alas! No. As suggested above, the recording and representation of Lambada cultural forms by élite historians does not do justice to the Lambada community or culture. What is the alternative?

A few outstanding scholars like Christoph von Fürer-Haimendorf with his work *Tribes of India: The Struggle for Survival* (1982) have brought a new element into tribal communities. His work presented an equitable and realistic analysis of the present situation of the Indian tribes. He took examples from a few failures and some successes of government policies in addressing tribal issues. Edgar Thurston's work on the Lambadas was the first which gave a natural picture. His foremost work, *Castes and Tribes of Southern India* (Thurston and Rangachari 1993), depicted Lambada cultural history based on mythological stories and census reports. He also emphasized the Lambada clan system, their geographical spread to the south and their socio-economic conditions. He said that the Lambadas are basically a trading class and played an important role during the time of the Moghuls.

Kumar Suresh Singh's current work, *The Scheduled Tribes* (1994), brought out some unimportant results, but never talked about an oppressed community. In his work he did not talk about socio-economic life, political life or historical problems. What he focused on was numerical data that are included in the Constitution of India. G. S. Ghurye and Mahasweta Devi have followed in the footsteps of eminent scholars. G. N. Devy founded a tribal research institute and is now working on tribal issues. In his works, he mainly focuses on the hill and remote tribes, the *adivasis* and aborigines of India, their cultural practice and their livelihood (see Devy 2002). However, all these works were written from anthropological and geographical perspectives; they contain mythology but not objective history.

Most of these works on tribes as outsiders have not discussed the tribal societies analytically; even as insiders those emerging from the Lambada tribal community have not done this. Most of these works are not considered prominent in Lambada tribal history but are seen as a gathering of general information. Only a few scholars have undertaken challenging work on the tribal societies.

Paul Thompson argues:

> [O]ral history is not necessarily an instrument for change; it depends upon the spirit in which it is used. Nevertheless, oral history certainly can be a means for transforming both the content and the purpose of history itself. It can be used to change the focus of history itself, and open up new areas of inquiry; it can break down barriers between teachers and students, between generations, between educational institutions and the world outside; and in the writing of history — whether in books or museums, or radio and film, it can give back to the people who made and experienced history through their own words, a central place (1978: 3).

Lambada narratives are memorized by them and handed down from one generation to another in oral form. They cannot be treated as straightforward historiographic material, because restored history is still not history. This is still history as memory or legend, myth or fable. It explains the past not as 'events' but as 'experiences', i.e., 'experiential history' vs 'objective history'. In this chapter, I would like to introduce the aphorisms of the Lambada community and show the richness and uniqueness of their culture. I want to see how and how far these forms of life and thought resist historicization, and to ask how this resistance implies the notion of understanding another culture.

The challenge of oral history lies partly in this essential social purpose of history. Therefore, the social purpose of history will be served only when the historians and anthropologists give up their written work and start focusing on oral forms on a large scale. Hence it is proper to say that the oral literature of the Lambadas has been a reflection of their contemporary society.

Until very recently the tribal community's history had been ignored by historians, partly because their lives have so often passed undocumented and they have been confined to peripheral areas. On the basis of existing oral tradition we can comprehend the past history of tribal communities of India. Therefore, my study is a construction of the experiential history of the Lambada community, of that which comes from past oral experience using both oral history forms and available written forms as their history.

The earliest aphorisms were a collection of medical sayings by Hippocrates. During the Renaissance, the term aphorism referred mainly to mnemonic sayings. Dr Johnson then defined an aphorism as 'a maxim; a precept contracted in a short sentence; an unconnected position' (quoted in Morson 2003: 409). Therefore, we see that an aphorism must be brief and should be centred on a moral topic. But, this definition is broad, as it can also include other forms of short expression such as maxims and witticisms.

John Gross gives us a narrower definition that would possibly make an aphorism different from other forms of short expressions. He tells us that it is often malicious, but also sometimes consoling and it can stand alone (quoted in ibid.). But finally, we see that aphorisms have no clear definition; they often overlap with many other terms for short expressions such as the slogan, witticism, maxim, or dictum.

Then how are we to understand the difference between the various kinds of short expression? It is basically a question of genre. In order to understand what an aphorism is, we need to compare it with other forms of short expression such as the dictum. We see that short forms can always be expanded into longer forms as they both express a view of experience in life. For example, Voltaire's philosophical parables are said to have been expanded forms of aphorisms. Oscar Wilde's plays can also be seen as expanded witticisms. We see that Tolstoy admired the great aphorist Lao Tzu and translated his aphorisms. He also produced an anthology of short expressions in his later years.

Now, let us first look at how an aphorism is similar to or different from a riddle. Most of the Greek stories were centred on a riddle. In the case of Oedipus, the riddle or puzzle is not a sign from god, but merely a trap. The Greeks believed that god never showed them the path or the solution, but merely pointed towards the goal. But as we get closer to it, the horizon seems to recede forever. This is what leads to a feeling of despair in mortals, as in the 'Myth of Sisyphus'. But eventually we feel that even though we have not reached the final goal, with each step we acquire more knowledge. An aphorism is a god's sign and a mystery.

The only difference between the two is that the riddle has an answer and can be solved. Whereas, once you interpret an aphorism, the mystery only deepens further. In Greek mythology, Oedipus is known for his riddle-solving abilities. The Sphinx sat outside Thebes and asked all the travellers who passed by to solve a riddle. If the traveller failed to solve the riddle, then the Sphinx killed him or her. If the traveller answered the riddle correctly, then the Sphinx would destroy herself.

'What goes on four legs in the morning, on two legs at noon, and on three legs in the evening?' Oedipus solved the riddle and the Sphinx destroyed herself. The solution: a man, who crawls on all fours as a baby, walks on two legs as an adult, and walks with a cane in old age. Of course, morning, noon, and night are metaphors for the times in a man's life. Such metaphors are common in riddles. But, we see that if life were merely a riddle, then all our problems could be solved. Instead, life is a mystery and that is exactly what an aphorism is.

Well, let us now look deeper into what an aphorism is. Pascal says, 'We shall all die alone' (Morson 2003: 421). There is no doubt that we are all born alone and we also have to die alone. The only choice we have is the people with whom we share the few years that we live on earth. All aphorisms are different in tone, language and form, but all of them share one thing in common: what is most precious is far beyond our reach.

Lambanis express their feelings in the form of aphorisms such as 'Kaanema Dam Chainpani Gatla Chadan Nachu Ko Kachae'. The aphorism shows us that the world is dim, but not completely obscure. We endlessly grope in darkness, but there is a way to truth which can be translucent. God speaks through us and shows us the path to take.

Lambada Aphorisms

The Lambadas speak Goar-boli, which belongs to the Indo-Aryan family of languages and was influenced by Rajasthani, Telugu, and many other local languages. It has no script or independent history. Though it does not have a script, it keeps Lambadas culturally and socially united. Wherever they live, they understand their language without any difficulty though their language consists of many borrowed words and expressions from other local languages. But when they speak to their relatives, they speak in the Lambada language, i.e., Goar boli. It is difficult to find a Lambani who cannot speak in this language.

The narrative aphorisms certainly occupy an important role in the traditional poetic forms of Lambada folk literature. The Lambada aphorists narrate the aphorisms in their stylistic way. Generally, they narrate the aphorisms of the heroism of the great at gatherings like an engagement ceremony, a marriage celebration, political meetings, or work in the fields to entertain or show their abilities to the relatives. There is no limitation to the length of an aphorism; it may be shorter or longer according to the narrators when they deliver it at the meeting. The Lambadas come together to listen and enjoy the deliveries concerning heroism and tragedy.

The Lambada aphorisms cover a great range of topics and can give expression to the various kinds of feelings and emotions. The aphorisms of Lambadas may be classified into different types:

(*a*) Traditional Aphorisms
(*b*) Religious Aphorisms
(*c*) Social Aphorisms
(*d*) Romantic Aphorisms

Traditional Aphorisms

The Lambada relate different kinds of aphorism during the celebration of rites and rituals. Some meaningful aphorisms are recited about their foolishness and idleness. These kinds of aphorisms are recited mainly at marriage celebrations. Basically, Lambada people use the aphorisms to demonstrate human and moral values.

> *Lakhe lakhene parvana bheju lakhe lakhene paruvana bheju*
> *Kholuto kuri kuri tholuto turi turi*
> *Aar mangniya aar nayak kha kha vujii khyee khacha*
> *Aanga ghaluto sukkar laraghaluto gohal meetoj meeto*
> *Aanghero julam khun ditto aavar nayak.*

This gathering of people all are aware of what is going to happen in front of the Thanda Nayak.[1]

> O Nayak, I am telling some truth, which will be good for both of your families when you become a blood relationship. I will give you a coconut with sugar and jaggery, its sweetness will make you so happy with this relationship. No one knows that what the future is. O Nayak (Mangniya), accept the sweet dish and enjoy it.

The use of rhythmic words is very meaningful in the tradition. After the negotiation between them, the function starts with the distribution of sugar and jaggery. This is known as *Golkhayero* (an engagement)

---

[1] This is part of my research work. I have collected from different places and translated all the aphorisms as I am an insider of this community.

which means the eating of jaggery. Words like *sakkar* (sugar), *goal* (jaggery) and *toparrow* (dry coconut) demonstrate the importance of the Lambadas' social ritual and cultural identity.

Religious Aphorisms

The life of the Lambada people is mainly religious. They submit themselves to different kinds of gods and goddesses, such as the family god, the village god and the ancestors. They believe that the stone, the earth and the tree are the gods for their family. The aphorisms, which are concerned with gods, goddesses, cultural heroes and great personalities are called 'Religious Aphorisms'. The following aphorisms explain the characteristic religious style of the Banjaras.

> *Aagal bagal tho nanjar ghoteche, Aagal bagal tho nanjar ghoteche*
> *Vachha dinoche vyathudu ghote, Chal chalya manmaseri ghagai*
> *Chal chaya manmaseri ghager, Muti ka mal jada kham*
> *Soloi boti punchika na puchi, Aamath karlora kayak.*

O Nayak, this is the place where you can pray to the god and goddess of your family, and take blessing from them. The boy came with the goat for your happiness giving it to us in the name of Grandfathers. There is flora and fauna. O Nayak, there is a delicious meat curry made of goat's blood (*Solai Botti*) for everyone to have and enjoy.

This implies a ritual importance where marriage takes place. The woman's family and his relatives offer a goat in the name of the bride's grandfather which is served to all relatives at the time of marriage. This is called as Ghoater Nokta.

The significance of the sayings of the Lambadas is imaginative and narrative. Generally, the Lambanis' marriage rites start at the bridegroom's house and continue at the bride's house before ending up at the bridegroom's house.

Social Aphorisms

The Lambada aphorisms give clear pictures of their bravery and heroism. Originally, the Lambadas hail from the Rajput families of Rajasthan. They roamed as tradesmen supplying food grains. They could not avoid leading an adventurous and heroic life. Therefore, they were forced to protect their families and were prepared to fight their enemies. There are some aphorisms which reveal their heroic lives and their social ties.

Mate mantram chetae kariya
Aaj gharema savara aangharema
Khavunu pivunu bhagvan denu.

This aphorism tells them to behave themselves and to be tough. One should not boast because god knows one's ability. The aphorism endeavours to explain human limitations, i.e., one should not be over-ambitious and should not talk much because no one is immortal. (The aphorism literally explains that depending on their ability god will be gracious to them. So, one should have patience.)

God makes you wait but he does reward you.

Romantic Aphorisms

There is no dearth of romantic aphorisms in the folk poetry of the Lambadas. Their natural life is filled with delight, fun, and irony, which show their romantic nature. These romantic aphorisms are delivered especially during the Teej and Holi festivals.

Khal khal bandhu pagadiya mod mod bandhu peta
Bhare sabham hath pakadu ma bhukiyro beta.

I am the son of the Bhukiya clan, standing in this crowded gathering and wearing the long turban. I am ready to propose and get married to you.

Theen ghamerro patelia banavura veera Peediya deedara.

O Brother, the sacred wood (*Peediya*) gives us blessings. Now we will make you a Nayak for three villages.

The above line originates in the Banjara culture as seen from the wood (*Peediya*) which is given to one of the boys in the celebration. The girls play with him and take it back from the boy. After getting back the wood, they make fun of him and enjoy themselves with it.

This rite is performed at the Nayak's house. The festival is symbolic of the emotional life of the Lambadas. There is a prolonged programme of dancing and singing for nine days. The girls have a dominant role but men have a partial role.

Conclusion

In spite of their having their own culture, rich tradition and heritage, the Lambanis were economically, socially, educationally, and politically retrograde. Even though some steps were taken to improve their conditions, these did not lift them to development. Even after 50 years of independence the economic conditions of Lambanis had not improved.

The present living conditions of Lambanis who live in remote areas are pathetic and undeveloped, and the people remain untrained. It is difficult to find people who work on their behalf. During the course of my work, I have observed many things which reveal the deprived conditions of Lambanis. And I came to know that they are still experiencing poor conditions like not having roads, a proper drainage system, electricity and the practice of selling girl children continues in *thandas* (hamlets).

For their experiential progress and development, I have started examining how the mainstream society deprives the community politically and culturally. Therefore, my study on the aphorisms looks at the debate between experiential history and objective history, where the experiential history is found in the aphorisms and the objective history is attempted by so-called outsiders such as historians, sociologists and anthropologists, who have engaged with the community for their research work on the tribes. The chapter was also an attempt to deal with the inability of these researchers to understand the Lambada culture.

References

Devy, G. N. 2002. *Painted Words: An Anthology of Tribal Literature*. New Delhi: Orient Longman.

Morson, Gary Saul. 2003. 'The Aphorism: Fragments from the Breakdown of Reason', *New Literary History*, 34: 409–29.

Singh, Kumar Suresh. 1994. *The Scheduled Tribes*. New Delhi: Oxford University Press.

Thompson, Paul. 1978. *Voice of the Past: Oral History*. London: Oxford University Press.

Thurston, Edgar and K. Rangachari. 1993 [1909]. *Castes and Tribes of Southern India*. New Delhi: Asian Educational Services.

von Fürer-Haimendorf, Christoph. 1982. *Tribes of India: The Struggle for Survival*. Berkeley: University of California Press.

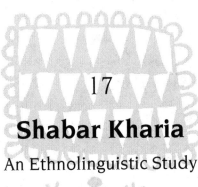

17

Shabar Kharia

An Ethnolinguistic Study

Narugopal Mukherjee

Ethnolinguistics, as defined in *Encyclopædia Britannica Online*, is a part of anthropological linguistics

> concerned with the study of the interrelation between a language and the cultural behaviour of those who speak it. Several controversial questions are involved in this field: Does language shape culture or vice versa? What influence does language have on perception and thought? How do language patterns relate to cultural patterns? These questions, which had been posed earlier by the German scholars Johann Gottfried von Herder and Wilhelm von Humboldt and their followers in the idealist-romanticist tradition, emerged again in the United States as a result of the discovery of the vastly different structure of American Indian languages, as delineated by the American anthropological linguists Edward Sapir and Benjamin L. Whorf. They noticed, for example, that Eskimo has many words for snow, whereas Aztec employs a single term for the concepts of snow, cold, and ice (*Encyclopædia Britannica Online*).

Ethnolinguistics thus brings onto a common platform the linguistic and cultural specificities of a community and shows how tradition, cultural practices, rites and rituals, and general life-style influence the language of an ethnic community. In short, it is a combination of ethnology and linguistics. Without elaborating further the conceptual part of ethnolinguistics let me pick up the pragmatic part of it. And here the ethnic community that deserves proper attention, both at the levels of theory and praxis, is the Shabar Kharia group.

It was in 1966 that Shabar Samiti, a social welfare group was founded at Kuda village in Purulia district and thereafter the community demanded the attention of social activists and scholars as well. In 1969, the then Prime Minister Indira Gandhi met with the representatives of this ethnic group and listened to the long history of deprivation and exploitation of the tribe.

This chapter will be an investigation of the ethnic and linguistic features of Shabar Kharia, one of the four most primitive tribes of West Bengal, the other three being Toto, Birhorh and Lodha. This is a language which does not even have a script and is yet to be recognized as a language. The language is on the verge of extinction as the native speakers of that language are switching over to some other languages for day-to-day communication. At the level of theoretical linguistics the phonological, morphological, syntactic, and stylistic features of this primitive language will be investigated, and at the level of ethnolinguistics the socio-cultural aspects of the tribe as reflected in the use of language will be explored.

Shabar Kharia and Kharia are not synonymous; rather there are a lot of differences between the two in respect of their linguistic, ethnic and topographical features. Kharia people in general constitute a comparatively powerful ethnic group spread over almost the entire part of eastern India, and more particularly, in three states — Jharkhand, Orissa and West Bengal. They comprise three tribes — the Dudh Kharia, the Dhelki Kharia, and the Hill Kharia. The first two groups speak an Austro-Asiatic language, Kharia, but the Hill Kharia people have switched over to an Indo-Aryan language, Kharia Thar. No language development has been traced out of the last group, i.e., Kharia Thar. The people belonging to Hill Kharia community, as mentioned earlier, are also known as *Pahari* (Hilly) Kharia or sometimes even Shabar Kharia. People from outside call them Kharia but they prefer to identify themselves as Shabar. This group has been unique in their language, culture, and social position.

The focus in this chapter is not on Kharia in general but Shabar Kharia in particular. In West Bengal, people belonging to this community are mainly found in West Midnapur, Bankura and Purulia districts. During the colonial regime the Shabars were labelled as a 'criminal tribe' under the Criminal Tribes Act 1871, and still suffer from social stigma and ostracism in modern times. In the district of Bankura, the Shabar Kharia people reside mainly in Ranibandh block, Sarenga block and Raipur block. Approximately 195 families with 1,100 members altogether belong to this community in Bankura district. They are spread over the three blocks mentioned above and, to be concrete, in the villages of Katiam, Jovi, Mohul, Baganpara, Banshkanali, Bethla, Dhakua-Buribandha, Khajuria, Gunpura, Boroda, and Kullyam. These people do not even find two square meals a day. Hunting, animal husbandry and working as agricultural labourers are their main occupations.

The traditionally forest-dwelling ethnic people are not used to agriculture, and rely on the forests for their livelihood. In recent years, with the spread of the Naxalite rebellion in the area, the police often restrict their access to the forest. In 2004, five Shabars of Amlasole, in Midnapore district, died after starvation for months together, shocking the entire nation. Later the Durbar Mahila Samanway Committee (DMSC) started a school in the area, funded partially by sex workers from Kolkata. In June 2008, the Shabar community suffered from severe flooding in many of the villages in West Bengal. Subsequently, large amounts of aid from Catholic missionaries were available.

Because of their acute poverty and starvation and because of domination from outside these people have not been able to retain their linguistic and cultural identity and in no way are connected with the re-awakening of ethnicity or 'new ethnicity' as labelled by J. W. Bennett (quoted in Paulston 1986: 130). Lachman M. Khubchandani says with reference to the tribal awakening in general: 'In the wake of democratization, economic mobility, and mass media exposure, many tribal communities in isolated inaccessible areas are gradually opening up for intense interaction with the non-tribal world' (1993: 530). Again, Andrew M. Greeley (1974) observes:

> One of the most extraordinary events of our time has been the resurgence of tribals in a supposedly secularized and technocratic world. Science and economic rationalization had been expected to reduce, if not eliminate, man's attachment to ancient ties of common ancestry, common land and common faith, but suddenly ties of race, nationality and religion seem to have taken on new importance (quoted in Edwards 1985: 99).

'Ethnicity and nationalism are vital forces in group identity', says S. Imtiaz Hasnain (1993: 522). He firmly believes that 'religious and ethnic groups' are not 'destined to disappear', rather, along with their language, they constitute 'a basic component of our social structure' (ibid.). This awakening, however, has led to a situation of conflict and confrontation with the dominating groups and even among the small linguistic and ethnic communities. Hasnain thus observes:

Fresh awakening emanating from growing awareness of ethnic conscious-ness has resulted in a sudden shift in paradigm from *equilibrium* to *conflict* perspective. In the former sense, ethnicity is construed as a group cultural phenomenon in which a group identifies itself with [some common bonds] . . . while the latter holds competitive and confrontationist perspective with an emphasis on the recognition of differentiation and conscious desire to maintain one's identity (Hasnain 1993: 522).

But the Shabar Kharias have not been introduced to this ethnic resur-gence. In the post-Independence era there might have been a pronounced and gradual increase in the overall ethnic and racial consciousness of the tribal people, but these people remained subjugated linguistically, cultur-ally and politically.

Until very recently, the Shabar Kharia people, however, have not been so eager to maintain their identity. Ethnic consciousness has never been so serious amongst the tribal population of this territory. Probably because of their urge to become a part of the so-called mainstream com-munities, or because of some other socio-political and socio-psychological factors, the Shabar people started ignoring their native language and switched over to either Alsike, the language of the Santals, the most powerful of the primitive tribes, or Bangla, the dominant language of the state. S. Imtiaz Hasnain points out: 'It has been observed that depending on the focus of social mobilization, i.e., ethnicity and nationalism, the linguistic consequences for social groups in language contact situation [vary] ranging from language death, language spread, language shift, and language maintenance' (ibid.: 521). In the case of the tribe under discus-sion, language maintenance has always been an unknown phenomenon. There has been a gradual loss of linguistic consciousness in the case of the tribal people belonging to this community. The language has experi-enced the common fate of most of the minority languages. In spite of 'the common religious, linguistic, and cultural bonds and shared norms, artifacts, values, and beliefs, the linguistic consequences of these minor-ity linguistic groups have either been language death or language shift' (ibid.: 526). Anvita Abbi rightly says:

> Kharia [in general] poses an interesting example where socio-economic pressures force some of the speakers to become bilinguals as well as to some to give up their mother tongue completely. On the one hand, the socio-linguistic factors force the language to have gratuitous borrowing; on the other hand, language contact situation exerts the pressure on the language to acquire complex and not simple structures (ibid.: 547).

As in the case of any other community Shabar Kharia has its linguistic and cultural specificities too. The section that follows shows certain unique features of the language[1] as well as of the ethnicity of the community.

Phonology

Shabar Kharia, like most other indigenous languages in India, has a strong approximant /R/ which in some cases even tends to gain further strength and is made a trill. Let us look at the following examples:[2]

ekhOR (now)
kOkhOR (when)
kisOR (why)
TOR (deep)
gaRha (ditch)
shiaNR (clever)
kichukhOR (some time)
guNRa (to count)
daR (pulse)
ThaR (plate)
huRiD (turmeric)
paiNR (water)
TaR (palm)
kukOR (hen/cock)

These are only a few of the hundreds of words with this strong consonant. This recurrence of the approximant suggests the toughness and the hardship that the people have to go through in their day-to-day living. As I said earlier, life is very hard for them. They work throughout the day for almost nothing. Nature does not have too much of herself to offer to them and both central and state governments are indifferent to their problems. Their voices remain unheard even in this post-colonial time. In different discourses of ethnicity or in subaltern studies reference is made to them, but nothing is going to help them lead a decent and comfortable life. They remain the Other; their position always remains marginalized.

---

[1] The data for the purpose were mainly obtained from Mandal (1989: 54–56); and Devi (1996: 76–84), and they were translated by the author.

[2] See Appendix for a list of symbols used to refer to Shabar Kharia and Bangla sounds.

The nasalized consonants and the strong approximant /R/ together mark the sounds associated with the weapons used in everyday life inside the forest and suggest their essential primitivism as well as their favourite pastime — hunting. Hunting has been their passion as well as a bare necessity. The forest is their home as well as their hunting ground. 'Hunting' has been a powerful metaphor for them. They hunt for food as well as for identity. The following examples with nasalized consonants and /R/ as well once again suggest the roughness of life. Territorial hazards along with stigma and disgrace make them produce harsh sounds.

kaNR (arrow)
dhoNR bauNsh (bow)
bORo Tabla (spear)

Even the names of the body parts bear the roughness and toughness of life:

muR (head)
aNguRia (finger)
gaNRia (back)
eRi (foot)
cuR (hair)
khuNthu (shoulder).

The smoothness of fingers, feet, or hair is missing here and instead the coarseness of life is hinted at.

This harshness of sounds is found in words relating to nature too. Words like *beRa* (sun), *paiNR* (rain), *boNR* (forest) amply illustrate the point. Words in connection with animal husbandry have this harshness too, as in *chagOR* (goat), *bheda* (sheep), *kaRa* (buffalo), *kukOR* (hen/cock).

It is obvious from the examples given that nasalization is a very common feature in this indigenous language. Personal pronouns like *muiN* (I), *hauNm* (we), *tuiN* (you) are nasalized in most cases and this suggests the kind of life this ethnic community passes through. This roughness and toughness of sounds is a testimony to their traditional nomadic character. They don't have fixed dwelling places; they roam about the jungle in search of food and forest produce. Outside the jungle they do not have enough access since, as already suggested, they are traditionally treated as criminals.

Morphology

Being essentially a synthetic language Shabar Kharia abounds in verbs going through the process of affixation. It incorporates several syntactic and semantic modifiers in agreement with the verb used. The semantic content is well communicated through syntactically distinct forms. The suffixes like '*-nos*' ('-ing'), used in the second person, as in *kuthik jaTnos* ('Where are you going?'), *-iTOnu* (used as present progressive marker and in the first person, as in *amhOr onusthanta arOmbho koriTonu* ['We are starting the programme']), '*-am*' (used as future time marker, as in *mui pez kham* ['I shall eat rice']), '*-nai*' (used as present progressive marker or future time marker and in the third person, as in *Ekta maROS asiTnai* ['A man is coming']), '*-ak*' (used as future time marker and in the second person, as in *ekhOR Ekta gan kurbak* ['Now you will sing a song']) are so frequently used in the language and suggest the shrinking of the morphological structuration of the language. '*-am*' and '*-ak*' are frequently occurring participles attached to verbs with reference to different persons and numbers. Let us have a look at the following verb formations:

'*-am*' formations	**'*-ak*' formations**
muiN kham (I shall eat)	*tuiN khabak* (you will eat)
haNum goDhim jam (We'll go to take a bath)	*hebak* (will be)
muiN kam kuriT jam (I'll go to work)	*gan kurbak* (will sing a song)
ekhOR muiN hatk jam (Now I'll go to market)	*cunbak* (will continue)
hauNm pOrob DikhiT jam (We'll go to see the fair)	*asbak* (will come)
hauNm mama ghOrOk jam (We'll go to the maternal uncle's house)	*cuni gemaki* (has/have gone)

As in Bangla, another synthetic language, in this language too, the postpositional particles like '*-e*' are attached to the nouns and separate prepositional or postpositional words or phrases as used in English, an analytical language, are not required. Thus, *bONRe jhaRe* (in the jungle) does not require any separate postpositional word; the particle '*-e*' is attached to *jhaR* and plays the role of English preposition 'in' ('in the jungle'). The domination of Bangla is very pronounced here and it exemplifies yet another case of reduction in morphological structuration. Anvita Abbi, while referring to Kharia in general, points out:

This process of reduction in morphological structuration could either be due to Aryanisation of the language, or due to internal change, or both. Whatever may be the reason, the language is going through a change and the language is undergoing a linguistic shrink as far as its morphological structuration is concerned. However, the shrinking in morphological structuration, contrary to general belief, has given rise to complex syntactic structure akin to Aryan languages . . . The phenomenon goes against the theory of language minority loss. Complexity of structures has never been associated with the language decay or language obsolescence (1993: 546).

Syntax

At the level of syntax also Shabar Kharia is very close to its neighbouring language, Bangla. Quite unlike English, Subject–Object–Verb order is usually followed in its structures. However, there is enough flexibility in collocation. There could be any kind of inversion depending upon the demands of the given situation. The following examples illustrate the point:

> *TONhOr nam kis?*
> Your name what?　　　(What is your name?)

The same sentence may be reproduced as:

> *kis nam TONhOr?*　　or even,　　　*nam kis TONhOr?*
> What name your?　　　　　　　　　Name what your?
> *muiN paiNR kham*
> I water drink　　　(I shall drink water)

An inversion in word order is quite permissible:

> *paiNR muiN kham*　　or even,　　　*kham paiNR muiN*
> drink I water　　　　　　　　　　　drink water I

This flexibility in the use of language suggests the liberty that the tribal people enjoy in the lap of nature. This apparent indiscipline in the field of linguistics testifies to their inherent unrestrained life. They are traditionally labelled as savage, barbaric, unruly, and that is what they are accustomed to. That is their way of life, and nobody, under any circumstances, can change their ethnic features. Their language thus speaks of the undercurrent of life prevailing there.

A unique feature of the language is the use of *nai*. In Shabar Kharia it is used both as a negative marker and as a progressive tense marker.

muiN peẓ kham nai (I shan't eat rice)	(Negative)
Ekta maROs asiT nai (A man is coming)	(Progressive)

Contrarily, in Bangla *nai* can be used only as a negative marker, as in *ami bhaT khabo nai* (I shall not eat rice). Here Shabar Kharia is different from Bangla and herein lies its indigenous feature. When *nai* is used as a progressive tense marker in Shabar Kharia the root verb normally takes '-*iT*' ending.

mOhOr muR DukhaiT nai	(I have a headache)
mOhOr pet DukhaiT nai	(I am having a stomach pain)
mOkO kalha nagiT nai	(I feel cold)
nani buRi peẓ khaiT nai	(The grandmother is eating rice)
bauko bONRe jaiT nai	(Father is going to the jungle)

An interesting feature of Shabar Kharia is its absence of relative structures. In fact, in other Kharia versions 'the introduction of relative syntax is a recent phenomenon' (Abbi 1993: 548) and in Shabar Kharia it is almost non-existent. The following example illustrates the point:

koNR	*koNR*	*gaotu*	*kOTO*	*maROs*	*asa,*	*nijOr nijOr*	*slip*	*kOrain*
which	which	from village	how many	men	have come	personal	slip	collect

(People/men who have come from different villages are requested to collect their slips/receipts)

The English relative pronoun 'who' is missing here and so is the relative syntax.

This language abounds in conjunct verbs like Bangla *kaj kOra* ('to do work' instead of 'to work'). Probably because of the influence of Indo-Aryan languages, Bangla in this particular case, the Shabars extensively use conjunct verbs. Let us pick up some examples:

ekhOR	*Ekti*	*gan*	*kurbak*
now	a	song	do

(Sing a song now)

amhOr	*onusthanta*	*arOmbhO*	*koriTonu*
our	programmes	start	doing

(We are starting our programme)

kis	*kuriT*	*jam*
what for	to do	shall go

(What for shall I go?)

Stylistics

The people belonging to this community use almost all stylistic features to bring about necessary changes in their production of language. Topicalization, collocation, foregrounding, underlexicalization, cohesion — all these stylistic features are very much present in this language. They 'divorce words from their usual partners', as Peter Barry says in a different context, 'and provide unlikely new partnerships between words which we would never have imagined getting together' (2008: 217). A sentence like '*TOhOr gaor nam kis?*' (What is the name of your village?) can be topicalized or foregrounded depending on the meaning to be conveyed and accordingly the emphasis is shifted. It can also be contracted so that the one word '*gaor?*' ('village?' meaning 'which village?') can convey the sense well.

Ethnicity and Cross-cultural Domination or Power Politics

As I mentioned previously, the people belonging to this community suffer from social stigma and ostracism as they are traditionally treated as criminals and outlaws. They do not get jobs anywhere because of their 'criminal' background. They have been marginalized through the ages and no rehabilitation programme has been undertaken for them. It is purely a power game that has kept them away from the privileged section of life — linguistically, socially, and culturally. The poverty and starvation that they experience in their daily life and the social stigma that they have been subjected to find very touching expression in a poem by Mahadev Shabar (quoted in Devi 1996: 76):

hamOk aDim shObOr byaDh jaTi	(We are the primitive Shabar tribe, the hunters)
bONRe jhaRe ruiha kuiRa baDhi	(We go round and pick up eatables from the forests and shrubs)
bONROR sOmpODei ruiha baNci	(We live on the treasure of the forest)

. . .

bharoTe jOkhOn anak british sOrkar	(During the British Raj)
khaiRaR name Di genai Ekta upohar	(A gift was given to the Kharia)
uta hiTnai khaiRa bunTe OporaDhi	(The Kharia people are always treated as criminals)
hai re Obujh athar KhaiRa jaTi hamOk ajoW acho pacho Di	(Alas! The innocent Kharia tribe, you are still lagging behind)
ajoW oi upohare kOTo jaTi DoSe biR DoSe	(Whether responsible or innocent still that gift)
kakoW DoTo piti mOrai, kakoW DoTo jele	(leads to someone being beaten or sent puri to prison)
hai re Obujh athar KhaiRa jaTi hamOk ajoW acho pacho Di	(Alas! The innocent Kharia tribe, you are still lagging behind)

The community has almost lost its linguistic identity since the language is on the verge of extinction. It is because of urbanization and modernization through Bangla and again because of the resurgence of Santali as a dominant language among the minority languages that Shabar Kharia as a language is endangered.

Jhumur songs and the Tusu festival have been the indigenous features of this language. Even in Tusu songs the deception or the deprivation that the people have been subjected to finds a pertinent expression in a poem by Nebi Shabar (quoted in ibid.: 79):

kOTo pati kOTo neTa	(So many parties so many leaders)
asche bhai Dine Dine	(coming every day)
Tobu mora poRe achi	(still we are left behind)
vote kachorer oDhine	(dependent on votes and administration)

The same sense of deprivation and calumny imposed upon them is discernible in Bholanath Shabar's poem (quoted in ibid.: 80–81) depicting the plight of the Shabars in general:

kuThao curi dakaTi hene shuiTe hOY	(If there is burglary or dacoity anywhere nobody can sleep in ruined huts)
pache police asi Dhuri ni jaTo sObaike	(lest police should come and pick up every one)
kiskuriba haY! khaRia! shObOr bhai!	(Nothing to do! Alas! Shabar brothers!)
hamOr baNcar upaY nai	(We have no way to survive)

This general feeling of helplessness can be noticed everywhere, be it their literature, their festivals, or their day to day living. They are scared of their very identity as Shabars. The expression '*shObOr bhai!*' (Shabar brothers!) is an attempt to remain integrated, to share the common lot.

In different festivals and celebrations the native language is used and manipulated in various ways and thereby it adds to the local colour, the indigenous culture of the tribe. The very life-style of these people is reflected in the language used and thus different sociolinguistic functions are traced out.

Very recently, as a result of the Maoist activities, socio-psychological factors are contributing to language identity and infusing in them a feeling of ethno-linguistic identity and language loyalty. Hopefully, this almost extinct language will rediscover its ethnic heritage and find an alphabet of its own to project itself to people around the globe.

Appendix

List of symbols used to refer to Shabar Kharia and Bangla sounds:

Consonants	Key words (Shabar Kharia/ Bangla)
k	*ke* (who), *ki* (what)
kh	*khawa* (to eat), *khuni* (murderer)
g	*gan* (song), *gObeSOna* (research)
gh	*gham* (sweat), *ghOnta* (bell)
c	*cawa* (to want), *cOla* (to walk)
ch	*chele* (boy), *chOY* (six)
j	*je* (who), *jeta* (which), *jOkhon* (when)
jh	*jhOR* (storm), *jhamela* (hazard)
t	*tOk* (sour), *taka* (money)
th	*thanda* (cold), *math* (ground)
D	*DEkha* (to see), *Dami* (valuable)
Dh	*Dhar* (loan), *DhOs* (slide)
n	*na* (no), *newa* (to take)
T	*Tara* (they), *Tini* (he)
Th	*Thala* (plate), *Tham* (stop)
d	*daka* (to call), *dakTar* (doctor)
dh	*dher* (eough), *dhal* (shield)
p	*pawa* (to get), *paNc* (five)
ph	*phera* (to return), *phOl* (fruit)
b	*baba* (father), *bOsa* (to sit)
bh	*bhalo* (good), *bhOY* (fear)

m	*ma* (mother), *mee* (girl)
r	*rasTa* (road), *raT* (night)
l	*lok* (man), *lOmba* (long/ tall)
s	*sona* (to hear), *DOs* (ten)
h	*hOwa* (to be), *haspaTal* (hospital)
R	*bORo* (big/large), *keRe newa* (to snatch)
N/M	*TaNra* (they + honorific [nasal]), *caND* (moon)

Vowels

O	*hOwa* (to be), *bhOY* (fear)
OY	*bhOY* (fear), *jOY* (victory)
a	*ami* (I), *amra* (we)
aw	*naw* ([you] take), *jaw* ([you] go)
ai	*bhai* (brother), *Tai* (so)
aY	*khaY* ([they] eat), *jaY* ([they] go)
ae	*DaNRae* (standing) [formal]
aii	*Daii* (responsible), *sOjjasaii* (bed-ridden)
i	*Tini* (he), *bikal* (afternoon)
io	*Dio* ([you] give), *nio* ([you] take)
ie	*nie* (taking), *gie* (going)
ia	*tia* (parrot), *sial* (fox)
u	*Tumi* (you), *cup* (stop)
e	*newa* (to take), *Dewa* (to give)
ee	*mee* (girl), *chele* (boy)
ea	*beara* (attendant/boy), *cear* (chair)
ew	*ghew ghew kOra* (to bark), *newa* (to take)
ei	*ei* (this), *sei* (he + Emphatic particle)
oi	*boi* (book), *hoi* (am)
o	*Tora* (you), *ora* (they)
ou	*nouka* (boat), *douRa* (to run)
oa	*soa* (to sleep), *roa* (to sow)
oe	*hoe* (through), *boe* (blowing)
E	*bEbohar* (behaviour), *bEsTo* (busy)

References

Abbi, Anvita. 1993. 'Language Contraction, Language Shrink, and Language Conflation: A Case Study of Kharia', in Mrinal Miri (ed.), *Continuity and Change in Tribal Society*, pp. 542–53. Shimla: Indian Institute of Advanced Study.

Barry, Peter. 2008. *Beginning Theory*. New Delhi: Viva Books.

Devi, Mahasweta (ed.). 1996. *Bortika*. July–December.

Edwards, John. 1985. *Language, Society and Identity*. Oxford: Basil Blackwell.

Encyclopædia Britannica Online, s.v. 'Ethnolinguistics'. Encyclopædia Britannica, http://www.britannica.com/EBchecked/topic/194306/ethnolinguistics (accessed 13 February 2011).

Greeley, Andrew M. 1974. *Ethnicity in the United States*. New York: Wiley.

Hasnain, S. Imtiaz. 1993. 'Linguistic Consequences of Ethnicity and Nationalism in Language Contact Situation: From Equilibrium to Conflict Perspective', in Mrinal Miri (ed.), *Continuity and Change in Tribal Society*, pp. 521–29. Shimla: Indian Institute of Advanced Study.

Khubchandani, Lachman M. 1993. 'Tribal Identity in a Plurilingual Milieu', in Mrinal Miri (ed.), *Continuity and Change in Tribal Society*, pp. 530–41. Shimla: Indian Institute of Advanced Study.

Mandal, Namita. 1989. *Bankura Kendrik Mallabhumer Upabhasha*. Kolkata: Kolkata Pustak Bipani,

Paulston, Christina Bratt. 1986. 'Linguistic Consequences of Ethnicity and Nationalism in Multilingual Settings', in Bernard Spolsky, (ed.), *Language and Education in Multilingual Settings*, pp. 117–52. Clevedon, UK: Multilingual Matters.

18

Narratives of *Home*

The Contemporary North-East Experience of (Un)belonging

Esther S. Narjinari

Towards the end of the popular Frank L. Baum's children's classic tale, *The Wonderful Wizard of Oz* (1900), young Dorothy Gale, after having had a whirlwind of an adventure, runs to Aunt Em gushing out the truism, 'I'm so glad to be at home again!' (ibid.: 111). This obvious illustration of a traditionally perceived understanding of home as an uncontested space that is safe and secure has fortunately been challenged and problematized by feminist writings as well as by post-colonial and diaspora studies.

One major reason why the notion of home often gets politicized is because of the fluidity of meaning that it offers. For writers like Biddy Martin and Chandra Talpade Mohanty, 'being home' and 'not being home' are two modalities that can show how *home*, a metaphor for feminism is not all encompassing as it is generally perceived. Analyzing Minnie Bruce Pratt's autobiographical narrative, they offer the supposition that there are 'discrete, coherent, and absolutely separate identities — homes within feminism, so to speak — based on absolute divisions between various racial, or ethnic identities' (Martin and Mohanty 1997: 294).

What succeeds in the article by Martin and Mohanty (ibid.), as Rosemarie Buikema suggests, is the way the traditionally bourgeois and somewhat patriarchal notion of home associated with dominant discourses is problematized. The community is thus seen playing a major role in transforming *home* from a mere physical space to a major site of belonging and identity (quoted in Nyman 2009: 24–25) where 'one is in and the Other is kept out' (George 1996: 27).

For the writers of diaspora and post-colonial texts again, the trope 'home' is also a metaphor of the self, and by extension, of the nation. Especially for the diaspora writer, 'being home' and 'not being home' captures the very essence of the diasporic experience of displacement. But Jopi Nyman problematizes it further when talking about how fictions of diaspora are not only mere lamentations for the home left behind but '[r]ather, they are texts actively redefining the migrant's sense of self and home' (Nyman 2009: 26). Therefore, 'homesickness' in these fictions does not only play a major role in making the absence of being 'away from home' felt, but it is also the reason why 'exciting and exquisite attempts' at reconstructing 'identity in new locations' are initiated bringing multiplicity and hybridity into what were earlier perceived as monocultural spaces. In this way, narratives of diaspora become 'critiques of pure origins and of national identity' (ibid.).

To elaborate on this a bit more, Jopi Nyman refers to theorist Avtar Brah's notion of 'homing desire' and quotes Nikos Papastergiadis's reflection on the ambiguous nature of *home* in modernity to help explain Brah's concept.

> The search for home is neither a nostalgic retreat to a familiar past nor a defensive reaction against the brutalities of the present. The meaning of home is now found in the future-oriented projects of constructing a sense of belonging in a context of change and belonging (Papastergiadis 1998: 9).

Putting us in a clearer perspective, Nyman refers to Susheila Nasta's contextualizing of the 'homing desire' in the context of diaspora literature. According to Nasta, this homing desire involves attempts to reconstruct home in other spaces and can be defined as 'a desire to reinvent and rewrite home as much as a desire to come to terms with an exile from it. Diaspora is therefore as much settlement as displacement' (Nasta 2002: 7–8).

For the purposes of this chapter, however, I would like to refer to some key ideas from Douglas Porteus' concept of the 'Territorial Triad' of satisfactions when talking about the ethological concept of territoriality in my exploration of how north-east writers write about home. I would also like to show how Martin and Talpade's second modality of 'not being home' is further problematized for some writers of the north-east. However, the scope of this chapter is limited for pragmatic purposes. Rather, the attempt has been to sample a few texts to see the deconstruction and defamiliarization of the concept of *home* for the writers of this often and much essentialized region.

Porteus understands the concept of 'home' as being the 'territorial core of all societies' (George 1996: 21). This is because every society tends to build itself around such a concept of *home* and what it offers to its inhabitants and the family for the sake of survival. According to him, most attempts to create territorial models

> have involved creating a home-base model, usually, and significantly located centrally within the various layers of spatial territory. As the nexus of individual and family activity, home is the goal of almost half of the daily trips taken by urban residents and is also the single core space in which, according to time-budget studies, the individual spends the greater part of his day (Porteus 1976: 386).

These three essential territorial satisfactions are namely security, stimulation and identity which can be extended to encompass the entire community. These satisfactions are however made possible when we personalize and defend this space. This 'personalization' not only takes on the personality of its occupant but also may confer 'psychic security on the occupant of a home' (ibid.: 383). In that way *home* becomes the symbolic self. This connection between self, identity and home is seen further elaborated by him when he says,

> Beyond the individual's private space within the home, the home itself becomes a vehicle for expressing identity through manipulation of its external appearance. Cooper, using a Jungian psychoanalytic approach, sees the house as a symbol of the self . . . Jung suggested that the individual's house is a universal, archetypal, symbol of the self. The house reflects how the individual sees himself, how he wishes to see himself, or how he wishes others to see him. The house, then, is a means of projecting an image both inwardly and outwardly (ibid.: 384).

Thus, for Porteus *home* is 'a major fixed reference point for the structuring of reality' (ibid.: 386).

But what relevance do some of these ideas have for contemporary north-east writers when writing about *home* consciously or unconsciously in their poems?

To the untrained eye, even a cursory glance at these texts reveals how strongly they are embedded in their respective regional, cultural, and racial contexts. They are accounts that are a result of lived experience. Sharing their borders with China, Bangladesh and Myanmar, the seven landlocked states of the north-east — Arunachal Pradesh, Assam, Manipur, Meghalaya, Mizoram, Nagaland and Tripura — seem to have more in common with neighbouring countries culturally and racially rather than with 'mainstream' Indians. Within the Indian fabric, the people from these states are often seen as 'outsiders' or even 'local foreigners' as little is known about them within India. This is not to say that societal modes of representation do not take these communities into account. Some form of accountability is present but largely these representations are often essentializing and stereotypical. Apart from everyday encounters with constant racial slurs like 'chinky', individuals from the north-east region are often subject to questions like, 'Are you from Manipur or Nagaland? Do you eat cockroaches?'. And if the north-eastern person happens to give the name of another state, the next question would obviously be, 'But where are you *really* from?'.

The north-eastern community in India thus lives largely under the shadow of being misunderstood, mistreated in covert ways and made to feel marginalized. Such a state of existence is primarily a result of homogenizing or stereotypical narratives disseminated by the media and by hegemonic discourses. This is one reason why when average north-easterners decide to move away from what they know as the place where they belong, to the larger 'Indian' cities for a better education, jobs or even to escape from the politics of terror back home, they often experience a sense of being 'unhoused'. Practically stripped naked and made vulnerable to questions about identity, place of origin and different culture which, when growing up, were never experienced as an issue, become one when contact with other Indian cultures and languages is made in the cities outside of the north-eastern part of the country. The desire to 'return' home' is felt strongly. But like the diasporic immigrant, 'return' is almost never made possible. For some, it may even take years. This is often because militant activities in the north-eastern states for a separate homeland among other related social injustices or economic marginalization crushes this desire to live an ordinary, mundane life that most of us take for granted. 'What is banal is the terror and the corruption' (Nongkynrih and Ngangom 2003: ix) in these insurgent-infested north-eastern regions. Within such a context, there is also

> [t]he uneasy coexistence of paradoxical worlds such as the folk and the westernized, virgin forests and car-choked streets, ethnic cleansers and the parasites of democracy, ancestral values and flagrant corruption . . . [that] make this picturesque region especially vulnerable to tragedy (ibid.).

The four poems that I will now analyze thus reveal how the notion of home as a physical space and as a metaphor can demonstrate the psyche of (un-)belonging of the north-eastern community. Not only are the three territorial satisfactions brutally denied, but this invasion and destruction of physical space in turn is symbolic of the destruction of the very self, of the identity of not only the common north-eastern individual but of the entire community as well.

'Home' for many of these writers remains an elusive concept. More than a safe haven, it is a site of intense physical oppression and terror. For Yumlembam Ibomcha's 'Story of a Dream' (2003), 'not being home' (Martin and Mohanty 1997: 296) as expressed through a dream narrative, is unlike that of Pratt's case where recognizing one's state of defamiliarization is a result of a previously held illusion of coherence and safety brought about by 'the exclusion of specific histories of oppression and resistance, the repression of differences even within oneself' (Ibomcha 2003). Here no specific 'Other' histories of oppression and resistance have been kept out, but rather one's own history of oppression and brutalities has invaded the confines of the very walls that were meant to keep these oppressions out. The *home* cannot hope to remain the major fixed point of structuring reality. Instead the very foundations of this reality are demolished. As Buikema offers in her reading of Abdelkanel Benari's work, 'rather than emphasizing a place', the destruction of the home, 'marks the loss of stories, cultural memories, and myths, and creates a redefined sense of "homesickness"' (quoted in Nyman 2009: 25). The only option left for a north-eastern writer to deal with this loss is to fictionalize the carnage, to locate the narrative within a 'dream sequence'. For attempting to make sense of the madness could probably result in a complete breakdown and an eternal incoherence or even deafening silence.

He ends the poem with a rhetorical question: 'Who else will dream/ such a dream?' (Ibomcha 2003: 80). The underlying presumption being that only those who had to witness and those who had to live through the nightmare can be haunted by such horrific images.

The terror that has 'invaded' the boundaries of what was once secure and safe is depicted in the second stanza where he dislodges the pleasant beginning with the horror of murder and the shedding of the innocent blood of children and other unfortunates, turning the *home* into a site of carnage where the innocent blood of children and others has been shed. In fact, the parallel that the poet draws between 'children' and 'rats' goes to show the worthlessness of the value of life before such acts of vengeance. Note that these lines are intended to shock us: 'entrails spilling', 'bodies of children lie about like rats run over by vehicles'. The value of life in these lines has been rendered worthless, even negated.

> I was having a dream, a very pleasant one,
> It began almost like a nightmare.
> It was our home, quite dark inside;
> On the floor of the house, their entrails spilling,
> bodies of children lie about
> like rats run over by vehicles.
> I tread cautiously, taking long steps.
> But walking on running blood
> My soles are sticky anyway (Ibomcha 2003: 80).

In the next two stanzas, the poet demonstrates the inhumanness and the unreality of it all by describing each frightening experience in positive terms. So the bullet that strikes the speaker's cheek becomes 'as silky as the caress/of a young woman's tender hand!' (ibid.: 81). The onslaught of bullets is interpreted by the speaker as 'June's deluge', like 'grapes almonds raisins' and the sound of gunfire is likened to 'the soothing strains of the flute the sitar the violin' (ibid.: 80).

The nightmare has been translated into a carnivalesque rhetoric where

> 'parties of young women/their hair redolent with the scent of herbs/and faces blooming with joy . . . /The elderly too walk all spruced up/as if going to a wedding./Women on their way to the marketplace,/women returning, greet each other cheerfully,/and laugh together joyfully' (ibid.: 81–82).

The poem ends on an escape mode from reality which is rather sadistic. 'This is all a dream / I'm dreaming. I know, while I'm still asleep/ but even if I know it, I don't want to wake up' (ibid.: 82). The killings and the carnage have demolished not only the walls that were built to protect, but have rendered the inhabitants unable to even attempt any kind of defence of their space. The only possible defence is escapism. Furthermore, this same carnage has resulted in the defamiliarization of the *home*, ridding it of its character, its very identity. The 'horror' is no longer kept outside but has been felt within the confines of what was once safe.

This dream-narrative is similarly used by Robin S. Ngangom from Meghalaya to depict images of slaughter and the pity of it all. However hard he may try to avoid it, his 'soles' will be 'sticky anyway' (ibid.: 80). But where Ibomcha seem to consciously want to locate his narrative of murder within the dream state and escape into an alternate reality, Ngangom's response is to 'harden' himself inside to not feel the pain and the injustice to the point where 'I lost my tenuous humanity' (Ngangom 2003: 154).

His decision to suspend his rationality and sense of right and wrong in an attitude of passivity can be found in the following second stanza from the poem:

I ceased thinking
Of abandoned children inside blazing huts
Still waiting for their parents.
If they remembered their grandmother's tales
Of many winter hearths at the hour
Of sleeping death, I didn't want to know,
If they ever learnt the magic of letters.
And the women heavy with seed,
Their soft bodies mown down
Like grain stalk during their lyric harvests;
If they wore wildflowers in their hair
While they waited for their men,
I didn't care anymore (ibid.).

By universalizing his cry of pain, the poet is not only lamenting the loss of a family but also of the many families of the community — and with it the loss of cultural memory. Even if the poet may have decided to let his sense of truth be burnt with the raging fires coming from the homes and to let his 'uneasy manhood' (ibid.) be buried along with it, by imprinting those images in the lines of his poem, he shows on the contrary his sense of disquiet, shame, and horror. The fact that injustice prevails is something that he cannot ignore, especially when 'the victors / and their victims grew in number' (ibid.).

On the one hand, we have poems of murder and carnage where in the crossfire between militants and those who parade around as the gatekeepers of peace, the innocent bystanders are the ones who have to pay with their lives. Yet, for some others, the inroads of invasion are seen couched in the rhetoric of modernizations that the government brings into these regions. In 'The Conquest' (2003), Desmond L. Kharmawphlang initially refers to his homeland using terms that evoke the images of untouched beauty and purity. The beauty of the place that he 'belongs' to is proudly stated in the very first few lines of the poem:

> I never get tired of talking about my
> Hometown.
> In summer the sky is pregnant,
> Swollen with unborn rain.
>
> Winter arrives, with a tepid sun
> Touching the frozen hills, the dream-boats on lakes (Kharmawphlang 2003: 134).

However, this narrative of the purity of the homeland is ruptured by the narrative of conquest motivated by self-interest in the name of modernization. He gives us a historical account of how these regions have been vulnerable since the past to the self-interests of others. The British, when they came, they did so 'with gifts of bullets, blood-money and religion' (ibid.). From then on, '[a] steady conquest to the sound of/guns began' (ibid.). But after a brief lull in these occurrences of invasion came 'those from the sweltering plains/from everywhere' to further ravage the already 'stricken land', the 'teeming soil' and its 'bruised children' in the guise of modernization (ibid.: 134–35). What is seen here again is yet another instance of the covert destruction of the *home* and by extension of the north-eastern communities as the 'territorial core' of the society that the poem represents. The failure of these modernization projects is pointed out by the poet as having failed in the last line: 'You Know,/ yours is a truly metropolitan city' (ibid.: 135). These lines go to show the irony of what a developed city actually turns into. What is 'metropolitan' here is probably the 'stricken land' and its 'bruised children'.

Paul Lyngdoh's 'For Sale' (2003) develops this image of invasion even further. The act of 'invasion' is shown to have resulted in a situation where its members have been denied the 'sanctuary of their 'homes' and to be able to call it their own. Thus, it is not only the land that has been invaded, but along with it the average north-easterner's home — and with it their traditional values and way of life — by the incessant, ruthless, and at times meaningless modernization and developmental projects decided by those in power.

Lyngdoh creates this image of the land — his homeland — as a commodity that could be easily sold in the marketplace of politics and commerce. By using words like 'battered' and 'autistic' to describe his homeland, Lyngdoh attempts to show the vulnerability of his 'homeland' and to establish the language of extorting the land of its riches.

> For sale
> This battered, autistic land with its lucre-laden earth,
> Our precious minerals, medicinal herbs, rare orchids, and trees and fields
> and waters,
> All these, and all else (ibid.: 145).

The image of 'nothingness' and a land made barren, stripped of its ability to regenerate, are what is observed in these lines. His poem jolts the reader out of his/her complacency into realizing that along with the land and its natural resources, the people themselves and their integrity and self-respect, especially 'our young, nubile girls, beautiful like the land itself', 'our cumbersome anachronistic tribal roots', 'our pride, values, work culture, our sense of shame, our collective conscious' are all up for sale (ibid.). The poem ends with the harsh truth according to the poet speaker that: 'No contact number is needed/our agents are everywhere/ you can meet them on the streets' (ibid.).

If *home* is a representation of the self and of one's identity and by extension of the community which creates the sense of belonging, these poems then show how the invasion and destruction of these homes is symbolically an invasion and destruction of the very core of the north-eastern community. Not only are the physical spaces demolished and made barren, but these destructions also mark the rupture of the cultural memories and stories that these spaces once held, and in its turn, 'creates a redefined sense of "homesickness"' (Buikema 2005: 184):

> Homesickness is the desire for a home . . . is a desire to come home to the magic of stories, a longing for the feeling of community that emerges through the actual telling. The telling, in the sense of dwelling in the same discourse, in the same linguistic house, ceases. It ceases because the craft of narration is strongly dependent on the extent to which the experience may be reported and thus shared (ibid.).

The north-eastern writer writing about *home* sees this act of violation not only in measurable physical terms but also at a much deeper level where the very existence of the community, its history, world views and values have been constantly threatened even to this day. Rebuilding seems to be an impossible attempt, for the structure of the building itself has been demolished and with it what it contained.

And so for some north-east writers, they are only able to weave into their texts vivid images that are evocative of the trauma that the region and its people have gone through and for some is still a reality today. Perhaps these writers may never be able to write about *home* in the same manner as writers like Marjorie Waters can, who see the house as an extension of their selves that is secure, comforted and enclosed in a warm inside while keeping the perennial 'darkness' out always threatening to invade.

> Night fell and brought a chill to the air outside. I built a fire in the stove, drank tea that smelled of oranges and spice. I warmed my fingers round the cup and thought of how my house would look to passers-by, drowsy and content, with soft rectangles of light on the ground below the windows, a breath of smoke from the chimney. She's come back, they would say as they walked through the dark night. She's home again (Waters 1991: 13).

References

Baum, Frank L. 1900. *The Wonderful Wizard of Oz*. Chicago: George M. Hill.

Buikema, Rosemarie. 2005. 'A Poetics of Home: On Narrative Voice and the Deconstruction of Home in Migrant Literature', in Daniela Merolla and Sandra Ponzanesi (eds), *Migrant Cartographies: New Cultural and Literary Spaces in Post-Colonial Europe*, p. 177–189. London: Lexington Books.

George, Rosemary Marangoly. 1996. *The Politics of Home: Postcolonial Relocations and Twentieth-Century Fiction*. Cambridge: Cambridge University Press.

Ibomcha, Yumlembam. 2003. 'Story of a Dream', in Kynpham Nongkynrih and Robin S. Ngangom (eds), *Anthology of Contemporary Poetry from the Northeast*, pp. 80–82. Shillong: North-Eastern Hill University (NEHU) Publications.

Kharmawphlang, Desmond L. 2003. 'The Conquest', in Kynpham Nongkynrih and Robin S. Ngangom (eds), *Anthology of Contemporary Poetry from the Northeast*, pp. 134–35. Shillong: NEHU Publications.

Lyngdoh, Paul. 2003. 'For Sale', in Kynpham Nongkynrih and Robin S. Ngangom (eds), *Anthology of Contemporary Poetry from the Northeast*, p. 145. Shillong: NEHU Publications.

Martin, Biddy and Chandra Talpade Mohanty. 1997. 'Feminist Politics: What's Home Got To Do With It?', in Robyn R. Warhol and Diane Price Herndl (eds), *Feminisms: An Anthology of Literary Theory and Criticism*. Brunswick, NJ: Rutgers University Press.

Nasta, Susheila. 2002. *Home Truths: Fictions of the South Asian Diaspora in Britain*. Hampshire: Palgrave.

Ngangom, Robin S. 2003. 'Native Land', in Kynpham Nongkynrih and Robin S. Ngangom (eds), *Anthology of Contemporary Poetry from the Northeast*, pp. 154–55. Shillong: NEHU Publications.

Nongkynrih, Kynpham and Robin S. Ngangom. 2003. *Anthology of Contemporary Poetry from the North-East*. Shillong: NEHU Publications.

Nyman, Jopi. 2009. *Home, Identity, and Mobility in Contemporary Diasporic Fiction*. Amsterdam and New York: Rodopi.

Papastergiadis, Nikos. 1998. *Dialogues in the Diasporas: Essays and Conversations on Cultural Identity*. London and New York: Rivers Oram Press.

Porteus, J. Douglas. 1976. 'Home: The Territorial Core', *Geographical Review*, 66(4): 383–90.

Waters, Marjorie. 1991. 'Coming Home', in Chandra Mohan, Vinay Sood, N. K. Bhasin, Sudarshan Sharma and Rajeswari Sunder Rajan (eds), *Contemporary English: An Anthology for Undergraduates — I*. New Delhi: Oxford University Press.

About the Editors

G. N. Devy is Professor, Dhirubhai Ambani Institute of Information and Communication Technology, Gandhinagar, and Founder, Bhasha Research and Publication Centre, Baroda (Vadodara), Gujarat, India. He is also a literary scholar and cultural activist who writes in three languages — Marathi, Gujarati and English — and has received prestigious literary awards for his works in all three languages. Between 1973 and 1996 he taught at the Maharaja Sayajirao University at Baroda, but gave up his academic position to take up conservation of threatened languages in India. Between 1978 and 1996, Devy held several fellowships such as the Rotary Foundation Fellowship, Commonwealth Academic Exchange Fellowship, Fulbright Fellowship, THB Symons Fellowship and Jawaharlal Nehru Fellowship. His major publications in English include *In Another Tongue: Essays On Indian English Literature* (1993), *Between Tradition and Modernity: India's Search for Identity* (1997), *Painted Words: An Anthology of Tribal Literature* (2002, edited), *Indian Literary Criticism: Theory and Interpretation* (2002, edited), *A Nomad Called Thief: Reflections on Adivasi Voice and Silence* (2006), *Indigeneity: Culture and Representation* (2008, co-edited), and *Voice and Memory: Indigenous Imagination and Expression* (2011, co-edited). *The G. N. Devy Reader* containing four of his book length essays was published in 2009.

Geoffrey V. Davis is Chairperson, European Association for Commonwealth Literature and Language Studies (EACLALS) and was formerly Professor of English, Rheinisch-Westfälische Technische Hochschule (RWTH) Aachen University, Germany. He is the co-editor of the Rodopi Series on 'Readings in the Post/Colonial Literatures in English', under which 140 volumes have been published so far. He was also previously Chair of the International Association for Commonwealth Literature and Language Studies (ACLALS). His published works include *Theatre and Change in South Africa* (1996, co-edited), *Beyond the Echoes of Soweto: Five Plays by Matsemela Manaka* (1997, edited), *Voices of Justice and Reason: Apartheid and Beyond in South African Literature* (2003), *Staging*

New Britain: Aspects of Black and South Asian Theatre Practice (2006, co-edited), *Towards a Transcultural Future: Literature and Human Rights in a 'Post'-Colonial World* (2008, co-edited), *Indigeneity: Culture and Representation* (2008, co-edited), and *Voice and Memory: Indigenous Imagination and Expression* (2011, co-edited).

K. K. Chakravarty is Chancellor, National University of Education Planning and Administration (NUEPA), New Delhi, and Vice Chairman, Delhi Institute of Heritage Research and Management, India. He has been an Indian Administrative Service (IAS) officer and a distinguished scholar in the fields of culture studies and archeology. Previously he was Director, Museum of Man, Bhopal, and Member Secretary, Indira Gandhi National Centre for Arts, New Delhi. Apart from numerous essays and journal articles, his recent works include *Restoring Human Culture and Biospheric Environment: A New Museum Movement* (2003, co-edited), *River Valley Cultures of India* (2005, co-edited), *Traditional Water Management Systems of India* (2006, co-edited), *Indigeneity: Culture and Representation* (2008, co-edited), and *Voice and Memory: Indigenous Imagination and Expression* (2011, co-edited).

Notes on Contributors

♋

A. O. Balcomb is Professor, School of Religion and Theology, University of KwaZulu-Natal, South Africa. He holds a PhD in Theology and has a particular research interest in the influence of Pentecostalism both in South Africa and further afield on the African continent. He has taught at the Akrofi-Christaller Institute for Mission and Culture in Akropong, Ghana, every year since 1995. His publications include *Third Way Theology: Reconciliation, Revolution, and Reform in the South African Church during the 1980s* (1993) and numerous articles in theological journals.

Eckhard Breitinger is Emeritus Professor, Institute for African Studies, University of Bayreuth, Germany. He read English, History and Archaeology at German, British and Swiss universities. He previously taught at the University of the West Indies, Kingston, Jamaica; the University of Tübingen; the Kwame Nkrumah University, Kumasi, Ghana; the University of Paris III: Sorbonne Nouvelle, Paris; and the Paul Valéry University, Montpellier. He has published articles on post-colonial literature, theatre and performance; has contributed to reference works with Cambridge, Oxford and Columbia University Presses; and has published monographs on Gothic novels, American radio drama and film, and political rhetoric. He is the editor of the Bayreuth African Studies Series, and has translated plays and poetry. His theatre photographs have been exhibited internationally.

Vibha S. Chauhan is Associate Professor, Department of English, Zakir Husain Delhi College, University of Delhi. Her research interests lie in the area of local cultures and oral narratives of non-urbanized communities. She has surveyed, written and published several articles about social codes like caste and gender and their complex interaction with creative articulation. She is also deeply interested in Indian classical music and has co-authored the biography of Siddheshwari Devi, the legendary singer of the *Benares gharana*. Proficient in Hindi, Bhojpuri and English, Vibha Chauhan is a published novelist in Hindi. She also regularly publishes poetry in all three languages, besides being an active translator.

Mohan Dharavath is Senior Research Fellow, English and Foreign Languages University, Hyderabad, India. Born and brought up in Warangal, Andhra Pradesh he belongs to the Lambada community. He graduated in Life Sciences from Nizam College, Osmania University, and did his postgraduate work in English at the English and Foreign Languages University, Hyderabad. His areas of interest are Adivasi and Dalit studies, Indian literature, post-colonial studies and translation. In 2011 he spent six months at the University of Dresden, Germany on a Deutscher Akademischer Austausch Dienst (DAAD [German Academic Exchange Service]) fellowship studying different levels of research on the Indo-European Tribes. Apart from attending conferences and seminars at universities in India, he has also presented papers at the University of Cambridge and the Universidad de Granada, Spain.

Birte Heidemann is Postgraduate Research Assistant, English and American Studies, Faculty of Humanities, Chemnitz University of Technology, Germany. She studied English and German Literature at the University of Bremen and at the National University of Ireland, Maynooth. She is currently completing her dissertation on the concept of liminal space in contemporary Northern Irish literature and film. Her research interests are in post-colonial theory, contemporary Northern Irish literature, Black and Asian British literature and film studies.

Dolores Herrero is Senior Lecturer in English and Post-Colonial Literatures, Department of English and German Philology, University of Zaragoza, Spain. Her main research interests lie in cultural, film and post-colonial studies, and Australian and Indian literature and film in particular. Apart from a number of essays focusing on various literary and cultural issues, her published works include *Margins in English and American Literature, Film and Culture* (1997, co-edited), *Between the Urge to Know and the Need to Deny: Trauma and Ethics in Contemporary British and American Literature* (2011, co-edited), and *The Splintered Glass: Facets of Trauma in the Post-Colony and Beyond* (2011). She was the editor of *Miscelanea: A Journal of English and American Studies* from 1998 to 2006.

Joseph McLaren is Professor of English, Hofstra University, New York, US. A specialist in African, Caribbean, and African-American literatures, his publications include numerous articles on literary and cultural subjects. His published works include *Langston Hughes: Folk Dramatist in the Protest Tradition, 1921–1943* (1997), *Pan-Africanism Updated* (1999, co-edited), *African Visions* (2000, co-edited), two volumes of the *Collected Works of Langston Hughes: The Big Sea* (2002, edited) and *I Wonder As I Wander* (2002, edited). He is also co-author with legendary jazz saxophonist-composer Jimmy Heath of Heath's autobiography, *I Walked with Giants* (2010).

Judith Misrahi-Barak is Associate Professor, Paul-Valéry University, Montpellier, France, and currently teaches English and Post-Colonial Literatures. Her publications include articles on Caribbean writers and the Caribbean diaspora, as well as chapters in edited collections, most recently in *Voices and Silence in the Contemporary Novel in English* (2009, ed. V. Guigney); *Hybridation Multiculturalisme Postcolonialisme* (2009, ed. D. Lasalle, H. Ventura and K. Fischer); and *Littérature et esclavage* (2010, ed. S. Moussa). She has organized several international conferences with invited writers. She is General Editor of the series *PoCoPages* in the collection 'Horizons anglophones' published by the Presses universitaires de la Méditerranée. The most recent volume is *India and the Indian Diasporic Imagination* (2011).

Macaulay Mowarin is Associate Professor and Head of Department, Department of English and Literary Studies, Delta State University, Abraka, Nigeria. He took his BA in English at the University of Ilorin and obtained both his MA and PhD in English Language at the University of Ibadan. He has published articles locally and internationally. His main research interests are in morphology, syntax and sociolinguistics.

Narugopal Mukherjee is Assistant Professor of English, Bankura Christian College, University of Burdwan, West Bengal, India, and has been teaching at both postgraduate and undergraduate levels for the last 12 years. He has to his credit a number of research papers. He attended various national and international seminars and conferences and has a keen interest in applied linguistics, classical literature, and Indian writings in English. He is Executive Editor of the *Wesleyan Journal of Research*.

Helen Oronga A. Mwanzi is Associate Professor, University of Nairobi, Kenya. Born in Esirulo, Kenya, she is a speaker of the Lunyore dialect of the Luhya Language. She holds a PhD in Literature Studies and a Diploma in Education. She taught in high school for seven years before registering for an MA in Literature at the University of Nairobi. She enjoys teaching literature, carrying out field research in oral literature, writing both creative and non-fiction work, singing and dancing.

Esther S. Narjinari is currently a doctoral candidate at Jawaharlal Nehru University, New Delhi. Her dissertation, entitled 'In the Shadow of Alien Lands: Literary Representations of the "Refugee" in Contemporary Literature' examines recent refugee fictions produced in the developed nations by writers from the developing world focusing on the importance of stories and storytelling, and the narrativization of lived experiences for the creation of personal agency in a context of powerlessness. Her work explores themes such as (un)belonging, identity, representation, processes of othering, and post-coloniality. She previously worked with the Department of English, Lady Shri Ram College for Women, New Delhi, and has also taught academic writing at the Asian University for Women, Chittagong, Bangladesh. Her article 'The Weaving of Bodo Women's Identity in their Traditional Folk Songs' was published in *Indigeneity: Culture and Representation* (2009, ed. G. N. Devy, Geoffrey V. Davis and K. K. Chakravarty).

Britta Olinder was Associate Professor, University of Gothenburg, Sweden, where she taught English literature for over 30 years. She has edited collections on post-colonial, especially Canadian and Irish, literature and has published books and articles on Restoration drama, particularly John Dryden; African and Australian writing; Irish authors such as John Hewitt, Anne Devlin, Christina Reid, Deirdre Madden, Eavan Boland, Paula Mehan, James Joyce; Canadian authors like Aritha van Herk, Janice Kulyk Keefer, Marian Engel and Gloria Sawai; and Indian writers, notably R. K. Narayan, Anita Desai and Shashi Deshpande.

Mumia Geoffrey Osaaji teaches post-colonial literature at the University of Nairobi. He holds a Master of Arts and will complete his PhD in African Literature at the University of Nairobi in 2012. Osaaji has published over 15 articles and articles in local and international refereed journals and books, including *Research in African Literatures* (RAL) and

Literature for Our Times (2012, ed. Bill Ashcroft et al.), and authored *Style in African Literature* (2011). Besides his literary interests, Osaaji is also a renowned expert on human rights and programme planning and evaluation.

Cecile Sandten holds the Chair of English Literatures, Chemnitz University of Technology, Germany. Her research interests are in postcolonial theory and literature, children's literature and literature for young adults, Indian English literature, Black and Asian British literature, Shakespeare and comparative perspectives, as well as adaptation studies, media transfer and urban studies. Her publications include *Broken Mirrors: Interkulturalität am Beispiel der indischen Lyrikerin Sujata Bhatt* (1998), *Transcultural Re-Readings of Postcolonial Shakespeare Adaptations* (forthcoming), *Zwischen Kontakt und Konflikt: Stand und Perspektiven der Postkolonialismusforschung* (2006, co-edited), *Transkulturelle Begegnungen* (2007, co-edited), and *Industrialization, Industrial Heritage, De-Industrialization: Literary and Visual Representations of Pittsburgh and Chemnitz* (2010, co-edited). She is currently working on an interdisciplinary research project entitled 'Postcolonialism in the Metropolis'.

T. S. Satyanath is a retired professor who taught comparative Indian literature and Kannada language and literature in the Department of Modern Indian Languages and Literary Studies, University of Delhi. Comparative literature, translation studies, folklore studies and cultural studies are his areas of interest. He has an MA in Kannada Language and Literature from Bangalore University and MA and MPhil degrees in Linguistics from the University of Delhi. He also holds a PhD in comparative Indian literature from the University of Delhi. He has published nearly 60 research papers in English and Kannada.

Chris J. C. Wasike is Lecturer in Literature and Cultural Studies, Masinde Muliro University of Science and Technology, Kenya. He recently completed his PhD in African Literature at the University of the Witwatersrand, South Africa. He has published various articles on Bukusu funeral folklore and masculinities in a number of journals. His other research interests include popular Kenyan music and East African drama and media.

Michael Wessels is Lecturer, Department of English, University of KwaZulu-Natal, Pietermaritzburg, South Africa. He has published widely in the fields of oral literature and cultural studies, and has written a book, *Bushman Letters: Interpreting /Xam Narrative* (2010). His current research interests include performance and social meaning, and contemporary religious identities. He worked as a school teacher in the rural areas and townships of southern Africa for many years, before becoming a founder member of an intentional community, based on principles of organic farming and the use of renewable energy. He still lives in this community with his partner and two children, surrounded by pristine mistbelt forest and grassland.

Index